· Our Fight ·

OUR

Writings by

FIGHT

Veterans of the
Abraham Lincoln
Brigade

SPAIN 1936–1939

Edited by
Alvah Bessie (1904–1985) and
Albert Prago

Introduction by
Ring Lardner, Jr.

MONTHLY REVIEW PRESS
with the Veterans of the Abraham Lincoln Brigade

Library of Congress Cataloging-in-Publication Data

Our fight.

   1. Spain—History—Civil War, 1936–1939—Participation,
American. 2. Spain—History—Civil War, 1936–1939—
Personal narratives, American. 3. Spain. Ejército
Popular de la República. Brigada Internacional, XV
—Biography. 4. Soldiers—Spain—Biography. I. Bessie,
Alvah Cecil, 1904–   . II. Prago, Albert.
DP269.47.A46096 1987   946.081   87-5562
ISBN 0-85345-725-5
ISBN 0-85345-724-7 (pbk.)

Monthly Review Press
155 West 23rd Street
New York, N.Y. 10011

Manufactured in the United States of America

10 9 8 7 6 5 4 3 2 1

You came to us from all peoples, from all races. You came like brothers of ours, like children of undying Spain; and in the hardest days of the war, when the capital of the Spanish Republic was threatened, it was you, gallant comrades of the International Brigades, who helped to save the city with your fighting enthusiasm, your heroism and your spirit of sacrifice.

—La Pasionaria

Contents

• The DECISION and the JOURNEY •

• The FIRST BATTLES •

• The ARAGON OFFENSIVE and the RETREATS •

• The EBRO OFFENSIVE and the WITHDRAWAL •

· The WAR GOES ON ·

Preface

Bernal Díaz del Castillo, a soldier in Hernán Cortés's collection of rugged adventurers, wrote an astounding version of the "True History" of the conquest of New Spain. Historians feel indebted, for his invaluable contribution was the only contemporary writing other than official histories and letters. As we approach more modern times we find that memoirs, poems, diary entries, and letters by war veterans increase in quantity. History and literature are often enriched by the contributions of nonprofessional writers who provide insights and interpretations not easily available to the professional author.

This collection, however, is not just another to be casually added to the body of nonprofessional writings about just another war. Its uniqueness lies in the uniqueness of the war and the collective uniqueness of the men and women who were volunteers in the historically unprecedented International Brigades in Spain. A natural consequence is an unusual collection of writings, and I feel especially privileged to have served as one of the editors.

Since 1939, the Veterans of the Abraham Lincoln Brigade have had a house organ, *The Volunteer*, which, these past few years, has been under the inspired editorship of Ben Iceland. It was he who dreamed of having an anthology of the writings of his fellow veterans published, and for several years he discussed his pet project with his editorial committee: four fellow veterans—

11

our national secretary Abe Smorodin, Irving Weissman, Theodore Cogswell, and me.

Discussion finally led to execution, and the dream approached realization with the appointment, by the national executive board of VALB, of Alvah Bessie as editor. All of us are proud and honored that he had undertaken this task. He was not only a novelist and screenwriter; he was also a fellow veteran who had refused to kowtow to homegrown fascism and had then, as one of the Hollywood Ten, been imprisoned and blacklisted for his staunchness. He devoted the last year of his life to working on this anthology, which he believed was one of VALB's most important projects. His death occurred with tragic abruptness in July 1985, and I was appointed his successor.

All the material included in this anthology was written by veterans, with three exceptions. Ring Lardner, Jr., who wrote the introduction, was the brother of a veteran. Langston Hughes visited the fronts and hospitals in Spain, was very moved, and went on to move so many with his impassioned poetry. And Ernest Hemingway—perhaps more than any other American writer, he made invaluable contributions to the cause of Republican Spain. Unless otherwise noted, all the contributions included here appeared in *The Volunteer.*

Throughout Europe public recognition has been given, in various ways, to the contributions made by each nation's volunteers in Spain. But in the United States not only has such recognition been lamentably absent, but our history has been virtually obliterated. It is therefore my fervent hope that the publication of *Our Fight: Writings by Veterans of the Abraham Lincoln Brigade* will bring additional honor to the American participants. It is also hoped that in the not too distant future the Veterans of the Abraham Lincoln Brigade will be honored by our fellow citizens, by the people's institutions, and perhaps even by our government.

I want to thank the editorial committee of *The Volunteer,* whose members gave me moral support. Theodore Cogswell, upon whose professional expertise I could rely, was a particular help, and his death in February of this year was a loss to all of us. I also want to thank the national executive board of VALB, whose encouragement was always welcome and greatly appreciated.

Without the patience and advice of my wife, Ruth, this project could not have been completed.

But in the end this book is dedicated to the men and women, Spaniards and the volunteers of the International Brigades, who died in the good fight, 1936–1939, and to those who died continuing the good fight.

—Albert Prago

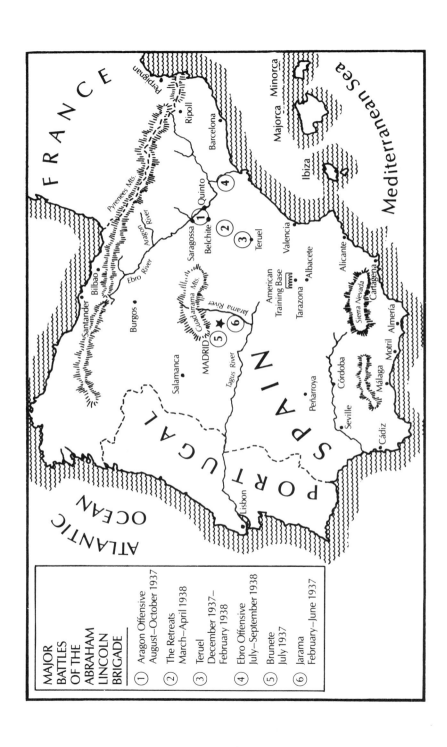

FRANCE

Perpignan

Ripoll

Barcelona

Minorca

Majorca

Mediterranean Sea

Ibiza

Pyrenees Mts.

Quinto

Aragón River

Saragossa ①

② Belchite

③ Teruel ④

Valencia

Alicante

Ebro River

Bilbao

Guadarrama Mts.

Jarama River

American
Training Base

Albacete

Tarazona

Cartagena

Santander

Burgos

⑤ MADRID ⑥

Sierra Nevada

Almería

Salamanca

Tagus River

Córdoba

Motril

Málaga

SPAIN

Peñarroya

ATLANTIC
OCEAN

PORTUGAL

Seville

Cádiz

Lisbon

MAJOR
BATTLES
OF THE
ABRAHAM
LINCOLN
BRIGADE

① Aragon Offensive
August–October 1937

② The Retreats
March–April 1938

③ Teruel
December 1937–
February 1938

④ Ebro Offensive
July–September 1938

⑤ Brunete
July 1937

⑥ Jarama
February–June 1937

· Ring Lardner, Jr. ·

Introduction

In the course of his reelection campaign in 1984, Ronald Reagan encouraged Americans to join the "Contras" harassing Nicaragua from their Honduran sanctuary. He cited the Abraham Lincoln Brigade in the Spanish Civil War as a precedent although, he added, they "were, in the opinion of most Americans, fighting on the wrong side." These words were an exceptionally glaring example of the president's problem with getting his facts straight—the problem that prompted his Press Secretary Larry Speakes to coin the phrase "presidential imprecision." The truth of the matter is that American public opinion during that war rose from 65 percent in favor of the legal government in 1937 to 76 percent in 1938—about the same percentage, incidentally, that in the spring of 1986 opposed the president's campaign against the legal government of Nicaragua.

When Mr. Reagan visited Spain in May 1985, right after the monumental misjudgment of Bitburg, Spanish newspapers quoted his line about the Lincolns, and the *Boston Globe* commented editorially on the reaction there:

> For democratic Spaniards, the implications of such a judgment were frightening and offensive: if the Abraham Lincoln Brigade was on the wrong side, then Reagan believed the fascists were on the right side. . . . The hundreds of thousands who marched through the streets of Spanish cities last Sunday to protest against Reagan's visit could hardly be blamed for seeing a link between his

15

view of Hitler's warriors as victims and his belief that fascists fighting for Franco were on the right side. Hitler, after all, also fought for Franco.

Spain was where Hitler first went to war against democracy in Europe. At Guernica, his air force dropped the first bombs on a civilian population, experimenting with "strategic" terror. When the Western democracies failed to come to the aid of the Spanish Republic, they gave Hitler a shameful sign of their failure to comprehend or resist the forces of fascism.

President Reagan, who lived through the 1930s and 1940s, seems oblivious to the lessons of that era. At this late date, no democratic leader should still be so blinded by anticommunism as to recapitulate the fatal mistakes of that time.

The mistakes of that time sprang from a somewhat different rationale in the United States than in the European democracies, but the results were the same. France, with a "Popular Front" government similar to Spain's, was dissuaded from its initial impulse to help by Tory Britain's argument that no one should help either side and the outcome be determined by Spaniards alone. So a "nonintervention" agreement was signed by all the European powers and the flagrant violations of it by Germany and Italy were ignored for two years, culminating in the outright appeasement of the Munich Pact. Give Hitler everything he says he wants, the British and French reasoned, and there will be no grounds left for a second world war.

In the United States, too, the policy toward Spain was determined in large measure by the desire to avoid war. But we had the special geographical delusion that even if Europe went to war, we could stay out of it by a steadfast refusal to take sides. We passed a neutrality act, and under its terms maintained an embargo against selling armaments of any kind to either side in Spain. This policy ignored the fact that one side was the democratically elected government of the country, with the same right as any other sovereign nation to buy what it needed from its fellow democracy. It also ignored the fact that the participation of Italy, Germany, and Portugal in Franco's rebellion made it as much a foreign invasion as a civil war. And, compounding the error even further, it failed to consider how the success of a fascist coup in Spain could influence events in Latin America.

According to Sumner Welles, undersecretary of state from

1933 to 1943 under a series of politically selected chiefs, "Of all our blind isolationist policies, the most disastrous was our attitude toward the Spanish Civil War."

In his memoir *My Mission to Spain,* Claude Bowers, our ambassador to Spain at the time, related that he was called to Washington for consultation during the final agony of the Spanish Republic and that he took the occasion to review the opinions he had been submitting to the State Department all along:

> 1. That after the first days of considerable confusion, it was plainly shown to be a war of the Fascists and the Axis powers against the democratic institutions of Spain.
> 2. That the Spanish war was the beginning of a perfectly thought-out plan for the extermination of democracy in Europe, and the beginning of a Second World War with that as the intent.
> 3. That the Nonintervention Committee was a shameless sham, cynically dishonest in that Germany and Italy were constantly sending soldiers, planes, tanks, artillery, and ammunition into Spain without an interference or real protest from the signatories of the pact.
> 4. That Germany and Italy were using Spanish towns and people for experimental purposes in trying out their new methods of destruction and their new technique of terrorism.
> 5. That the Axis, in preparation for the continental struggle, was using Spain to see how far it could go with the silent acquiescence of the great democracies, and to test their spirit, courage and will to fight in defense of their ideals.
> 6. . . . That our interests, ideologically, commercially and industrially, were bound up with those of democracy in Spain, whose government we recognized as the legal constitutional government, and that the victory of Franco would be a danger to the United States, especially in South America. . . .
>
> I found President Roosevelt seated at his desk in the White House residence, more serious and graver than I had ever seen him before. . . . Before I could sit down or utter a word, he said: "We have made a mistake. You have been right all along."

Why did it take as enlightened a statesman as Franklin Roosevelt so long to adopt the view held by the majority of Americans with clear-cut opinions about the struggle? The answer seems to lie in the fact that most of the public either did not know or did not care enough about who stood for what in Spain for that to count among the issues that shaped their voting decisions. A determined Catholic minority, on the other hand, was specifically taught by the church hierarchy that the loyalist government in Madrid was the agent of the Antichrist. Political opportunism often yields to a resolute bloc of voters rather than an unorganized majority view.

The minority that did feel deeply for the loyalist cause came nowhere near the Catholics in number but more than matched them in intensity. Three thousand men, mostly very young and single, seamen and students the two largest groups among them, enlisted as fighting men, and 40 percent of them lost their lives in Spain. Supporting them at home, beyond their friends and families, were the Communist and Socialist parties, the more militant trade unions, and an overwhelming majority of academics and intellectuals of all kinds. The League of American Writers published the results of a poll in a pamphlet called *Writers Take Sides*, and the count was 410 for the Loyalists, 1 for Franco, and 7 neutral.

Under a legal embargo that forbade any transfer of arms but allowed Texaco and Standard Oil to ship 3 million tons of oil (presumably for pleasure travel) to Franco on credit, the only meaningful assistance we could provide was medical supplies. Seventy fully equipped ambulances were sent with money raised by the Medical Bureau to Aid Spanish Democracy. A couple of them came from Hollywood; at Warner Brothers, where I was working in 1937, we collected contributions from all departments, and I collaborated with John Huston to enlist such major stars as Cagney, Bogart, Davis, and Muni. Reagan was on the lot at the time, but if we approached him I do not remember it. I think that despite his professions of liberalism in those days, he was not considered a likely prospect for a cash donation.

When my brother Jim came out from New York on the occasion of my marriage in February of that year, we heard about the first contingent of American volunteers arriving in Spain and going into action almost immediately on the Jarama front. We talked about that struggle and the larger conflict looming in Europe, and Jim told me of his plan to be transferred to the Paris edition of the *New York Herald Tribune*. There, he hoped, he would be writing about matters of more consequence than a weary round of banquets, funerals, and trivial murders. We had been raised in a journalistic tradition, and it was understood between us that while you naturally had your private opinion about the merits of democracy versus fascism, you also had an obligation to remain sufficiently detached from the struggle to be able to record objectively what you saw and heard.

The rest of 1937 did not go too badly. It was infuriating that the European democracies and the United States continued their refusal to sell arms to the Loyalists, but you still hoped the policy would be reversed, and meanwhile the Soviet Union was providing part of what was needed. There was a battle at Guadalajara in which the antifascist Italians of the Garibaldi Brigade routed a superior force of Mussolini's regular army troops. Then came a successful offensive by government forces at Brunete that helped secure Madrid, and another one in Aragón that began well and resulted in at least a standoff. At the end of the year there was a distinct victory at Teruel.

But with the beginning of 1938 our hopes began to fall apart. A fascist counteroffensive retook Teruel, and by the end of winter a wide retreat was under way along the whole northern front. The Fifteenth (mainly English-speaking) International Brigade, which had played a vital part in the Aragon offensive, was routed and disorganized along with the rest of the Loyalist forces in the northeast. We began to realize there was no way to prevail against the fascist superiority in planes, tanks, and other equipment without a change in the policies of the Western democracies.

At this discouraging point Jim wrote from Paris that he was going to Spain to write a series of pieces about the American volunteers that could later be collected into a book. Ten days after his arrival in Barcelona, having visited the Lincolns at the front and seen his story cut to few lines in the *Herald Tribune*, he insisted, over considerable resistance, on joining the battalion as a recruit. Five months later, on the night before the International Brigades were withdrawn from the war, he was killed in action.

The Lincolns Jim joined included only a fraction of the original battalion that had been assembled fifteen months earlier.

The casualties at that first, fierce battle of Jarama and other bloody campaigns after had been replaced by a steady stream of new volunteers and finally, after the Aragon disaster, by very young and very raw Spanish recruits.

The Americans who went to Spain came from all over the country and a variety of social and political backgrounds. Although the Lincoln Battalion was organized by the U.S. Communist Party and a large number of the volunteers were members, there were also substantial representations from the Socialist and Democratic parties and from among the politically unaffiliated. In view of the open participation on Franco's side of the Nazi Condor Legion and the Luftwaffe, it is not surprising that about 40 percent were Jewish. Approximately one hundred were black, including Captain Oliver Law, who, shortly before his death on the battlefield, took over command of the Lincoln Battalion, the first black officer in U.S. history to lead an integrated military unit.

Closely allied with the Lincolns—to the point of overlapping personnel at various stages of the war—was the Canadian Mac-Kenzie-Papineau Battalion. This unit numbered 625 men at full strength, drawn from a total force of about one thousand volunteers from Canada.

Women, mostly nurses but including a few technicians, truck and ambulance drivers, were in the majority in the American Medical Unit. The first group of seventeen, headed then and throughout the war by Dr. Edward Barsky, sailed from New York in mid-January 1937, just three weeks after the first contingent of 96 fighting men. After some Franco partisans in the State Department were overruled in their effort to bar all travel to Spain, even for humanitarian purposes, about 120 more nurses, doctors, dentists, technicians, and drivers went over to reinforce and expand the original unit.

About eighteen hundred of the Lincolns survived to return to the United States, some only after being held in the stark conditions of a fascist prison for months after the war was over. Most of the able-bodied veterans served honorably, and a few with great distinction, in the armed forces during World War II. In the four decades since, they have been in the forefront of resistance to McCarthy-era repression, of civil rights battles in the

1950s and 1960s, of opposition to U.S. intervention in Vietnam, and of continuing efforts toward a rational nuclear policy.

Today they are especially concerned with support for Nicaraguan independence, moved perhaps by the grim irony that Washington has assumed the role played by the Rome-Berlin Axis in a remarkably similar situation half a century ago.

· Langston Hughes ·

Tomorrow's Seed

Proud banners of death,
I see them waving
There against the sky,
Struck deep in Spanish earth
Where your dark bodies lie
Inert and helpless—
So they think
Who do not know
That from your death
New life will grow.
For there are those who cannot see
The mighty roots of liberty
Push upward in the dark
To burst in flame—
A million stars—
And one your name:
    Man
Who fell in Spanish earth:
Human seed
For freedom's birth.

· Ernest Hemingway ·

On the American Dead in Spain

The dead sleep cold in Spain tonight. Snow blows through the olive groves, sifting against the tree roots. Snow drifts over the mounds with the small headboards. (When there was time for headboards.) The olive trees are thin in the cold wind because their lower branches were once cut to cover tanks, and the dead sleep cold in the small hills above the Jarama River. It was cold that February when they died there and since then the dead have not noticed the changes of the seasons.

It is two years now since the Lincoln Battalion held for four and a half months along the heights of the Jarama, and the first American dead have been a part of the earth of Spain for a long time now.

The dead sleep cold in Spain tonight and they will sleep cold all this winter as the earth sleeps with them. But in the spring the rain will come to make the earth kind again. The wind will blow soft over the hills from the south. The black trees will come to life with small green leaves, and there will be blossoms on the apple trees along the Jarama River. This spring the dead will feel the earth beginning to live again.

For our dead are a part of the earth of Spain now and the earth of Spain can never die. Each winter it will seem to die and each spring it will come alive again. Our dead will live with it forever.

Just as the earth can never die, neither will those who have ever been free return to slavery. The peasants who work the earth where our dead lie know what these dead died for. There was time during the war for them to learn these things, and there is forever for them to remember them in.

Our dead live in the hearts and the minds of the Spanish peasants, of the Spanish workers, of all the good simple honest people who believed in and fought for the Spanish Republic. And as long as all our dead live in the Spanish earth, and they will live as long as the earth lives, no system of tyranny ever will prevail in Spain.

The fascists may spread over the land, blasting their way with weight of metal brought from other countries. They may advance aided by traitors and by cowards. They may destroy cities and villages and try to hold the people in slavery. But you cannot hold any people in slavery.

The Spanish people will rise again as they have always risen before against tyranny.

The dead do not need to rise. They are a part of the earth now and the earth can never be conquered. For the earth endureth forever. It will outlive all systems of tyranny.

Those who have entered it honorably, and no men ever entered earth more honorably than those who died in Spain, already have achieved immortality.

The
DECISION
and the
JOURNEY

In 1936, the world was still in the throes of the Great Depression. Many tens of millions of people were hungry, homeless, and unemployed. In Italy and Germany, the fascists had destroyed democracy, and were violently crushing all public opposition to their repressive policies. Elsewhere, as in Eastern Europe, reaction was on the rise.

The rebellion of Franco and the fascists against the newly elected government in Spain drew the battle lines between democracy and fascism. And when the Nazis, as well as the Italian and Portuguese fascists, sent troops, technicians, planes, and other war matériel in support of Franco's generals, it became apparent to many that a second world war was possible.

The threat to world democracy and the growing menace of world war brought 40,000 anti-fascist volunteers from fifty-three countries to fight on the side of the young Spanish republic. Their coming was a "reflex of the conscience of the world," wrote Vincent Sheean. The excerpt from Robert Colodny's The Struggle for Madrid *gives a brief history of all the International Brigades and describes the role they played in the war. We then turn to the 2,800 Americans who went to Spain between 1936 and 1938 and joined the Abraham Lincoln Battalion (in the United States mistakenly called Brigade). The motivations—personal and political— that spurred these young volunteers to risk their lives were many, but, as we see here, common to all was a deep-seated hatred of fascism.*

The Americans went in small groups, beginning on December 26, 1936, when the first ninety-six left the port of New York, and continuing until the early spring of 1938. The majority had reached Spain by the fall of 1937. Almost all had great difficulty getting there—many climbed the Pyrenees, sometimes in the dead of winter, while others went by sea, or tried to. When they arrived, they were organized into battalions of approximately 500 people; three or four battalions comprised a brigade. The first American battalions were part of the Fifteenth Brigade, one of the five International Brigades. In this section, the volunteers describe the decision to go to Spain and the perils of getting there.

—A.P.

· Robert G. Colodny ·

The International Brigades

The history of the formation of the International Brigades falls into two periods. The first begins on July 19, 1936, with the outbreak of the rebellion in Catalonia and ends on October 17, 1936. The second phase begins on November 5, 1936, and ends on March 23, 1937.

October 17 was the day on which the Spanish government opened the great base of Albacete as the headquarters and training ground of the foreign volunteers. On November 5, the first International Column left Albacete for the Madrid front. March 23, 1937, was the day on which the International Brigades stabilized the front at Guadalajara and fulfilled their mission of serving as a living wall behind which the Spanish Republic formed its Ejército Popular.

The origins of the International Brigades are vague, lost in the chaos of the July days when Franco's rebellion had been answered by revolution, and when the few "Leftist" foreigners in Barcelona, German and Italian émigrés, for the most part, joined the militia columns and marched off with them to the strange and often senseless operations waged by the Catalans in Aragon.

From the volunteers with the Catalan militia were formed the various "centuria" of language groups, the Thaelmann of the Germans, the Gastone-Sozzi of Swiss, Germans and Italians, a Slavic group, and the Paris Centuria of the Frenchmen, Belgians,

27

Englishmen; a few Americans and Scandinavians joined the groups of their choosing, usually through militia committees in Barcelona and Figueras. These centuria were the true precursors of the International Brigades.

The resistance of the Spanish Republicans to the rebellion of the generals had set off a political chain reaction in Europe whose ultimate result was the appearance of the International Brigades at the gates of Madrid. The first centuria were spontaneously formed by the men on the spot and these were continuously reinforced from France. The news that foreigners were fighting with the militia, that Germany and Italy were supporting the rebels, was spread across the continent by the socialist, communist, and anarchist press, and served to stimulate the flow of volunteers. That this took place before the Soviet government denounced the Non-Intervention Agreement and openly championed the cause of the Spanish Republic is an indication of the wide response the first armed resistance to fascism evoked in the European working class in general and among the German, Italian, Austrian, and Polish émigrés in particular.

The concept of the war in Spain as a crusade against fascism was born in the West, not in Moscow, and was concomitant with the proclamation of the crusade against Bolshevism in Iberia proclaimed in Berlin, Rome, Burgos, Lisbon, and the Vatican City. The political season was propitious for forming a legion to fight for the Republic (and another to fight for the rebels). The left had gone down to ignominious defeat in Germany in 1933; the Vienna workers had gone down fighting, but fighting alone in 1934, as had the miners of Asturias. The Popular Front policy proclaimed by the Third International at the Seventh World Congress in 1935 had led to electoral victories in France and Spain in 1936. That the Popular Front on a European or on a world scale should defend a Popular Front government under armed attack in Spain was simple political logic, and the implementation of this logic was first seen in Aragon in the summer of 1936. It was also not surprising that the German and Italian volunteers formed the hard core of the International columns and gave them the character that made them militarily potent.

The history of the Germans in Spain, as one of the British

volunteers has written, is the history of strong men who proved
and overproved their courage and endurance, their resistance to
pessimism and despair. It is the story of men who died or were
broken physically in doing this. They brought to the International Brigades an offensive spirit, a bitter desperate courage—
at rare intervals in war priceless, essential, but always costly.
They set an early example of what shock troops could be like.
They tried to do the impossible, and paid for it. And during the
early days in Aragon, in the futile fighting around Huesca, at
Tardienta, the Germans, in countless bayonet charges against
fortified positions, took their objectives, buried their dead, and
waited with a caged restlessness for the next day's orders.

The French, with a handful of Poles and Czechs, threw themselves into the desperate battle for Irún, and when that was lost
they came to Catalonia, adding their veterans and a reputation
for "hold at all cost" valor to the legends of the International
volunteers.

The Italians were in the field early. To the Gastone-Sozzi Centurion was added the Giustizia e Libertá Column, organized
mainly by Italian anarchists under the leadership of Carlo Ros-
elli. This unit had its baptism of fire at Monte Pelayo in Aragon
on August 29, 1936. They brought with them to Spain a courage
and sense of discipline no less great than the Germans, but they
brought also a sense of fraternity that tempered their valor, that
was more understandable to the Spanish soldiers, and though
they, too, died almost to a man, their influence in Spain and
throughout the Brigades was greater than that of their German
comrades.

From the beginning the physical as well as spiritual headquarters of the volunteers was Paris. Here the illegal political
parties of Eastern and Central Europe had their centers of political organization, their press, and their greatest concentration of
émigrés. At No. 8 Rue Mathurin-Moreau in the Maison des
Sindicats, the first volunteers were provided with the credentials and directions for the journey to Barcelona. German and
Italian Communists, the latter headed by Mario Nicoletti
(Giuseppe di Vittorio) and Nino Nanetti, directed the recruitment of volunteers and elaborated the ideological justification

for the formation of the International Brigades. Here, the first Polish unit, the Dombrowski, sewed onto its battle flag the slogan: "For Your Liberty and for Ours."

When the Army of Africa moved on Toledo, some of the volunteers left the Catalans and their private war in Aragon and went to Madrid to join the Communists' Fifth Regiment. In September Vittorio Vidal, Luigi Gallo (Longo), and Pietro Nenni were in Madrid, and the Gastone-Sozzi Centurion, an International Brigade in miniature, was fighting with the militia before Maqueda, Almorox, and Chapinería, stiffening the resistance, forming a nucleus around which beaten units reformed, and continued to fight.

In the first days of September, an Italian émigré officer, Randolfo Pacciardi, came to Madrid to discuss with the Republican government the project of forming an Italian legion, independent of all political parties, that would fight under the control of the Republican General Staff. Having been introduced by Luigi Longo, the Italian Communist leader in Madrid, to Prieto, Pacciardi was taken by Prieto to see General Estrada, the chief of the Republican General Staff. Estrada was favorable to the plan, but Largo Caballero rejected the idea of foreign volunteers and thus postponed the formation of the International Brigades by six critical weeks.

Talavera de la Reina fell; the Army of Africa rolled on through Maqueda to Toledo. The Soviet delegate to the Non-Intervention Committee denounced the violations of the agreement by the Germans, Italians, and Portuguese; but still Moscow refrained from any unilateral action in Spain. At the end of September Maurice Thorez, the head of the French Communist Party, flew to Moscow to plead the Spanish cause before Dimitroff, chairman of the Comintern, and members of the Soviet Political Bureau.

The same decision that sent Soviet freighters loaded with tanks and planes toward Spanish ports increased the flow of foreign volunteers to Paris and Barcelona. The Comintern decided to sponsor the raising of an army of trained soldiers for the Spanish Republic. And on the same day that Stalin's telegram to José Díaz was printed in *Mundo Obrero*, Largo Caballero commissioned Diego Martínez Barrio, the president of the Spanish

Cortes, civil governor of Albacete, with orders to form the International Brigades and to create a base of supply for the Madrid front. Albacete became a secret city and its very name disappeared from Spanish news dispatches.

The far-flung organizations of the Comintern and Profintern, supplied with money by the Soviet government and the Spanish Republic, began a systematic recruitment of military personnel for the army forming in Albacete. At the same time that General Goriev's staff arrived in Madrid, a Comintern staff headed by Palmiro Togliatti (Ercoli) and André Marty reached the Spanish capital and began the work of shaping the polyglot collection of volunteers into an offensive shock unit. The former had been for years a high official serving on the executive committee of the Comintern; the latter, the leader of the mutiny of the French Black Sea Fleet of 1919; was a Communist deputy from Marseilles. Marty, assisted by Luigi Longo, the inspector general of the International Brigades, and by di Vittorio, the political commissar, took over the control of the units in Albacete. Hans Beimler, the one-time chief of the Communist delegation in the German Reichstag, Vittorio Vidal, the political commissar of the Fifth Regiment, and Ludwig Renn (Arnold Vieth von Golssenau), once of the Saxon Guards and lately an inmate of a German concentration camp, formed the general staff of the Albacete base.

Recruits now poured into Albacete by the hundreds. European governments attempted to halt the traffic, but were only able to slow it down. Switzerland made even the discussion of the Spanish struggle a penal offense. Belgium gave sentences of fifteen years to men apprehended in transit to Spain. Scandinavian parliaments banned travel to Spain, but the crowded Copenhagen-Paris line was dubbed the "Red Express," as volunteers took it to avoid travel through Germany. From Eastern Europe, where the governments were friendly to General Franco, hundreds of men moved along an illegal railway leading from the Balkans to Vienna, from Vienna to Zurich, and thence to Paris. This underground railroad from the east was organized by Joseph Broz, later Marshal Tito.

To command the International Brigades, the Soviet government sent one of its best officers, General Gregory Stern, who fought in Spain under the nom de guerre of Emil Kleber. Gregory Stern was a former officer of the Austrian army who, after imprisonment in Russia during World War I, joined the Red Army in 1917. He advanced rapidly in the General Staff Academy, directed the Hamburg insurrection of 1923, commanded an army corps of the Chinese Red Army, and later the Soviet Far Eastern Army that decisively defeated the Japanese at Lake Chasan in 1935. With Kleber came General "Paul Lukacz," the Hungarian author and army officer whose real name was Mata Zelka, the German army officer Colonel Hans Kahle, the German author Gustav Regler, and a large number of men experienced in the techniques of civil war and revolution.

In Albacete and in neighboring towns such as Tarazona and Madrigueras, the International Brigades began to train with the few score obsolete machine guns, rifles, mortars, and artillery pieces that could be spared from the collapsing Madrid front. The plan was to use these volunteers as the offensive fist to strike from southwest of Madrid toward Toledo. But the sudden collapse of the front after the failure of the October 28 offensive altered the plan. After Getafe fell, it was decided to rush the International Brigades to Vallecas to meet the rebel drive that was expected to strike against the capital from the south. For this purpose three battalions—the Edgar André, with a hard corps of veterans from the Thaelmann Centurion from Aragon, the Rakosi company of Hungarians, and a section of British machine-gunners; the Commune de Paris Battalion, composed of French and Belgians; and the Slavic Dombrowski Battalion were grouped together as the Eleventh International Brigade.[1]

André Marty had wished to keep his battalions in Albacete to complete their training, as only a minority had fought in the world war. He had told those who had demanded to be sent to the front: "We are preparing for war, not for massacre. When the First International Brigade goes into action, they will be properly trained men, with good rifles, a well equipped corps." He had told them much else: that the peril theatening Madrid was less great than that which had threatened Leningrad; that the Spanish People's Army had not conquered fascism, not for lack of courage, but because they lacked three things essential for victory—political unity, military leaders, discipline. These things, Marty had reiterated, the International Brigades would have, and these things the International Brigades would bring to the Spanish army.

André Marty was a stern disciplinarian. Some men thought he was merciless. But the task of transforming a collection of revolutionaries from thirty countries into a disciplined fighting force required a hand of iron, and this Marty possessed. He and his staff saw in the international volunteers the cadres of the army that would not only save Madrid but turn Spain into the graveyard of European fascism. The General Staff conceived of an instrument that through its example would change the raw, brave, but undisciplined levies of the Republic into a regular disciplined army.

But time was running out. The enemy was at Carabanchel. The time for training was over. Marty addressed the Eleventh International Brigade:

> Here on the battlefields of Spain, there are no *croix de guerre* to be won, no stock of Victoria Crosses for the widows of dead heroes. Be brave, my comrades, but no false heroics. We are here to kill fascists, not to commit suicide in front of them.
>
> Soldiers, comrades, my friends from all countries, bear your weapons with love and strength. Defend the cause of this people, and you will be defending the cause of all peoples.

On November 5, the Eleventh International Brigade, 3,500 strong, left Albacete. On November 7, it was quartered in Vallecas. A few hours after the capture of Varela's orders, the Brigade was assigned its battle stations for November 8.

November 8–November 15

> Madrid has passed into history and people to come will read the story of her defense as the story of Troy is read by people today. She stood uncaptured for over two years, more than half-encircled by the enemy and the enemy could not break through. The war had swept by her on both sides; history was being made elsewhere. The city herself had already passed into history, but she held firm with stubbornly reared head, and when finally the game was up and she was delivered into the enemy's hands by her military commander,

her mission was accomplished. She had given her lesson of resistance to other capitals.

—Lorna Lindsley

Unaware that this plan of operations had been carefully studied in the offices of the Madrid General Staff, General Varela continued to drive his troops against the barricades of Madrid. But the carefully designated lines of march of the various columns were roads of death, as the meager firepower of Madrid was concentrated in the exact path the rebels attempted to follow. "He who does not believe in victory is a coward!" So read the leaflets distributed throughout the city on the night of November 7. The militia and the worker-volunteers accepted the slogan and obeyed the orders of Miaja's commanders. A battalion of women went into action in front of the Segovia bridge. The children built barricades, and in sectors where Rojo's reorganization could be completed, the militia counterattacked, duplicating in Casa de Campo the maneuvers of November 7.

Varela could not accept the complaints from his commanders. He called for more artillery, more tanks, hoping that the continous barrage would open the way, that the morale of the defenders would dissolve in the drum fire of the German batteries. The planes of the Condor Legion entered the battle, concentrating their cargoes on University City, whose magnificent buildings began to crumble.

The artillery commanders of Varela directed the corps batteries on the suburb of Argüelles, the Moncloa, against the Paseo de Rosales. The losses of the militia rose alarmingly. The unarmed reserves, waiting in obedience to Rojo's orders in areas behind the front lines, had their ranks thinned by the shells that fell beyond the closely locked lines of fighters. Hand-to-hand fighting raged in Casa de Campo, at the approaches to University City, beyond Villaverde. The few Republican batteries were silenced; only rifles, machine guns, and homemade bombs broke the waves of attacking Moroccans and Legionnaires.

The fifth column, hearing the rising crescendo of rebel artillery and aerial bombs, maintained its offensive, firing into crowds, hurling grenades under the cover of aerial attack, sowing rumors that the city was about to fall; that the cemetery was choked with corpses; that Miaja had sent emissaries to rebel headquarters. These rumors flew across the world from rebel headquarters and reappeared in the great metropolitan press of London, Paris, Berlin, New York.

The Madrid radio transmitted every two minutes mobilization orders to the city's population. And the city obeyed, filling the gaps torn in the lines of the defenders. The wounded remained in the trenches, as did the dead, the corpses strengthening the parapets. The lines bent dangerously before University City. But they did not break.

General Miaja issued a proclamation to his troops:

> Militia and soldiers:
> The enemy forces, supported by all arms, are attacking Madrid. I expect that none of you will retreat a single step, for from me you will receive only the order to advance.
> —Your General Miaja

The will of Varela was as inflexible as that of Miaja. He repeated his order to the column commanders. Lieutenant-Colonel Delgado Serrano was ordered to break through to the Model Prison at all costs. The command was passed down to the Moroccan troops of the First and Second Tabors of the Regulars of Alhucemas. Artillery was shifted to support the column, and the Africans, charging with fixed bayonets, heedless of losses, broke through the Republican lines, crossed the Manzanares, and advanced toward the coveted objective. News of the breakthrough was flashed to the Ministry of War, and General Miaja and his General Staff rushed in cars to the breach in the Republican front. The general went up to the top floor of the half-wrecked edifice that was under heavy fire and watched the retreat of his troops through binoculars. Then, drawing his pistol, he stumbled through the mounds of shattered masonry and confronted the troops that had left the trenches: "Cowards! Cowards! Die in your trenches! Die with your General Miaja!"

The lines were re-formed. The Moroccan vanguard was wiped out. The general wished to remain on the firing line, but was literally dragged back into his staff car by Lieutenant-Colonel Rojo and returned to the Ministry of War. The front held; but Madrid was bleeding to death.

The radio reiterated the Junta's appeal for more men at the front. Speaking in accents that transcended the parochial issue of the life or death of the city, Fernando Valera, a young deputy of the Cortes, phrased the call to arms in apocalyptic sentences:

> People of Madrid! History has presented you in this hour with the great mission of rising up before the world as the obelisk of Liberty. You will know how to be worthy of so exalted a destiny. You will tell the world how men defend themselves; how peoples fight; how Liberty triumphs. You will tell the world that only a people that knows how to die for Liberty can live in freedom.
>
> People of Spain! Put your eyes, your will, your fists at the service of Madrid. Accompany your brothers with faith, with courage, send your possessions, and if you have nothing else, offer us your prayers. Here in Madrid is the universal frontier that separates Liberty and Slavery. It is here in Madrid that two incompatible civilizations undertake their great struggle: love against hate; peace against war; the fraternity of Christ against the tyranny of the Church. . . .
>
> Citizens of Madrid! Each of you has here on this soil something that is ash; something that is soul. It cannot be! It shall not be that impious intruders trample the sacred tombs of our dead! The mercenaries shall not enter as heralds of dishonor into our homes! It cannot be! It shall not be that the somber birds of intolerance beat their black wings over the human conscience. It cannot be! It shall not be that the Fatherland, torn, broken, entreat like a beggar before the throne of the tyrant. It cannot be! It shall not be! Today we fight. Tomorrow, we conquer. And on the pages of history, Man will engrave an immense heart. This is Madrid. It fought for Spain, for Humanity, for Justice, and with the mantle of its blood sheltered all the men of the world. Madrid! Madrid!

Sometime before noon, Sunday, November 8, the vanguard of the Eleventh International Brigade marched up the Gran Vía of Madrid. Dressed in corduroy uniforms, with blue berets, carrying rifles, steel helmets hanging from their belts, the tramp of their boots sounding in perfect unison, the volunteers of the Edgar André, Dombrowski, and Commune de Paris battalions moved toward the front.

Each section was preceded by its officers, carrying swords and revolvers. Behind rolled a small convoy of trucks loaded with machine guns and ammunition. At the rear trotted two squadrons of French cavalry.

The commands cracked out in the clipped Prussian voice of

Colonel "Hans" and were repeated in French and Polish. To the Madrileños watching from the sidewalk the promises of the commissars had come true. The Russians *had arrived*, and they greeted the foreigners in their street with shouts of "Vivan los rusos! Salud! Salud!" The International rang out in various languages, and the shout in Spanish: "Uníos, Hermanos Proletarios!" Unite, Proletarian Brothers! Madrid was ignorant of the origin of the battalions that marched up the Gran Vía. But that help had come, that the city no longer fought alone—this Madrid knew. The radio broadcast the news across the city, the voice of Dolores Ibárruri carrying the information to Mola's headquarters: "Resist, because from Valencia and Catalonia, legions of fighters are coming to aid us. We have the effective aid of Russia!"

By nightfall, the Dombrowski Battalion of the Eleventh Brigade was in the line at Villaverde, the machine-gun section of the Edgar André was in position in the Hall of Philosophy and Letters in University City, the rest of the Germans and the Commune de Paris Battalion in the Casa de Campo.

In the Casa de Campo, where the fighting was most severe, the volunteers were spread out among the militia, one International Brigade soldier to four Spaniards. This was more than an injection of enthusiasm to raise morale. The militia followed the example of the foreigners, digging foxholes, firing their machine guns in short bursts, seeking the natural cover of the park's rolling, wooded terrain. The chorus of Republican guns rose, more certain, more accurate. And the tired, thinning columns of Varela felt for the first time the deadly cutting edge of machine guns expertly managed in open country. Puzzled, but resolved to obey their general's orders, the Army of Africa returned again and again to the charge, but in the Casa de Campo they encountered a line that would not budge. Each outflanking move was countered by another on the part of the Republicans. In the early afternoon, the columns of Asensio and Castejón were forced to yield ground to Galán's Third Brigade and the Eleventh International Brigade.

The command of the northern sector of Madrid, Casa de Campo, and University City, passed into the hands of General Kleber, who set up his headquarters in the very center of the battle. He established a section of liaison officers, and through these men he transmitted his orders to the troops by means of notes written in pencil on slips of paper: "Resist—K." "Hold your position—K." "Advance to your left—K." These were obeyed without vacillation by the International Brigade commanders.

A company of Polish troops were ordered to take positions in the Casa de Velázquez in University City. The commander received a slip of paper: "Resist—K." For five hours the unit held its position until six men and the commander were left. When the relief arrived, the officer attempted to shoot himself, feeling that he had not protected his men. He was disarmed and taken to Kleber. A word, a handshake, and the Polish officer returned to action. The Casa de Velásquez became a symbol of the International Brigades, and later the Republican troops set the saga of November 8 to a dirge-like song.

There were Frenchmen in the Commune de Paris Battalion who had fought at Verdun, and to them "No Pasarán" recalled the "Ils ne passeront pas" of 1917. Germans of the Edgar André, some of whom had fought with the Crown Prince's army before Verdun, paced the counterattacks of the Eleventh Brigade that broke the charge of the Moroccans and won back the first few square yards of the Casa de Campo for the Spanish Republic.

"War received them with all its mortal pyrotechnics. At the end of the first hour they were fewer in number. This was their down payment."

The blood shed by the International Brigades had a double exchange value. It stopped Varela's army at the moment when the militia's lines were stretched to the breaking point. In dying scientifically, the volunteers showed the Spaniards how to save their own lives.

Madrid received the International volunteers with the simple fraternity born of the common danger that both shared. The people referred to the Germans of the Edgar André as "Our Germans." Hating the others, the city accepted the Internationals as though they had been born in the town's poor suburbs. They listened to half the languages of Europe being spoken in the streets and understood that the city had become more than the capital of Spain, being now linked by ties of blood to most of the nations of the earth. They heard the foreign accents and told each other: "Son de los nuestros." They are ours.

On the night of November 8, in the Teatro Monumental, during the hours when the militia and the International battalions were repulsing the attack of Varela's columns, representatives of the Republican, Socialist, Anarchist, and Communist parties sat on the same platform to celebrate the nineteenth anniversary of the Russian Revolution. Dolores Ibárruri made the main speech, which was broadcast by the Madrid radio:

> When the fascist revolt broke out, the people cried: "They shall not pass!" Today this slogan is implanted deeper than ever in the minds of the people. Today as yesterday, the people of Madrid are prepared to put it into effect. . . . We possess everything needed to enable us to pass to the offensive.
>
> Comrades, we must withstand the onslaught of the enemy for four days, perhaps eight days more. That will be enough to enable our heroic army to start the rout of the enemy's troops.
>
> Madrid is repeating the glorious deeds wrought by the Spanish people in the days when they fought for their independence. The slogan, "They shall not pass" will become a reality. The people of Madrid will make it a reality in the fight for victory.

The deputy from Asturias was optimistic. Trains and planes were bringing in cartridges for Madrid's rifles and machine guns. The International Brigade had brought a few batteries of artillery. Russian fighters were arriving at the air base of Alcalá de Henares. Catalan battalions, excellently equipped, had passed through Valencia and were expected in the capital within forty-eight hours. General Miaja had summoned battle-tested units from the Sierra Guardarrama; and from Albacete, the Twelfth International Brigade, hastily organized on the orders of General Kleber, and composed of the Thaelmann Battalion of the Germans, the André Marty Battalion of French, Belgians, and Swiss, and the Garibaldi Battalion of the Italians, had left for the Madrid front. The Twelfth International Brigade, supported by four Spanish brigades, was to strike against the right flank of the rebels from the direction of Arganda. The troops in Casa de Campo and north to Pozuelo would strike the rebel left flank and snap a pincers behind Varela's army, thus freeing the city from the horrors of siege warfare and trapping the attackers. As on the eve of Caballero's October 28 offensive, Madrid passed from the depths of despair to the optimism of victory. But between the plans on the drawing boards in the Ministry of War and the actuality of the battlefield, there was an abyss that was never bridged.

General Miaja's command extended only to the front of Madrid, and the resources of the Republic, despite the appeal of the capital, were not mobilized with sufficient speed or skill to destroy the Army of Africa, which was pinned down before the stones of Madrid's barricades.

A modern army could not be mobilized in twenty-four hours. For this, the transport, the matériel, and the technicians were lacking. The militia, recovering from the shock of four months of defeat and retreat, had held for the forty-eight hours demanded by Miaja on November 6. It had held because the resources of a city of 1 million had been mobilized in the last hours by the Junta and by Lieutenant-Colonel Rojo's General Staff; because the population of the city had mobilized itself upon the appeal of the radio and had formed the human wall that foiled Varela's overambitious plan of operations; because in the last hours of respite, the minimum of political unity required to turn Madrid into an armed community had been achieved; because at the moment when Varela's Moroccans and Legionnaires had made their desperate bid to move through Casa de Campo and University City and gain the wide avenues leading to the heart of the capital, while yet the Army of Africa retained sufficient numbers and cohesion—at this moment General Kleber's Eleventh International Brigade had provided both the moral spark, the fire power, and the blood to hold Madrid.

On November 9, couriers from General Pozas's Center Army Headquarters reached Madrid. Their mission: to discover who held the city. From Caballero and the High Command in Valencia came another courier who was received with great anxiety by the officers of the General Staff. Miaja's officers had sent frantic cables to Valencia requesting information on the timetable of arrival of arms, men, and food, all of which were running short in Madrid. The courier from Valencia, however, brought a message from the prime minister and minister of war that concerned none of these topics. Largo Caballero, on H-Hour plus seventy-two, requested only that the Madrid commander deliver to his messenger the tableware left behind by the prime minister's staff on the night of November 6. When General Miaja was informed of the mission confided to Caballero's envoy, he stated: "Tell the Minister from me that we who have remained in Madrid are still eating."

Having expected on the night of their departure from Madrid that the rebels would take the capital, neither Caballero nor Pozas had prepared detailed plans for the supply of the city; nor had they realized that in the event of the failure of the rebels to carry the metropolis by storm, Varela's army would be vulnerable to a well-planned counteroffensive. The Catalans, the Twelfth International Brigade, and a brigade of socialist militia from Levante had been sent toward Madrid, as had emergency supplies of matériel. But by November 9, only the battalion of "El Campesino's" peasant guerrillas, which had come down from the Sierra Guadarrama, had reached the city.

Throughout the day, General Varela, driven on by General Mola, maintained a remorseless pressure against the entire Madrid front. Column Nos. 5 and 2, the units assigned for feinting attacks on November 7, were strengthened from the reserves and thrown in deadly earnest against the Toledo bridge and the Princess bridge. Twice the Moroccan tabors broke through the lines and twice they were driven back before the gap in the front could be exploited by the rest of the rebel columns. In front of University City, the Eleventh International Brigade held on, its companies growing thinner under the unceasing fire of the rebel artillery. A few Soviet bombers came over the battlefield of Casa de Campo, hitting the column of Italian tanks moving toward the city.

Column Nos. 1 and 4, strengthened by units of the Civil Guards, continued their attacks in Casa de Campo, completing the conquest of Garabitas Heights and threatening to turn the northern flank of the Madrid defenders.

Faced with this crisis of the defense, General Kleber resolved upon a desperate expedient. He replaced the International battalions at University City and Villaverde with picked Spanish troops and regrouped the surviving units of the International Brigades in Casa de Campo. Without waiting for the promised reserves, for in so doing he would have gambled the life of the city, General Kleber, gathering what Spanish units he could spare from the other sectors as support, ordered his International battalions to attack.

Led by the Germans of the Edgar André, the Eleventh International Brigade pushed into the Casa de Campo at the northeast end, in the area where the Coruña highway ran into the outskirts of Madrid. At the same moment that the Internationals were advancing into what was a no-man's-land, the Moroccans were also advancing under the cover of a strong artillery barrage. The starry night turned cloudy, and the mists, swirling around the scrub oaks of the park, cut visibility to practically zero. Here, under the command of a Red Army general, veterans of all the revolutionary upheavals of postwar Europe, university students from Cambridge and Oxford, White Russians believing that the road to Moscow and home ran through Madrid, veteran soldiers and youths entering battle for the first time, advanced with fixed bayonets toward Varela's Army of Africa.

Well beyond the banks of the Manzanares, the two armies met, the Internationals ordered forward to the charge with the cry "For the Revolution and for Liberty."

Then, for the first time, the men of the Fifth Regiment fighting with the army of the Comintern saw the tabors of Moroccans and the banderas of the Foreign Legion break before the steady fire of machine guns and the line of bayonets, as company by company the men of Kleber pressed forward. Ridge after ridge of the great park was cleared as the battle went on throughout the night and most of the next morning. Verla's troops fell back slowly, leaving their mounds of dead under the ilex trees, leaving prisoners, carrying their wounded, but cheated of the coveted city that lay beyond the Manzanares River; robbed of the prize that would have meant glory to their commander, victory for the rebellion, loot beyond the wildest dreams of the African tribesmen, who had been promised the gold of the Bank of Spain in exchange for the German Reichsmarks of 1923 with which their pockets were crammed.

One-third of the foreigners who had paraded up the Gran Vía on November 8 were dead. Prematurely thrown into offensive operations due to the failure of the Republican High Command to rush reserves to the city, they had broken the back of Colonel Yagüe's northern attack group and won the time that was necessary to complete General Goriev's system of fortifications and Lieutenant-Colonel Rojo's reorganization of the militia. And if the price for this time won back from the chaos of the Republic's wasted months was high, the men who paid for it with their blood did so without bitterness. And the price paid was another down payment. In the weeks that followed, the price for each day of time won went up. And others came to pay it.

ROBERT COLODNY served in Spain until he was wounded at the battle of Brunete. Later he served in World War II in the U.S. Signal Corps, the Air Corps, and worked as a military historian, lecturer, and analyst of Axis radio propaganda. After the war he received a Ph.D. in history and philosophy and taught at the universities of California, San Francisco State, Wesleyan, Kansas, and Pittsburgh. He has published several books, including *The Struggle for Madrid* (1958), from which this selection is taken. He is now retired professor emeritus at the University of Pittsburgh.

· Bill Bailey ·

Swastika Off the *Bremen*

July 25— Word got down to the seamen's section from the district. All seamen were to gather at the French Workers' Club uptown the following day to discuss plans for a demonstration at the pier of the North German Lloyd. There, the S.S. *Bremen* was berthed, preparing to sail for Germany the same night. Well, at last we were going to do something, whatever it was. I met Robbie after receiving the word. "What's it all about?" I asked him.

"The district leadership worked out some plan. From the way I hear it, there will be a big demonstration at the front of the pier about an hour before the *Bremen* sails. We will try to get as many people aboard as possible. What's expected of them is as soon as the 'all ashore' whistle blows they're to form a corridor of people to the bow. One or two of our guys will rush up and grab the swastika, dash back through the line and bring it ashore where it will be turned over to the demonstrators to pour gasoline on it and publicly burn it. That's the plan."

"Who the hell worked out plans like that?" I asked, astonished.

"Some lunkhead who never saw a ship before, I suppose," he replied.

July 26— Following instructions we put on our best clothes. I looked good in my new suit and my panama hat that I had purchased two weeks before. The three of us, Pat Gavin, a big burly Irish seaman, Blair, and myself headed for the French Workers' Club. Since we were early we stopped at a restaurant close to the club for a sandwich.

"The plan sounds stupid," I told Blair.

"No one who knows ships would ever dare propose such an unthinkable plan," Blair said. "Just think for a moment what they're asking us to do. We may be lucky just to get aboard the ship, let alone walk ashore with their swastika."

"I suppose," chimed in Pat, "that they want us to fold it neatly before we take it ashore. Sounds like we're getting into another fiasco."

At the club we were joined by many others, some we knew and others we saw for the first time. No one had any control of who was walking into the building or sitting down in the small meeting hall. One thing was evident: everyone was nicely dressed, including the dozen or two women.

A member of the district leadership addressed the gathering of some fifty people. "This is the way we'll play it," he said. "Ten of our maritime comrades will be stationed on the main deck. When the "go ashore" whistle blows, just ten minutes before they pull in the gangway, two women," and he introduced the young women, "will handcuff themselves to the mast and throw away the key. Then the seamen will make a rush for the bow, haul down the swastika, race back to the gangway and get off the ship. The crew will be diverted from the flag by the shouting of the handcuffed women. There should be no problems. Once off the ship the flag will be handed to the chairman of the demonstration and it will be burned in front of the crowd. Comrade Burney will pass out a dime to each comrade who will board the ship. That's the cost of boarding as a visitor. Just remember, you have to make it appear that you're going aboard to see someone off. So act cautiously until you get on board and perform the job you're assigned to. If there are no questions, let's get down to the ship." Before we had a chance to question some parts of the strategy, the meeting was over and the crowd was on its way to the ship.

Pat Gavin was no Johnnie-come-lately to the struggle for human rights. As a youngster in Ireland, he fought on the side of the Irish Republican Army for Ireland's freedom against England's Black and Tans. Since his first days in the United States he had allied himself with the revolutionary struggle of the people and given a good account of himself at demonstrations or picket lines. He was always a good man to have at your side in the event of trouble. He walked with Blair and me to the pier.

The three of us had come to the conclusion that if by chance we were arrested, it would be less effective if we said we were Communists out to demonstrate against Hitler. Instead, if we said we were Catholics demonstrating against Hitler's terrorism against the German Catholics and other religious groups, that probably would be stronger and more effective. Since that was the plan we decided to follow, we cleaned out our pockets of all identifications and bought some prayer beads, a crucifix, and some sundry medals of various saints. As seamen we knew that the halyard ropes the swastika was attached to were strong; we would need something to cut them. A few safety-razor blades would do.

On the Upper West Side, for two blocks on either side of the pier, cars were looking for parking space, as hundreds of people slowly made their way to the ship. The *Bremen* stood motionless alongside the pier. Her bow jutted up, looming over the street. Large, powerful floodlights stationed in various parts of the ship directed their beams to one spot on the bow, the jackstaff, which held the Nazi swastika fluttering brazenly in the summer breeze. It seemed that all New York could look out their windows and see this flag lit up like a house on fire.

Some vendors had taken up positions at the gate of the pier, selling souvenirs such as little Nazi flags, buttons, pictures of the *Bremen*, postcards, etc. It was a carnival atmosphere from the gate to the gangway. Pat bought himself a Nazi button and pinned it on his coat. Blair and I bought little flags depicting some German castle with the word "Vaterland" written below the castle. It would all be good camouflage to make our appearance aboard the *Bremen* friendly and beyond suspicion. Making it appear that we were slightly drunk, and waving our banners, we made our way to the crowded deck of the *Bremen*.

Things took on a new perspective as we viewed our task from another vantage point. From where we were cordoned off to the bow and the swastika seemed like miles away. It would be impossible to carry out the original plan of someone going to the bow, grabbing the flag, and returning through a protective aisle of men to bring the flag ashore. Those who made these plans were fools with no conception of the deck of the ship. Crew members were lounging around the forward deck as many do prior to sailing. Besides the crew, there were three or four sea-breakers that would have to be hurdled. They were at least three feet high and ran the width of the forward deck. As if this were not enough, the jackstaff was held on top of a seven-foot rise on the bowsprit. It would take time to hurdle the sea-breakers and climb the bowsprit. The "planners" in their ivory tower were of the foolish belief that, once the action started, the crew would be most sympathetic to our cause and do nothing. Fools or dreamers!

We began to recognize some of the faces among the crowd that moved slowly and almost aimlessly in the short space near the gangway. Our watches said it was 9:20. In ten minutes the whistle would be heard. Bellhops and stewards would circulate in the passageways and along the decks saying loudly, "All ashore that's going ashore." This was the agreed upon signal for some of us to reach the bow. We moved closer to another small group that stood at the railing.

It was obvious to all of us aboard that for purposes other than sailing the original plan could not work. No, sir. No chance. Whatever we could agree on doing had to be put into effect within the next ten minutes. The demonstrators on the dock were growing in numbers and becoming louder. Within an hour their ranks had swelled from a few hundred to a few thousand and more were coming. Banners and placards by the hundreds were on display: "Free Ernst Thaelmann . . . Free Lawrence Simpson . . . Down with Anti-Semitism . . . Unite Against War and Fascism." The roar and the noise of the crowd attracted the crew members lolling on the forward deck. They all shifted over to the starboard or offshore side to better lean over and watch the demonstrators. That helped us adopt a new plan quickly. Some ten or fifteen of our seamen were on board. At the sound of the whistle, Bill Howe, George Blackwell, and Ed Drolette were to work their way up the starboard deck toward the bow. This should distract any crew members on the forward deck to move to the starboard side. Our small group on the port side would then try to make it to the bow, unhindered, we hoped. We took our positions, getting closer to the rail, knowing that only seconds remained.

The sharp, shrill blast of the whistle was met by a loud roar of the demonstrators on the dock. The summons of "All ashore that's going ashore" could be heard on the loudspeakers. Our men on the starboard side started to move forward. When "Low Life" McCormick, standing next to Blair and me, moved out of our group toward the bow, he was quickly grabbed by the officer at the gangway who said, "Sir, you're going the wrong way. The gangway is in this direction," pointing to the gangway. McCormick quickly brought up a right-hand punch that knocked the officer flat on his back in view of the crowd now pressing near the gangway to get ashore. Women screamed, and the captain and other high commanding officers who looked down from the bridge on this whole scene shouted orders to stop our men now racing toward the bow.

On the starboard side our men were slow in moving toward the bow. We on the port side had covered a greater distance and were now attracting the attention of the crew members who were leaning over the starboard railing. They started moving toward the port side. Halfway up that deck, McCormick was stopped again, this time by a young officer and a crew member. They argued some, but Blair and myself and Gavin could not afford the luxury of standing back to protect one member. We had to keep pressing forward.

Now it was Gavin's turn to come face to face with two members of the crew. He wasted no time in throwing lefts and rights at them. Blair and I raced ahead. Only a few feet more to the bow. By now, other crew members had discovered the men moving forward on the starboard side and a battle ensued. Crew members were appearing from all over the ship as the captain shouted orders over the loudspeakers for all crew members to get to the bow immediately.

A sailor grabbed Blair by the neck and tried pulling him down to the deck. Blair had uncovered one end of his fountain pen and was vigorously jabbing the pointed end of the pen into the face of the sailor. I felt the urge to stop and yank the German off Blair. The sailor seemed to be subduing Blair. Instead, I hurdled the last sea-breaker and grabbed the first rung on the short ladder leading to the bowsprit.

Pandemonium was all about me as I reached the top. The Nazi symbol was just a few inches from me. I drew a breath, oblivious of the thousands of screaming, yelling demonstrators now able to look up and see the action. In back of me I could hear the screams of the passengers, the barking of orders in German by the captain, and the blowing of police whistles as dozens of policemen were boarding the *Bremen.*

I grabbed the swastika and started to pull. The banner at first resisted, but then I heard the sound of the banner ripping along the seam. Still, it was hanging onto the halyard. I yanked some more. It would not part. I grew panicky. Time was getting short. Goddam this flag. It seems to be stronger than canvas. Why won't this rope part? I had to be careful, one misstep and I would be over the side into the Hudson River. I grabbed the Swastika more firmly, preparing to give it my all, when I noticed a pair of hands reaching up to grasp the top rung. My first instinct was to bring my foot down on the hands, thinking a member of the crew was coming to get me. But in the next second I recognized one our guys, Adrian Duffy, a short, wiry seaman reaching the top. "Hold the bastard tight," he shouted. A snap of a switchblade knife and quick slash at the rope. The flag was free. Quickly, I tossed it overboard as the roar of the crowd reached a deafening crescendo. When I turned to get off the bowsprit, Duffy was gone. I noticed that Blair was still receiving wallops from several crew members. I jumped down to the deck, stumbled when I tried to get up and fell forward. Two crew members grabbed me and pulled me to my feet.

A quick glance showed Blair lying stretched out on deck. I did not waste time after I delivered a blow to one guy that knocked him over one of the sea-breakers; the other panicked and stepped back a few feet. Looking for a safe way down the deck, I saw him again moving toward me. For a moment our eyes seemed focused on each other. For that split second I had the feeling he was telling me, "Good work, comrade, but I have to put up a front." I did not wait for any confirmation of such wishful thinking. As soon as he came within striking distance I swung out at him, catching him on the jaw. He fell back.

But a wallop in back of the head, another on the back, and I was down. I tried to get up and noticed three crew members standing over me. A kick in the solar plexus knocked the wind out of me, and then a kick in the forehead and I started to see varied colored lights and then another kick that caught me in the jaw. Stupefied, immobilized, I lay sprawled against the deck railing. It could not have been more than five or ten minutes when I was lifted to my feet and half dragged toward the gangway. Through swollen eyelids I could make out a mass of angry and stunned people blocking my way as cops shouted, "Open up, let us through."

A voice could be heard, "Why they're all young punks, probably college kids," and the crowd parted and I was once more on the dock.

I was taken toward a small booth, used by the ship's officers to validate the passenger tickets. Horrified, I saw one man lying on his back, blood over all his face. The cops dragging me shouted to the bloodied figure, "Is this the guy?"

The figure looked at me. "No," he mumbled.

Quickly I was taken out, walked a few feet from the booth, then taken back in again. "This is the guy, right?" said the cop.

The bloodied figure looked at me again. "No," he said.

After that I stayed in the booth and was told to sit down. "Low Life" McCormick was already there. His ear was badly bloodied, with blood running down the side of his face. Bill Howe sat next to him, and next to Bill, George Blackwell. Blair was dragged in, holding his stomach and bruised in the face. They dragged in Drolette and laid him almost at our feet. He had been shot and his mid-section was soaked with blood. He lay there moaning in pain, yet conscious.

I could hear the steel door closing on the pier as the gangway was pulled away from the ship. A series of whistle blasts from the *Bremen,* and she was pulling away from the dock. Where only minutes before hundreds of passengers and visitors had lolled on the dock, an equal number of policemen were now clearing the dock of all civilians.

Ambulances and doctors arrived, and quickly we were all

checked over. Blair was taken to the hospital. Drolette was placed on a stretcher and removed. The doctors threw a bandage on McCormick's ear. The medics wiped some blood off my face and commented that it wasn't necessary to take me to the hospital. The bloodied figure that lay on deck got the most attention. We found out that he was a Jewish detective by the name of Solomon. The cops carried him out with loving care, cursing us as they passed him to a special ambulance. With the wounded out of the way, the four of us sat in the booth contemplating our fate.

With over two hundred cops now occupying the pier, all sorts of possible dilemmas had to be considered. Knowing the brutality of the New York cops toward radicals was one thing. Knowing how they feel when one of their own is killed or injured is another. Here we were in a pier occupied only by cops, and every few minutes cops sauntered over to the booth to look in on us with a scowl of hatred on their faces.

One thing was certain. The way I saw the picture, we were going to get worked over. Who was there to say that we didn't receive our injuries while trying to escape? Almost three quarters of an hour had passed since the ship departed. What the hell are they waiting for? The suspense is killing.

Two cops from the harbor patrol walked into the booth, dressed in their blue overalls. The riot call must have brought the patrol boats to the scene. I had a cigarette in my mouth as this cop moved closer. He took a slow look at each of us. You could sense that he wanted some further provocation before striking out. He found it. "Who told you to smoke?" He then slapped the cigarette out of my mouth.

From my vantage point I could see through the window to the inside of the pier, where the cops had now formed a circle. A high-ranking officer in gold braid was speaking to them. We could not hear what was being said. Then the circle broke up and the cops lined up into two lines facing each other but staying at least two feet apart. "On yer feet, yer bastards," said a sergeant. We were escorted out of the booth and slowly made our way down the steps through the line of cops to the outside of the pier. The streets were empty of demonstrators. Only dozens of police cars and motorcycles were evident.

Into a large paddy wagon we were pushed, the door slammed

shut, and we moved out with motorcycles in front and more police cars in back of us. As our motorcade of New York's "finest" moved closer to the precinct station, they had to battle their way up the street, since the demonstrators had shifted from the pier of the *Bremen* to the police station, blocking the streets. Hundreds of cops had to converge on the demonstrators to clear a path to the door amid cries of "here they come."

Upstairs in the detectives' room we sat waiting for what was to come next. We could hear the demonstrators yelling and banging the lids of garbage cans. A detective at the typewriter got up to shut the window. "I wish it was legal. I'd love to turn a machine gun on them bastards," he said eyeing us. There had to be more to this than just sitting around. I could not visualize a detective getting "worked over" and we sitting here with all our limbs intact. I passed word to the others: This would be a testing of our convictions; it's usually the first one or two blows that are the toughest, but remember we are just anti-fascists pissed off against Hitler for what he did to Simpson and religious people in general.

A detective walked out of one of the side rooms, took a good look at each one of us, then told McCormick to follow him. They both entered the room, the door banged shut behind them. A few minutes later there came the sound of something banging against the wall, then the door opened and McCormick came barging out with the detective following him and kicking him as he hustled back to his seat alongside us. "What happened in there?" I asked McCormick.

"One bull wanted me to admit that we were all Communists and following orders to sabotage the *Bremen*. When I told him he was wrong, he gave me a few clouts and threw me out."

The streets had now been cleared of demonstrators. Quiet prevailed. Our "life history" had been taken down on paper by the clerk. Once again we were hustled into a police van and moved downtown to the central police headquarters, where we were lined up for fingerprinting and pictures. A white-haired police captain with a strong Irish brogue walked over to where we were sitting, and to each man he said, "And what would your name be?" Jotting down the names, he looked puzzled, then in a whisper that I could overhear, he told another policeman, "Why, they're all Irish! There's not a Jew amongst them."[. . .]

BILL BAILEY was born in New Jersey and has been a seaman and member of the National Maritime Union, sailing off both coasts and to almost every port in the world. He completed his working life as a longshoreman and member of the International Longshoremen's and Warehousemen's Union in San Francisco, and retired to spend his time writing. He has published many short stories and articles, and has appeared in several films, including *Seeing Red*, *The Good Fight*, and *On the Edge*. This piece is from his forthcoming autobiography.

· Tom Page ·

Interview with a Black Anti-Fascist

A: I wasn't getting my share of the pie. I just didn't have a job and I wanted a job. And not being . . . too well-qualified, there were very few jobs that I could do. I learned to wait on table. And, what else did I learn to do? Oh! How to rack balls in a pool hall. That kind of job . . . that paid nothing.

Q: Were you active? I mean, were you active in terms of opposing fascism?
A: In the unemployment councils—that's where I was particularly active. Going out on demonstrations—any demonstrations against war and fascism, I would be there! Over the subway turnstile, 'cause I didn't have a nickel! And go. . . . This is what I would do. And—the beautiful thing about that—the feeling of camaraderie, that everyone had a oneness, a singleness of purpose. Everyone—irrespective of their color, or their sex. [This is] a wonderful feeling . . . from being rejected to being accepted as a person. . . .

Q: Did you have to tell your parents about going to Spain?
A: Of course not! I mean, I was, I think I was twenty-one by that time. I didn't have to tell them what I was going to do, or why I was doing it. You know, Spain was an experience that I wouldn't forgo for anything. There, too, I got the feeling that I got at those demonstrations. Persons see me as me. Not as a black. They see me as an individual. And judge me as such. They judged me as

Tom Page, not as anybody else, or Tom Page, black. Just Tom Page.

Spain was the first time in my life I was treated as a person. . . . I was a man! A person! And I love it very much.

Q: Could you form really close relationships in Spain, was it hard to do that?
A: (sighs) Well, if you're living and fighting and dying with somebody, it gets kinda close, it doesn't take too long.

. . . Some of the wounded Spaniards whose mothers would bring me an egg when I was in the hospital. If you know the meaning of that . . . cause those people were starving, you know, and they brought me an egg. And I was—all torn up inside, cause I knew they were depriving themselves of food. And I thought [clears throat] . . . I knew I was doing the correct thing, I thought, "Here I am fighting for their country," they appreciated what I was doing, and this is one of their ways of showing it. . . .

Q: How did the Brigaders' consciousness of what was going on in the world show in the way that they fought?
A: When you are fighting in a people's army, you know, you are fighting . . . you are conscious of what you're doing, . . . you do this, not because you're drafted, conscripted, but because you volunteered. . . . That's why they're awful hard to beat. . . . There were no blacks who came back here who turned for the McCarthy committee or any other kind of committee. HUAC, the House Un-American Activities committee . . . no blacks ever testified before them. . . .

Q: So what feelings, when you think of Spain, what feelings do you retain? What comes up for you?
A: First, the feeling of warmth. Then the . . . feeling of human dignity . . . and the feeling of camaraderie. This was Spain's meaning to me. And I get very emotional about Spain. Probably I don't show it, but I do. . . . It's the first time in my life that I was treated with dignity . . . treated as a human being, as a *man!* [. . .]

Q: Tell us about the war.
A: Just like that! Tell us about war! War . . . I . . . you can't

describe war, war is something you have to experience for youself in order to get an accurate feeling about it. . . . The civilians . . . suffer more, I think, than soldiers. There's the bombing. . . . There's the hunger. . . . There's the cold weather. There's the hot weather. There's the wounded, who suffer miserably. There's the dead, who are probably the luckiest of all. What can I tell you about war? War's horrible. War is obscene . . . that's the only word I think that can describe war. . . . But you have to have war if you want to have any modicum of freedom, you have to protect your dignity, and if it takes war to do that, you have to have war. [. . .]

Q: So are you proud that you went?
A: Absolutely. . . . Absolutely. Yes. . . . As I said before, I hated to come back . . . hated to come back here, 'cause this is the home of reaction, where blacks are concerned, . . . 'cause I know them, being one myself. [Clears throat] Yes.

TOM PAGE was born in 1909. He was one of about eighty black men who fought in Spain. He served on the southern front and then in the major actions of the Aragon and Ebro offensives. After returning to the United States, he became a freelance photographer and then a technician for the New York Telephone Company. The excerpts included here are taken from a taped interview with the producer-directors of *The Good Fight*, the award-winning documentary on the Brigade made by Noel Bruckner, Mary Dore, and Samuel Sills.

· C. H. ·

To the Editor, *The Volunteer*

The wives whose men went off to fight in the Spanish war felt quite different from those whose husbands fought in wars throughout history when their own countries were involved. The ALB [Abraham Lincoln Brigade] men went to fight in a far-away war that seemingly had nothing to do with their own nation; they went voluntarily and in defiance of their government.

This couldn't help but cause mixed feelings, even though the wives shared the same beliefs as their husbands. One couldn't help but wonder why their love and marriage was secondary to some principles or ideals. Was the marriage shaky and in need of a respite? Were you less dedicated than he in your convictions?

The first news of the Republic's fight against fascism shook me in an objective political sense since it was a question of democracy versus military dictatorship. But I was appalled when my own husband suddenly determined to fight in that war. It immediately changed the war from an abstract intellectual political matter to a very personal and emotional situation. How could I take seriously that this man who was my husband would be so foolhardy as to volunteer?

Desperately I hoped to talk him out of it, and so did our friends and relatives. But we both had a good laugh when someone said with a perfectly straight face, "Of course you're anti-fascist, but do you have to take it so seriously?" Somehow that remark made me realize that I could no longer stand in the way or be dilettante about fascism. Yes, you had to be serious about it—enough to let your husband leave you and go to war.

Of course I knew nothing of the involved arrangements that had to be made, but I well knew the pain of breaking up our cozy little apartment and closing the door (temporarily? permanently?) on our life together. He left on the long and devious journey to Spain, I to the Midwest as a CIO union organizer; both too young to fully comprehend the course on which we had each embarked or the perils ahead.

Each day the newspapers were a barometer for my fears and apprehensions. Though I had to believe that their reports of the war were biased, it nevertheless filled me with gloom and foreboding. I lived from letter to letter, knowing that as of the last date on the envelope he was at least alive. But then letters came so infrequently and were so heavily censored that they were hardly reassuring.

The continuing blockade of Spain by the world's democracies added to my anguish and I tried desperately to aid protests against the blockade, even sending a personal cable to Leon Blum, urging him to lift the embargo.

Meeting other women whose loved ones were also in the International Brigade brought some solace, along with new friendships. But in the end, when there was no word for weeks or months, you anguished alone, especially as the end drew near for the Republic.

The mix of political convictions with emotional gut feelings is always tenuous and subjective at best. When youth is spirited and life experiences beckon, two or three years of separation proved too much for some relationships and they became unglued, another cost of political ideals and convictions. But in light of the spread of fascism and the world conflagration that followed, there is no doubt in my mind that the men who fought in the ALB were the best that humanity could offer in the struggle against evil. And I am still proud to have played a little part in that momentous panorama of our times.

C.H. is the wife of a volunteer who wishes to remain anonymous.

· Irving Fajans ·

Tourists to Lyon

"There were perhaps thirty other Americans already seated when Butch Johnson and I entered the room. We unfolded a couple of chairs and sat down in the back near the door.

We were pretty jittery. Coming to Paris to volunteer for the International Brigades, in the face of State Department opposition, had not been easy. Our passports had been stamped "Not Valid for Travel in Spain or China," and the week's stopover in Paris, while the committee in the Maison des Syndicats arranged the trip down to the closed French-Spanish border and over the Pyrenees, had increased the danger of our being picked up as "illegal volunteers" and either shipped back to the States or thrown into a French jail.

We fidgeted around for a while in uneasy silence. "What's holding up the works?" Butch whispered after a quarter of an hour had passed.

"How should I know?" I replied. "Although there is a story in the morning paper that the government won't open the frontier and will take additional precautions to prevent volunteers from reaching the border."

"Precautions my eye," Butch said. "We could have crawled down to the border on our hands and knees by this time."

Our conversation was interrupted by the appearance of the chairman of the committee, who proceeded in careful English to outline the difficulties that lay before us on our trip to the Pyrenees.

"The French people," he said, "are overwhelmingly in sympathy with the Spanish Republic. Unfortunately, and for reasons I will not go into, the government has seen fit to keep the frontier closed.

"Many Frenchmen have gone to Spain to fight and many others are cooperating in getting volunteers over the Pyrenees. However, France is filled with fascist agents who would desperately like to know how men are aided to join the Loyalists. Most are German and Italian, but some are French agents working for the Croix de Feu. It is for this reason that we must ask all of you to obey our instructions implicitly and conduct yourselves discreetly. Just last week, a group of Americans were arrested in Carcassonne and sentenced to forty days in jail.

"You are leaving for Lyon tonight. If you are questioned, you will say that you are American tourists who have come for the French Exposition and are traveling around the country waiting for it to open. One of your number, Comrade Johnson, will be given full instructions and he will be responsible for you during this part of the trip.

"You will be at the Gare de Lyon at 7:30. There will be many other volunteers of other nationalities taking the same train. Under no circumstances will you speak to anyone. If there should be any difficulty, look for Johnson and he will tell you what to do.

"Just a last few things before I give you your railroad tickets. It is an overnight trip and the train has no dining car, so I suggest you provide yourselves with some food. Your luggage should be sent home, but if you wish, you may bring it here and we will forward it to Spain when the border is opened. Also, it might be a good idea to buy a beret and discard the hats you are wearing as they identify you immediately as Americans.

"If there are no questions, I should like to close this meeting by wishing you the best of luck. Will Comrade Johnson please remain for a few minutes?"

Everyone felt better. At least, we were moving in the direction of Spain. The businesslike instructions had quieted some of our uneasiness and the tourist story was certainly more plausible than any we had been able to devise for ourselves.

I got my ticket and some tags for the luggage and went out into the hall to wait for Butch, wondering what they could possibly be telling him. It would be pretty rough if we had to duck fascist agents and the Garde Mobile all the way down to the border.

In a few minutes Butch came out of the room. He scarcely saw me, so hard was he concentrating on the words he was repeating to himself.

"What are you mumbling about?" I asked, catching up to him.

"The password," he said. "I'm supposed to meet a guy in the station at Lyon and give him the password."

We returned to our hotel, stuffed some extra socks and toothpaste into our pockets, tagged our luggage, and checked out. On the way back to the Maison des Sindicats with our bags, we stopped and bought two berets.

"How do I look?" Butch asked, pulling the beret down over his right eye.

"Stick a paint brush in your hand and you're a dead ringer for Picasso," I said.

"Well, you're not exactly my idea of Pepe le Moko," he said, with another yank at the beret.

We dumped the luggage and walked in a leisurely fashion to the Gare de Lyon, stopping for a couple of beers and to get some sandwiches put up.

The station was crowded. We made our way to the Lyons express and took a position close to the entrance of a third-class coach. Soon little knots of two and three men gathered along the length of the train. All carried little paper packages of food. In addition, most had acquired bottles of wine and the corked tops peeked coyly out of their bulging pockets. And all, carrying out the instructions of the committee to the letter, had purchased berets.

Some secret stuff, I thought, looking at the clusters of blue-bereted heads. Any one mistaking us for tourists could also be convinced that Americans visited the Folies Bergère for cultural purposes.

"Not a weeping wife in sight," Butch said. "Let's get on the train before they trot out the band and play the 'Internationale.'"

We found a couple of seats in a compartment that was already partially occupied. No one said a word. Men in berets tramped up and down in the corridor outside, looking for empty places.

Finally, the train pulled out of the station. Still no one spoke. I fixed my attention on the little tassle on Butch's beret. An hour passed. Every time I moved my head, my neck creaked like a wicker porch-chair after a day in the sun. Suddenly a man burst into our compartment.

"Which one of you is Johnson?"

"Me," said Butch.

"Then come on, we've got a fascist in our compartment."

"How do you know?"

"No beret. Besides he's been asking a lot of questions."

"Save my seat," Butch said. "I'll be right back."

What would Butch do, toss him off the train? I lit a cigarette and leaned back. Time passed. The train whistled for a curve . . . once . . . twice. On the third screech, Butch returned.

"What's the score?" I asked with a sidelong glance at our fellow travelers.

"Nothing to nothing," Butch said. "He's probably the only legitimate passenger on the train. He lives in Lyon and was only trying to be sociable."

There were no further alarms and after a while I dozed off. It was just growing light when the sudden braking of the train jerked me awake.

"We're coming into Lyon," Butch said.

We got off the train and Butch hurried away to make his contact. The station was soon crowded by the detraining volunteers. The baggage porters who had hurried to the steps of the coaches, backed away incredulously, as man after man stepped down without so much as an overnight bag in his hand. Other early risers gave dubious welcome to the foot stamping, face massaging, clothes brushing, invasion *des touristes*.

Soon groups of men were leaving the station. Where was Butch? Standing near the station master's office, two gendarmes regarded us suspiciously. Where was Butch? Soon, only our group of Americans was left on the platform. I debated with myself whether to show some initiative and get the men out of the station and into a café, but before I had time to make a decision, Butch appeared, trailed by a small, blond-haired child, who couldn't have been more than six.

"This is Odette," he said. "She'll show us where to go."

"Are you kidding?" I said, studying the six-year-old Mata Hari.

"Don't worry, she's done this before. Her old man was the contact, but he's down with the grippe."

"Real conspiratorial stuff," I said.

We paired off at ten-yard intervals and trailed the child out of the station. At the end of the block, she turned down a narrow shop-lined street. We tagged behind, elaborately casual—tourists out for the morning air. I looked back. Stretching for a full block were pairs of blue berets.

Shopkeepers, raising their iron shutters, and black-shawled women with their market baskets watched our curious procession pass. Tongues clucked and heads shook. As we neared the corner, a woman detached herself and asked the child if anything was wrong. Odette backed away frightened and started to run.

"Come on!" Butch yelled. I turned my head. The whole line of berets started to bob up and down. Suddenly, she turned the corner. "Don't lose her!" Butch panted. I speeded up and rounded the corner. She was nowhere in sight. I ran a few more feet and stopped. Gasping for breath, the line accordioned up on me. We stood there for a moment at a loss as to our next move. The neighborhood, now fully aroused, eyed us with sympathetic amusement.

"M'sieu," the child's head appeared from behind a door to a stable, "Ici."

"Some secrecy," I said as we entered.

"Some tourists," said Butch, pulling his beret from his head and slapping it against the rump of a sad-faced horse.

IRVING (TOOTS) FAJANS was born in Brooklyn in 1915. Before he went to Spain he was an organizer for the Department Store Workers' Union. He went to Spain and was severely wounded in the battle of Brunete. After a period of convalescence he volunteered for the U.S. army and served in the OSS. After the war he was a film editor, and served as the VALB's executive secretary. He died in 1967. This piece is from *Heart of Spain*, the anthology of writings published by the VALB in 1952.

· Steve Nelson ·

Doing It the Hard Way

[. . .] We docked at Le Havre and took the train to Paris. I went to see Arnold Reid, who handled arrangements for getting volunteers into Spain. "Here's how we stand," he said. "They're shipping out as fast as possible, but we have to be careful. We can't risk a collision with the French government: we can't give them an excuse to shut us down. The borders are sealed, and if a volunteer's caught, it's jail and deportation. This damned nonintervention is making it difficult to get men across. Some of the boys have to wait a long time—too long. The Volunteers' Committee has them scattered around under cover. Ever hear of the Red Belt? Most villages around Paris—working-class districts on the outskirts—have Communist or Socialist mayors councils. They're taking care of most of our fellows. I think I can get you and Joe in soon, but don't count on it."

There were twenty-five men leaving in our group, of which Joe Dallet, who spoke French, was the leader. I had seen some of them on the boat coming over. The rest were strangers, but you could spot them. We were scattered throughout the railroad station in clusters of five—American tourists, most of us in our early twenties, wearing berets and carrying no luggage. Fine tourists. We stood around, conspicuously trying to be inconspicuous, eyeing each other and watching Joe. I was glad to be going with Joe and glad to be moving toward the frontier after only four days' delay in Paris.

The train announcer called our departure for Arles, and at Joe's signal, we rushed on board. Obeying earlier instructions, we spread out through the cars, two or three to a compartment. Joe and I found a place together near the middle of the train. He was full of excitement and responsibility. The men too were excited, and no one slept much that night. We kept telling each other we ought to sleep so as to be fresh for our hike over the mountains—for we all believed we would cross the Pyrenees into Spain the following night. Instead, we played pinochle and talked.

At dawn Joe noticed a peasant woman selling milk on the platform of a station where the train had halted. He bargained with her and returned triumphantly to the compartment carrying her whole supply, a two-gallon earthenware jar more than half full. All at once a horrified look came to his face. "Steve, everybody'll know I can't use this much milk myself! My God, I'll give the whole show away." But a brown-bearded man— already dubbed the "Professor"—had noticed some bottles in another compartment. The bottles were rinsed and filled with milk and passed around to the tourists. Within half an hour the milk was gone.

After an all-night ride we left the train at Arles, where a man in a yellow sweater stood on the platform, as Arnold had foretold. Joe stared at the man and gripped the right lapel of his coat. At this signal the man nodded and beckoned carelessly and walked away. Joe followed him. I followed Joe, the Professor followed me, and so on. Twenty-five men were strung out in single file, each one scared of losing sight of the man in front. It was an odd sight for the streets of a quiet little French town. Presently we realized we were making a show of ourselves, and we formed little groups of two or three, strolling carelessly. The man in the yellow sweater led us to the other side of town, where an ancient stone building stood beside a little stream.

It was the former poorhouse and had been fixed up for us. Joe learned that the mayor was one of us and that the little town of Arles was already taking care of seventy-five Spanish refugees besides all the volunteers that came through, all out of the people's own pockets. In addition to us, there were fifty other Americans awaiting their trip into Spain.

We were dismayed to find we had to stay overnight and that the others had been waiting for four days. Joe reassured us that if we had to stay a day or two, it was because it was necessary. There was no point in complaining.

We crossed the alley to an enormous building, stone below and clapboard on the second floor, where we were to sleep. The lower floor had been a stable. We climbed wide rickety stairs to the loft, and Lou Secundi, who was later to become transport officer for the International Brigades, came to greet us in his fluent Brooklynese. "Hiya, gang. Welcome to the Hotel des Anti-fascistes."

The "old-timers" gathered around to welcome us and show off the establishment. A potbellied stove stood on either side of the loft, and bales of straw were stacked against the walls. We were warned to be careful of fire. There were blankets in a corner, and the straw was to be our mattresses. There was not a light in the place, and everyone went to bed at dusk.

The first arrivals had established a routine of living, and Lou explained the rules at a joint meeting called immediately. "Now, guys, we got to make the best of this. After all, we're in for tougher things than this. I hope there'll be no complaining. You'll find there's an awful lot of work living in a place like this. In order to make things go smoother, we elected a house committee of three men. I suggest you fellows also elect three to that committee." We did that and settled in and waited.

Two days later our contingent moved out. We were taken by auto to another little town, nearer the Spanish border. Joe, I, and three others were quartered in the home of a French carpenter, a party member, whose wife greeted us like her own sons. All of us appreciated their kindness, but we wanted to get out of France.

Joe and some others were playing cards and the French woman was cooking lunch when a young man wearing leather puttees came in hurriedly and demanded to know who was in charge. Joe stood up. "I am." The man said, "All right, have your gang meet at the park right away. There'll be cars to pick you up. You're moving out."

"Wait a minute," Joe said. "Who are you? How do I know this is on the level?"

"It's all right," the man said. "I'm handling this district. I was going to Spain, but I got stuck here because I can speak French. I'm from Quebec. It's okay, man. Just get down to the park."

We loafed nervously around the park, trying to look like tourists. After a long anxious time, a taxi stopped, and its driver came quickly across the grass. He gave a signal with his right hand, and Joe answered the gesture. The man spoke in French, saying, "Five of you come with me." We got into the taxi and he banged the gears, just about lifting the car off the ground. Looking back, we saw another group of the boys piling into an old touring car.

One of the guys had never ridden in a taxi before. "Boy, this is good! Imagine going to Spain in a taxicab."

"Don't be a sap. How can we be going to Spain when we're bound east?" Joe pointed off to the right, where the Mediterranean lay.

But it was all right. We had come too close to the border and were being taken back to a little port where a boat would pick us up. Still, I didn't like going back the way we had come, with the border getting farther away instead of closer.

After an hour or so, the taxi stopped beside a long stretch of beach. There were a few little houses like summer cottages, with the windows boarded up, and a small stone pier stretching out into the water. We could see a village a mile or so away, and that was all. One by one other cars rolled up and stopped, until all twenty-five of us had been deposited on the beach. Each group as they arrived said the same thing: "What the hell is this? Where are we? Where's the boat?" And to each group Joe answered, "It'll be here. Take it easy." But Joe did not look easy. He was worried and glanced often out to sea. We were so conspicuous on the barren beach that anyone who saw us would know why we were there.

One. One-thirty. Two in the morning. We had been there since five the previous evening. Joe came over and whispered, "Maybe they can't find the place. Maybe they overshot us in the dark. If we're still here in the morning, all the gendarmes in France will be down on us." I said nothing, but Joe went on. "I got to do something," he said. But there was really nothing we could do.

Finally the boat came. The sleepers on the cottage verandas were kicked awake, and everyone ran for the pier, stumbling and falling in the soft sand and swearing excitedly. The boat was about thirty feet long, pointed at bow and stern, with a single mast and a one-cylinder engine. It was manned by two French fishermen. Joe, who had stood on the pier counting noses, was the last man aboard, and finally the boat began to move.

France was behind us. We were on a boat, and the boat was taking us to Spain. Some of the men shook hands solemnly, and others capered on the deck and cheered quietly. They stood around the deck trying to keep out of the way of the second boatman, who was setting the sail. They were anxious for him to get through with his work because Joe had told them that he would bring out food as soon as the boat was under way.

Joe was talking French to the man who stood at the tiller. From time to time he paused to translate hastily. The French comrades had been laboring over their engine since earliest morning. Moreover, the mayor of their village, a man unfriendly to the cause, had sent gendarmes to observe them, and it had been necessary to satisfy the gendarmes. They apologized for their lateness and brought greetings to the Americans from the comrades of their village. They wished us to know that this boat had been purchased with money raised by the party branch of their village—the gift of the French comrades to the Spanish people in their struggle. The men nearest the helmsman patted him on the back when they heard that. The boat represented a lot of money measured by the incomes of a handful of fishermen, railroad workers, teachers, and dock workers, and we knew that.

A dim glow came from the forward hatchway. Down in the hold, the second sailor had lit a lantern and was pulling out loaves of bread, long cylinders of sausage, round cheeses, strings of onions, and flasks of thin red wine. He arranged them on the floor of the hold, laying them on the gunnysacks in which they had been packed. He grinned up at the circle of heads peering hungrily over the hatch and motioned to us to come and eat. With the knife from his belt the sailor cut off chunks of bread, cheese, and salami; picked up a small, flat wine flask with a long spout projecting from it; and sprang up the ladder to the deck.

The helmsman said that they usually made the trip in six hours, but with the wind turning against us, they wouldn't be able to use the sail, and it would take longer. It would be light before we approached the Spanish town of Port-Bou.

I sat in the bow, straining my eyes to the right, trying to believe I could glimpse the looming mass of the Pyrenees. A streak of light showed in the east, and Joe called, "It's getting light. We'll have to go down in the hold pretty soon." The streak of light grew broader, and without orders from anyone, we went below. By common consent, in a common weariness, talking ceased, and some fell asleep.

Sunlight filtered through the cracks in the side of the boat and poured through the open hatchway. The air in the hold was thick with gasoline fumes from the engine and the smell of tar and old fish, onions, stale tobacco, and sweaty bodies. Some of the guys were bleary-eyed and others a bit cranky. Shorty Friedman yelled, "Hey! I can see the Pyrenees! *I can see Spain!*" He had his eyes glued to a crack in the planking. The others clustered around him, begging for a look, but he clung to his place. "Go find a peephole of your own. This is mine!"

At the knowledge that they were actually within sight of Spain, the men racketed around the cramped hold, talking and laughing. On deck one of the French sailors had spread fishing nets on frames. Occasionally he grinned down at the roistering Americans. Suddenly he called out to Joe in a sharp voice. Joe immediately commanded, "Something's happened. Everybody quiet."

We were still instantly. The hatch cover slid into place, leaving the hold in semidarkness. From somewhere outside we could hear the rapid throbbing of a diesel.

"Relax," I said. "It's probably a nonintervention patrol! The worst that can happen is we go to jail a while."

We heard a roar of chain slipping through a hawser hole. Joe groaned. "Oh God, they're anchoring! Quiet, everybody. Give me a chance to hear what's being said."

The French comrade, seated casually on the hatch cover, answered questions shouted at him from the patrol boat. Joe whispered translations. "They're asking him for his papers. The other comrade's getting them." Silence. The engines of both vessels were stopped. There was no sound but the lapping of the water against the side, and the heavy breathing of the men crowded in the hold. Then we heard a voice from the patrol boat. "What's he saying, Joe? What's he saying?"

"They want to know what cargo's being carried," Joe whispered. "Furniture, he says, furniture." Joe listened intently. "He's alongside now," he said. "Quick, scram over to the other side! Hurry!"

We crowded against the sides up into the bow, pressing away from the hatchway. We watched the hatchway and tried not to breathe. A streak of light appeared, and we could see the face of a French naval officer. The hatch cover slid back into place. "We're busted!" Joe said. He was still whispering, and none of us moved. "He's giving it to our comrade. 'Furniture!' he says, 'You're lying, Red; that's a fine kind of furniture. Here, catch this rope,' he says. They're going to tow us. Tear up everything you have—all the papers. I've got a list of some of the men who've gone to Spain. Grab some of the sheets—we'll have to eat this list, and do it fast."

Joe shouted in French toward the deck: "Comrade! Can we throw anything in the water?" He listened. "They say to stay down and not move. They're having to stand up there with their hands up. We're being towed to a French port. All you guys! Don't forget, we're American tourists! Everybody stick to that when they question us."

Tourists! Remarkable tourists, ragged, filthy, caught at dawn crammed into the hold of a fishing boat. I whispered to Joe, "We've got to change that story. We can't tell anybody we're tourists now. It's ridiculous."

"I know it's ridiculous. But we can't take it on ourselves to change the decision." Joe spoke aloud, and instantly the others were listening, their eyes intent on the two of us, to whom they looked for leadership.

"Circumstances have changed the decision for us. That cover was never meant for a thing like this. We must tell them we're volunteers for Spain," I insisted.

The men argued back and forth, but the roar of diesels had ceased. I cursed myself for not having foreseen the situation. We had thought of capture, worried about capture, ever since we got into the boat—and now, at the last narrow moment, we debated what to do in the face of capture. But there was no time. The boat was barely moving. "Listen. The French will support us," I argued. "It's our only chance. How can they organize a defense for a bunch of tourists?" I knew I had spoken badly, but some were nodding agreement. Joe, however, was still dubious.

The hatch opened, and we were ordered up on deck. I moved quickly to be first up the ladder. I was now convinced that we had to adopt new tactics.

A voice said, "Well, God almighty, what are we going to say?"

"Tell them the truth!" I answered over my shoulder as I climbed to the deck.

People were gathering on the pier and on the street nearby. They had seen the patrol boat coming in with the other vessel in tow and were curious. The crowd, composed mostly of men, kept growing. Nearly all of them wore blue shirts and dungarees, and many had bailing hooks stuck under their wide leather belts. I figured they were longshoremen, fishermen, and teamsters. They looked all right to me.

The French officer motioned us toward the gangplank, and the crowd moved closer, trying to get a better look at us. Near the gangplank I halted, snatched the beret from my head, and flung up my clenched fist. "Viva la República Española!" The men in blue shirts and dungarees roared back an answer: "Viva!" Their fists shot up, scores of them. Joe and the others behind me had their fists up too and were yelling. Joe bellowed, "Vive le Front Populaire!" and the crowd's answer shook the air. A gendarme ran up the gangplank and tugged at my arm, shouting. I followed him down the gangway through the ranks of the men in blue shirts and dungarees.

We marched through the cobblestone streets of the ancient town on our way to jail. Children ran into the streets, and women leaned from the windows or came hurrying from stores, shops, and little factories. We marched with our heads and fists up, and we grinned at them and shouted, "Long live the Spanish Republic! Long live the Popular Front!"

After a day in a crowded little jail in Port Vendres, where our boat had been impounded, the French police took us to the prison in Perpignan. The newspapers had headlined our arrests, accusing us of inciting the longshoremen of the port to riot and of defying the police and even the magistrate of the district. For three days we were kept with about fifty other prisoners in a small room pierced only by two tiny windows high up in the vaulted roof.

The American consul arrived on the fourth day, and Joe and I talked with him in the warden's office. He had little interest in our conditions and declined to inspect our cell. What he wanted was our passports, which we refused to give up.

After several days of confinement, I was feeling pretty helpless. On the fifth day, I was sitting on the floor, leaning back against the wall, idly watching Joe converse with a French prisoner on the other side of the room. They were crouching over a man lying next to the rusty coal stove that heated the cell. Joe suddenly beckoned for me to come over, "Look at this guy!"

The man on the floor, thin, dressed in ragged clothes, was scratching his left arm with a contrivance of pins. The arm was raw and bleeding. His shirt was unbuttoned, and his chest was a mess of festering sores. Joe called our guys together and said, "That guy by the stove's got syphilis or leprosy or something—I don't know. But if we get whatever's eating him, we're done for. No Spain. No nothing. Whatever it is, we've got to get him out of here."

We talked it over for a few minutes, and Joe translated our sense of urgency to the other prisoners. We then started banging on the iron doors to the bullpen, screaming for the warden. Within a half hour we had him in the cell looking at the sick man. The sight of the man's chest made the warden nauseous, and he had him taken to the infirmary.

Forcing the warden's hand was a real shot in the arm and won us the respect of the other prisoners, who were now willing to follow our lead. It was only the beginning. After listening to the warden berate us in both French and English, Joe and I presented a set of demands the men had agreed on. Flustered and unfamiliar with an organized presence in his prison, the warden relented. We secured an additional half hour in the yard each day and the right to empty the cans of filth from our cell twice daily and to disinfect them with lime and carbolic acid. Finally we won a transfer for half of the men to another, unoccupied bullpen. It was much like the other one, but it felt almost roomy after we had been jammed together for a week.

All the Americans had been transferred, and as soon as we were together, Joe called a meeting. "We've got lots of space now," he said, "and plenty of time. It looks like we'll be here for another two weeks, maybe longer. We can't just sit around. Anybody got any suggestions?"

I didn't, and it didn't seem as if anyone else did, but finally Shorty Friedman suggested that we organize classes with talks and discussions. The idea caught hold immediately, and before the day was out, the Professor, Shorty, and Tiny Sundstrom, a Finnish-American auto worker, our "school committee," had organized a set of lectures and classes. We set up a daily schedule of physical exercise, classes, free time, and chores and stuck to it more or less for the next two weeks. It was the only thing that made our confinement bearable.

After two weeks Joe and I were called out of the cell and told we were going to Ceret, about twenty kilometers southwest of Perpignan at the foot of the Pyrenees. The court sat there and we would be able to meet with a lawyer from the Popular Front Committee. We were handcuffed and chained together and were marched from the prison to the railroad station. Unshaven and dirty, we looked like pretty rough customers, but more than a few men and women in the streets saluted us with clenched fists and shouted encouragement in French. As we rode toward Ceret, I could see the mountains. I wondered how much of a job it would be to get over them—and if we'd get the chance to try.

We arrived at the courthouse, where small groups of townspeople were gathered. Because the magistrate had not yet arrived, the gendarme permitted us to walk up and down the sidewalk in the sun. Next to the courthouse was a house with a huge bay window facing the street. The window was open, and inside the room a woman was dusting a grand piano. She glanced at us and smiled, and Joe remarked that the piano was beautiful. She asked Joe if he played. He said he did; and at once the woman spoke to the gendarme, telling him to bring us into the house and take off our handcuffs. He saluted respectfully and obeyed; it turned out she was the wife of the local inspector of police.

Joe took off his coat, rolled up his sleeves, filled and lit his pipe, and sat down at the piano. He played some Chopin, a little ragtime, and finished off with the "Marseillaise."

A crowd including gendarmes, passersby, the assistant prosecutor, and other officials, gathered outside the open windows. When Joe finished playing, they applauded enthusiastically. A newspaper photographer came running up and begged Joe to sit at the piano again while he took his picture. Joe was pretty embarrassed about it, but it turned out well. The next day the local papers, even the reactionary ones, had editorials to the effect that the Americans, who at first appeared to be hardened criminals, proved to be men of culture, and they described the concert Joe had given in the police inspector's house. They couldn't figure it out. I couldn't figure it out either. I had known Joe for a long time, but I had not known that he was a talented pianist. I said as much to him on the train back to Perpignan.

He looked away uncomfortably and replied that there were things a lot more important than playing a piano.

"You've been holding out on me," I said.

Joe said, "Nuts! You think I want to go around impressing the comrades with what a hell of a superior guy I am, like a lot of these bloody bourgeois intellectuals? Make them think I'm better than anybody else because I had a chance to learn music— that they never did?"

I didn't answer. A lot of things about Joe became clearer. His "hard" manner. His way of speaking that was deliberately profane and deliberately ungrammatical. A rudeness that in another would have passed unnoticed but on Joe's lips had a faintly studied air. I had supposed this odd effect flowed from Joe's intensity, his earnestness of character, but I realized now that Joe's manner was a screen that I had never penetrated.

Joe was leaning forward, gazing out the window. There was a lot about him I didn't know, he said, a lot he never talked about. His father was rich, and he had grown up with all the advantages wealth could secure. He stared out at the mountains and started to describe his tour of Europe in 1928.

I could hardly believe what he told me. He had really done it in style—the best hotels, the finest restaurants, and fancy wine. In those days, he explained, he had just one idea in his head: a good time. "I traveled all over Europe, and I saw exactly nothing at all. I didn't know people existed. That brakeman, for instance—to me, he was just a part of the train, like the engine or the doors or the seats. Waiters were just flunkeys. Think of all the millions of lives that I passed by without ever knowing they were there! It was like living inside a soap bubble. I tell you, when I think of those days I just crawl all over!"

I promised Joe I wouldn't mention this to the other men, although we talked about it a number of times. The movement is entitled to the best in its people, and I think Joe realized that just being himself was his way to give it. Besides, most people like Joe who came into the movement and put on a blue shirt and a dese-dem-and-dose accent, speaking out of the sides of their mouths like they thought a worker would, just didn't cut it. It was better when they didn't pretend to be someone other than who they were.

On the seventeenth day after we were jailed, our entire group was taken to Ceret for the trial. Remembering the experience in the port, we were set for a demonstration as we marched through Perpignan en route to the station. But the police too had learned. Buses were drawn up before the jail; the Americans were hustled into them and driven to the train. Nevertheless a crowd had gathered at the station, and the train pulled out to the accompaniment of cheers and singing from the platform.

In Ceret the Popular Front Committee had mobilized the townspeople to greet us. They were lining the main street, crowding the sidewalks. The gendarmes directed the column into narrow back alleys where only dogs and stray cats would witness our passing. But to reach the courthouse it was necessary to enter the main street, and the crowds were waiting. They burst into a roar as we appeared: "Vive l'Espagne! Vive les Brigades Internationales!"

Three hundred people were crowded into the little courtroom, and through the windows I could see more people gathering outside. The judges, three bewigged gentlemen, were also aware of the gathering. They cast nervous glances over the courtroom, out the windows, and at the prisoners who sat before them. They were anxious to begin.

The judges agreed readily to counsel's request that Joe be allowed to speak for the entire group. Joe was asked two questions:

"You are Americans?"

"Americans and Canadians, yes."

"Why did you come to France?"

"In order to reach Spain, to fight in the Loyalist army against fascism."

The last words of his answer were lost in a storm of applause that swept the courtroom. The judges waved their hands for silence, the prosecutor frowned, and the gendarmes threatened to clear the courtroom.

There was no dispute on facts or on the law. The trial consisted of speeches by the prosecution and the defense. The Americans listened intently to the address given by Monsieur Gregory, their French attorney. They did not understand a word he said, but it was perfectly obvious that he was putting his whole heart into his argument. For the moment, he was the front line.

At the close of his address, we were removed to an anteroom while the judges considered their verdict. We crowded around our attorney, pounded his back, and exclaimed, "Bon! Bon! Very bon! Great going kid!" He smiled back at us, delighted by our praise. Within ten minutes Joe and the attorney were called back to the courtroom. Ordinarily all prisoners would have been brought back to hear the sentence, but the judges evidently feared a demonstration.

It was an agonizing wait till the door flew open and Joe rushed in, grinning from ear to ear. In a solemn voice he intoned. "For violating French laws and an international agreement to which France is a signatory, bumble, bumble, bumble, you are sentenced to twenty-one days in prison. Four more days to go, gang! And then eight days to get your fannies out of France."

Six days later, after finishing the sentence and spending a night in a hotel bathtub and a day hidden in a farmhouse outside of town, I was riding on the back of a motorcycle down dark bumpy side roads toward the Pyrenees. The Popular Front Committee had broken up our group, thinking it would be harder for the police to keep track of us. I had no idea where I was when my French cyclist eased to a halt and motioned for me to duck into the woods by the side of the road. I stumbled over something soft, and a Cockney voice cursed heavily.

"I'm sorry man," I muttered and lay down on the ground and

panted for a few minutes. I ventured quietly, "Any Americans here?"

"Steve!" A figure rose out of the darkness and pulled me down.

"Lewis!" Lewis from Chicago. We lay side by side, laughing and calling each other bad names because we were so glad to see each other.

Out of the darkness a voice called softly, "Vámonos, camaradas!" All around us shadows were rising out of the earth. I was amazed at the number, and Lewis told me there were thirty men in our party. They were mostly English and Canadians, with a sprinkling of Americans and others.

We walked through darkness, each man following the steps and heavy breathing of the man in front. We moved through fields, through what appeared to be a vineyard, and through another field to a river. A voice called softly, "Ici! Ici!" and the guide turned toward the voice. My eyes were growing used to the darkness; I could distinguish vague shapes now. The guide and the man who waited by the riverbank took up a long plank, a two-by-twelve, and thrust it out over the water. The guide trotted down it. I followed, not happily, teetering above the racing water.

The end of the plank rested on a rock midway across the stream, and a second plank was thrust out from the opposite shore. I made the crossing safely. The guide took me by both arms and pressed down as if fixing me to the earth—indicating that I was to stay there and wait until everyone was across.

We walked for half an hour, then halted, and the guide went down the line with Lewis as interpreter, speaking to each man separately. We were to keep contact at all times with the man in front. We were not to smoke or cough or make any sound. Whenever a halt was made, each man was to be in touch with the man behind him, and let him know when the line started.

Ten minutes later we stopped again, and the guide spoke quickly to Lewis. Lewis translated, "Pass the word back. We're going to go along between a canal and the river canyon. Hug the left. If you fall off the cliff, you could be killed."

I had heard in prison of a French youth bound for Spain who fell off a cliff and was injured in the fall to the river below. This must have been the place. I dropped willingly to my hands and knees and proceeded with the utmost caution. Beyond a sluice the guide waited anxiously. He seemed vastly relieved to have us safely past that spot.

The ground had tilted up sharply; we were really climbing now, climbing into the black wall of the mountains. The ground was soft and wet. The guide seemed to be leaping from rock to rock, and I tried to copy him, but I immediately missed my footing and sprawled full length in the mud. I seemed to be slipping much more than the others. The trouble, I decided, was with my shoes. They were good shoes, but they had rubber soles, and rubber soles were not good for wet climbing. All the others had been given *alpargatas*—rope-soled sandals that tied around the ankles and were strictly nonskid.

We shuffled cautiously along a ledge on the sheer side of the mountain. Word came up from the rear to stop, and the guide edged past us toward the end of the line. Lewis and I turned and looked down. The lights of Ceret were directly below: it was as if we had climbed a ladder out of the town.

The guide returned, cursing. Two men had missed a turn, and he was furious at their clumsiness. He set a stiff pace. We reached the end of the ledge and started climbing again. The hillside did not look so terribly steep to the eye, but it was steep to the legs and lungs.

We stopped to rest, and a fat little Dutch comrade sank down near me, groaning and panting. He was an older man of forty-five. He stretched his short legs before him and shook his fist at his feet. Lewis and I watched the Dutchman. When the time came to start, he had to struggle to stand up. Within ten yards other men began passing him. A tall Canadian whispered, "We got to go slower. The old boy can't keep up."

Lewis spoke to the guide, and they both went back to the Dutchman. I followed them. Lewis said, "Look, Comrade. We got to get across before morning. It's one o'clock now—ein Uhr. Only four hours. Must hurry. Mach schnell, ja? Wir mussen schnell machen or something. Versteh?"

The Dutchman looked from Lewis to the guide. "Go ahead," he said. "Go ahead, I try."

We climbed through another heartbreaking hour. The trees

were smaller here, and fewer. We crossed patches of soft snow, and then snow that was less slushy, and then we were walking on snow that was dry and frozen and there were no trees at all, only bushes, and the rocks were covered with deep moss. At the crest of a ridge, the guide halted us. "He says we can rest for ten minutes," Lewis said. "We've got to skin along another ledge."

The ledge widened and tipped steeply, and conversation stopped. Lewis called back encouragingly to the Dutchman, and the guide hissed sharply for silence. The ledge ended, and the ground fell away on either side; we had reached the top of the ridge. As soon as the guide stopped, we turned back to the Dutchman. He stood for a moment, staring straight before him. Then his knees buckled, and he toppled and fell forward.

The guide knelt beside the Dutch comrade for a moment and then sprang up. He whipped a long Catalonian knife from the sheath on his belt and with it cut and trimmed two saplings growing nearby. He laid the two poles side by side and spoke to Lewis. "He wants belts," Lewis said. "He's making a stretcher."

Five belts were offered. The guide chose the three strongest and swiftly looped them between the poles, at each end and in the center. He jerked his long black serape over his head, and threw it over the belts. The stretcher was ready. A sweater came flying out of the darkness and fell at the guide's feet; he grinned and pulled it on. I rubbed the Dutchman's face with snow. He stirred and his eyes opened, and we rolled him onto the stretcher. Lewis and I and a Canadian and a Londoner each took a corner. Feeling himself lifted, the Dutchman groaned in protest and tried to sit up; the guide thrust him down, and he lay back weakly and began to cry, pleading with the men to put him down, to leave him. "I no good," he kept repeating.

The weight of the stretcher pole on my shoulder was less than I expected. I looked up at the sky; it was blue-gray now, and the stars were fading. The guide waited for us and warned us to be silent. There was a patrol station close by. We went on, placing our feet down cautiously, trying not to breathe too loudly. The pole was now cutting into my shoulder. A hand touched my arm, pushing me aside. Without a word, four fresh bearers took over the strecher.

The guide called softly, "Camaradas! Adelante!" His voice was worried, and his anxiety affected the group. In the east the sky was perceptibly lighter, and I prayed that the sun would stay down just a little longer.

The guide rounded a great boulder, and the path suddenly became a narrow ledge. A tall Canadian, carrying one corner of the stretcher, cried out suddenly and disappeared over the bank. The Dutchman clutched the neck of the man on the other side to keep from falling. We thought the Canadian was killed; but in a moment he came scrambling up the ledge, swearing and raking snow out of his collar. But the Dutchman would not be carried any more. He went forward on his own short legs, supported between two other comrades.

It was not possible for us to run, but we jogged along, our breathing like that of hard-pressed horses. And still the guide danced before us, beckoning us on—faster—faster! He called out something, and Lewis sobbed, "Just five hundred meters, boys!"

Then we sprinted. The muscles in my thighs burned, and there was a sour taste in my mouth. Even the Dutchman, who had torn himself away from the men who supported him, was running. The sky was growing lighter.

The guide had stopped beside a heap of stones and was patting them, grinning. "España! España!" he called.

We halted by the pile of rocks and stared down the slope into the valley before us. It looked like the valley on the other side, the French side, but it was not like that valley because it was Spain. We stared down into the valley for a while, and the only sound was the gasping of exhausted men.

When we could breathe again, and before any man spoke, a big Welshman stepped forward. A blood-soaked bandage was wrapped around his ankle, where he had cut it on a rock, and his face and hands carried the blue marks of a coal miner. "Now, lads, this is a good time for a song, and I know a good song for this time." In a clear tenor voice he began to sing the "Internationale."

STEVE NELSON was born into the working class and achieved national attention during the Depression, when he organized the unemployed in Philadelphia and Pittsburgh. He was among the earliest of the Americans to fight in Spain and was wounded at the battle of Belchite. When he returned to the United States, his trade union and activist activities attracted the attention of local reactionaries, and he was indicted (under an obscure Pennsylvania "sedition" act), convicted, and sentenced to prison. After his release, he worked as a carpenter until he retired in the early 1970s. Now in his eighties, he is the beloved national commander of the VALB.

· Abe Osheroff ·

The *City of Barcelona*

We had been waiting in Marseilles for a week. By that time everybody in town knew who we were and where we were going. All sorts of people approached us and wished us well.

The border had been sealed tight, so we were to go by sea. On the eve of May 29, 1937, we received our marching orders. While Italian seamen from an adjacent freighter stared in disbelief, some 250 "passengers" carrying cheap paper suitcases, and many wearing berets, filed on board the Spanish freighter *Ciudad de Barcelona*. It would have been high comedy if not for—

Under "cover" of darkness, we set sail for Barcelona. There were some 250 men aboard, from all over Europe and some 50 from the United States. Among the Americans were Bill Cantor, Solly Davis, Murray Nemeroff, and myself. (I later learned of Carl Cannon and Bob Reed.) There was also Bob Schultz, captain of the Brooklyn College swimming team. Another man, named John Kozar, had been a seaman and a miner in Pennsylvania.

We sailed at midnight, and at crack of dawn it was clear that we were hugging the coast for safety. Somewhere around midday a lone Republican seaplane flew alongside. The pilot was gesticulating wildly and pointing to something in the water nearby. The warning was not fully understood or acted upon. Many of the men were below-decks . . .

I remember a loud, dull thud, and the whole ship sort of shuddered. In a matter of minutes, it tilted sharply and began to go down by the stern. Pandemonium followed as men raced to the very few lifeboats. I remember a loaded lifeboat overturning and crashing down on its occupants. I remember the screaming faces of men trapped at the portholes. And above all I remember some seamen tearing loose anything that could float and tossing it into the sea.

I dived into the water and began to swim away, to avoid being pulled down by the suction. Almost immediately, I felt guilt and swam back to help with the rescue of nonswimming comrades. Fishing boats were already on their way from the nearby town of Malgrát and the seaplane was floating nearby, nearly capsized by the numerous men clinging to its pontoons.*

As we came ashore, we found hundreds of villagers waiting with towels, blankets, and even some liquor. That evening there was a meeting in the Casa del Pueblo. Luís Companys came up from Barcelona and gave a welcoming speech. There were lots of other speeches, too. We were told that we could change our minds and go back home if we so desired. Only one man took advantage of that offer.

The next morning we boarded a train, amid fond farewells from the local inhabitants, and soon after we were in the railroad station in Barcelona. A brief stay in the Karl Marx Barracks and we were off for Albacete, and thence to the training town of Tarazona de la Mancha.

ABE OSHEROFF was born in Brooklyn in 1915. He was a neighborhood activist at sixteen, a student activist at City College, and then did some organizing for the CIO. He went to Spain in 1937. On his return he was a union organizer, headed the Communist Party's Jewish Commission, and worked in the South. He is a carpenter by trade and has helped build housing in Nicaragua. He has also made a documentary film on the Spanish Civil War entitled *Dreams and Nightmares*.

Note: There is some disagreement about how many men died in the sinking of that ship, and how many American volunteers were lost. Edwin Rolfe, volunteer, poet, and journalist, in the first history of the Lincoln Battalion ever published, reported that twelve Americans were lost. *New York Times* correspondent Herbert L. Matthews confirmed that figure. Sandor Voros, who was in the commissariat of the Fifteenth International Brigade, said there were fifty, and the U.S. consul in Barcelona claimed there were more than that.

Schultz drowned, trapped beneath deck. John Kozar was said to have swum ashore with a pound of coffee in a paper bag in his teeth. In World War II he shipped out on the Murmansk run, was torpedoed again, and froze to death in a lifeboat. (A.O.)

· Edwin Rolfe ·

Death by Water

On May 30, 1937, the small Spanish coastal
steamship *Ciudad de Barcelona* was torpedoed and sunk off the coast of Malgrat by a
submarine the Non-Intervention Committee
preferred to designate "of unknown nationality." More than a hundred volunteers,
twelve of them Americans, perished.

1

Nearing land, we heard the cry of gulls and
saw their shadows in sunlight on the topmost deck,
or coasting unconcerned on each wavecrest, they rested
after their scavenging, scudding the ship's length.

And we thought of the albatross—an old man going crazy,
his world an immenseness of water, none of it to drink;
and the vultures descending on an Ethiopian plain:
all of us were the living corpse, powerless, bleeding.

And suddenly the shock. We felt the boat shiver.
I turned to Oliver, saw his eyes widen,
stare past the high rails, waiting, waiting . . .
Others stumbled past us. And suddenly the explosion.

Men in twenty languages cried out to comrades
as the blast tore the ship, and the water, like lava,
plunged through the hull, crushing metal and flesh before it,
splintering cabins, the sleepers caught unconscious.

Belted, we searched for companions but lost them
in turmoil of faces; swept toward the lifeboats
and saw it was useless. Too many were crowding them.
Oliver dived. I followed him, praying.

In the water the sea-swell hid for a moment
Oliver swimming, strongly, away from me.
Then his voice, calmly: "Here, keep his head above."
We helped save a drowning man, kept him afloat until

dories approached. Looking backward, we saw
the prow high in air, and Carlos, unconcerned,
throwing fresh belts to the tiring swimmers.
Steam, flame crept toward him, but he remained absorbed . . .

2

On shore, later, a hundred of us gone,
we are too weak to weep for them, to listen to
consoling words. We are too tired
to return the grave smiles of the rescuing people.
Too drained. Sorrow can never be the word.

But beyond the numbness the vivid faces
of comrades burn in our brains: their songs
in quiet French villages, their American laughter
tug at responding muscles in our lips,
shout against ears that have heard their voices living.

Fingers, convulsive, form fists. Teeth
grate now, audibly. We stifle curses,
thought but unuttered. While many grieve,
their hands reach outward, fingers extended—
the image automatic—ready for rifles

until night brings us sleep, and dreams
of violent death by drowning, dreams
of journey, slow advances through vineyards,
seeking cover in wheatfields, finding always
the fascist face behind the olive tree.

EDWIN ROLFE was a newspaper correspondent and editor of *The Volunteer for Liberty*, the organ of the Fifteenth Brigade, but he insisted on enlisting with the Lincolns. His book of poems, *First Love*, is treasured by all veterans, and his unofficial history, *The Lincoln Battalion* (1939), earned praise from Ernest Hemingway and many others. The two poems in this volume are from *First Love* (rept. ed., Los Angeles: Edmunds Bookshop, 1951).

· Arthur Timpson ·

An Encounter with the Anarchists in Figueras

We did not have to wait long. In an hour a truck pulled into the yard. It was covered with one of those Conestoga canvas tops. Two men were in the cab. We got in the back. The canvas back drop was pulled down and we were told not to look out. The order surprised me. I had the feeling that volunteers for the war ought to be allowed exposure to the people. I remembered how the first trains from France went to Spain all covered with flowers. But I was a good soldier and said nothing out loud.

About an hour later the truck stopped with a lot of voices all about us. Then the back flap was pulled aside and someone with a very seamed face, topped by a leather cap, looked in, gave us a brief scrutiny, and closed the flap. I was sitting close to the rear and got a glimpse of a wall and a machine gun pointing carelessly in our general direction. Two more of the leather-capped men were with the gun. Our truck went ahead for another fifty yards. Then we got out. We were in an immense square with barrack-like buildings all around. There was the gate that we came through with two machine guns over the gate. A half dozen more of the leather caps were visible. None of them looked friendly. Someone, of the reception committee, I suppose, said, "Anarchists. We are POWs."

And so it was that on May 6, 1937, I became a prisoner in the fortress of Figueras. That fort had held off Napoleon. Famous place connected with history. Was it to be merely a matter of incarceration? A quick peek at the machine gunners on the wall didn't reassure me any. I suspected they would have no qualms over the prospect of using those two Maxims on us. But how come? Our reception committee had a man who seemed to be an authority. Strongly built, speaking with an accent, he asked us to follow him into one of the barracks. We sat down at tables and he ordered food for us. Then he introduced himself as the cantonment commander. Later I was to hear that he was a hero in the war, and that he was Armenian. He told us that the Anarchists were getting impatient with the Republicans, Socialists, and Communists who were running the war, and hampering the Anarchists in the spreading of their gospel. The Anarchists were keeping all the weapons they could get, borrow, or steal, and hiding them in Barcelona, and that they had decided to strike out on their own and take over the country. It seems there was some battling going on in Barcelona, and the Anarchists had seized Figueras and the fort. He went on to say that it was quite serious, and the fascists were interested and eager to fan the flames. A Franco plane had made a turn over Figueras that very morning. He also hoped that no one inside these walls would excite the lads on the wall. We all averred that we would behave. He said we could rest a bit after eating; then we would be called to go to the parade ground for drill. He also said to go easy on the Spanish wine for it was raw and had a fierce and sneaky wallop.

We got rice, one bowl. The rice was brown and boiled in olive oil, making it porridge-like. Spanish bread rather heavy in taste. The food didn't make much of an impression on me. It was to be much later that the monotony of the food got on the nerves now and then, and it was a bit of an inner struggle to keep the nerves from exploding. My time for eating cats, dogs, lizards, and horses was still in the future.

The day turned out to be a dull day of drill and hanging around the barracks. We got word that the Anarchists had pretty much given up the grandiose ideas they held of taking over Spain. Even in Barcelona they were laying down their arms. Our leather caps never changed their expressions, however. And we were still prisoners. Some sort of argument must have taken place the next morning, for we were all asked to come out and drill in large formations with the other three hundred men who had been waiting shipment south. And we were told to sing. The Germans sang beautifully. The British and we were not so artistic. We heard a short speech from the commandant in which he hinted that though we meant no harm to anyone here, we would conduct ourselves as men if pressed by anyone. I suspected this was a form of warning to the leather caps who might have threatened our people. The leather caps must have taken umbrage but nothing happened. The Germans marched and sang; we tried to march. Eventually we were all dismissed. The leather caps must have gotten the point about their private war having had a disastrous ending all through Republican Spain.

In the afternoon we were all called out for exercise in the field. The leather caps must have relented in full, for the machine guns were now pointed to the outside, instead of into the compound. The outside of the barracks were solid walls. The compound and the barracks had been cut into the top of the hill, for the walls showed only a low outline. Looked formidable. We were about a third of the way downhill. There we were assigned to groups that took up a rough line facing uphill. We were to attack up the slope, scrambling and lying prone by turns. But before we got going we had an air alarm. A plane had come in from the sea and was making a turn over Figueras. A series of whistles and loud calls had us all flatten along the sides of the arroyo we were in. The plane went away and we started our campaign to reduce the fort. The next morning, May 9, we loaded onto trucks and left the fort. The trucks took us to the town of Figueras. There we moved hurriedly over several tracks in the freight yards, and loaded into a string of cars without an engine. There we waited for hours. The day was darkening rapidly when the train finally left. And so we proceeded to Valencia and finally Albacete, where we would be processed and assigned to the John Brown Battery, an artillery outfit.

ARTHUR TIMPSON left for Spain in 1937. After crossing the Pyrenees, he—like most of the Americans—went to the ancient fort at Figueras, where, in May 1937, the Anarchists were briefly in control. In this piece he described his unusual experience there. He was then assigned to the John Brown Artillery Battery and eventually became its commanding officer. He died in 1976.

· Albert Prago ·

Jews in the International Brigades

Paris was the main relay station for antifascists on their way to Spain 1936–38. It took Bobrus Nissenbaum about five months to get to Paris from Warsaw. Bobrus was one of many volunteers coming from Eastern Europe who encountered special difficulties getting out of their own country in the first place and then in traveling across Europe to France. As a Jew, Bobrus had additional compelling reasons for risking imprisonment and even death for the opportunity to take up arms in the International Brigades to fight against fascism.

Since the war in Spain that began in July 1936 was a war of fascism against democracy, the participation of Jews in the International Brigades takes on a very special and added significance.

Fascism against democracy? The fascists would have had us believe otherwise. "Our war is not a Spanish civil war, it is a war of Western civilization against the Jews of the entire world. The Jews want to destroy the Christians who, according to them, 'came from the devil.'" So explained General Queipo de Llano in a radio broadcast October 10, 1936, almost three months after he and the other fascist generals headed by Francisco Franco had rebelled against the Spanish Republic.

A war "against the Jews of the entire world?" From many tragic experiences some people have learned not to ignore or underestimate the power of such demagogy. Anti-Semitism was a potent weapon, an integral part of the Nazi-fascist catechism, one major feature of which equated Jews and Communists. Recall that, as Vincent Sheean wrote in *Not Peace but a Sword*, just before the betrayal at Munich the German press was screaming that "Prague was the 'Jewish center' of the world, that it was governed by the 'Russian Bolsheviks,' that the 'International capitalists' (also Jewish) had collaborated in this curious enterprise."

This absurdity was believed by Germans and by the "Sudeten" Germans in Czechoslovakia, who also were led to believe that photographs of Spanish women and children killed by German bombs were of Germans killed by Czechoslovak bombs. And that, to quote Sheean again, the "Spanish Republic was a Jewish Communist attempt to conquer Europe for Bolshevism." Had not Hitler proclaimed repeatedly that "the British, French and Americans were dishonest profiteers and warmongers dominated by Jews"?

A campaign against the Jews—of the entire world—in Nazi logic was equivalent to fighting Communists, and vice versa. To argue that the war in Spain was one of fascism versus communism means missing one of the distinguishing characteristics of Nazi fascism: anti-Semitism.

The International Brigades became the vehicles through which Jews could offer the first *organized armed resistance* to European fascism. Their combatant role in Spain proved that they could fight well, and that as early as 1936 they were actively resisting fascism. Not all went passively to the concentration camps and crematoria.

There are scores of books in many languages about the war in Spain, including many about the International Brigades. Some make the barest reference, two lines or so, to Jews in Spain. There is only one book on the Jews in the International Brigades, written in Yiddish by the Polish-French Jew David Diamant, published in Warsaw in 1967, and also a work, unfortunately not available in this country, by Joseph Toch, an Austrian Jew. There have been many articles in periodicals and some pamphlets written, mainly in Yiddish, Hebrew, and Slav languages, that deal with some aspects of the Jews in the International Brigades. I know of no book or pamphlet written in English that deals with this important matter. This silence of forty years in the English-speaking world is strange.

How many Jews were there in the Brigades?

Estimates of the total number of volunteers vary from 40,000 to 45,000 men and women from 53 countries. Estimates of the number of Jews range from 7,000 to 10,000; not less than 15.5 percent and perhaps as much as 17.5 percent of the Brigaders were Jewish. (Estimates are derived from statistics provided by several scholars including Alberto Fernandez, a Spanish Catholic, in "Judíos en la Guerra de Espana," published in Madrid in *Tiempo de Historia,* September 1975—while Franco was still alive! Fernandez asserts that 22 to 25 percent of the Brigaders were Jews!) [. . .]

Many of the Jews who came from England, Canada, France, and the United States did not identify as Jews. They went to Spain as internationalists, as humanists, as antifascists, as communists—and while they may not have denied their Jewish heritage, they did not go to Spain identifying as Jews. This is particularly true for the American Jews.

The exact number of American Jews is not known. Robert Rosenstone in *Crusade of the Left,* culled apparent Jewish surnames from a list of 1,800 and concludes that 30 percent of all American volunteers were Jews. From a similar, independent study I have made of some 2,000 names, I can support Rosenstone's estimate of 30 percent. Therefore the total number of American Jews is probably between 900 and 1,110.

After sifting the evidence and taking into account the many difficulties involved in this census, the estimate that about 16 percent of all Brigaders were Jews seems reasonable.

Even before the formation of the International Brigades, the first members of which arrived in Spain in October 1936, there were a number of volunteers. The very first were those foreigners who were present in Spain at the time of the fascist uprising in July 1936. Some were political refugees, as was Emanuel Mink. Others were members of athletic groups, mostly from several European countries, present in Barcelona to participate in the Workers' Olympiad being held in protest against the World Olympics scheduled for August in Hitler's Berlin. Many of these antifascist athletes volunteered to fight immediately after the fascist outbreak.

The Palestinian "Hapoel" was one such sports association, almost all of whose members joined the Popular Militia and took part in the fighting in Barcelona in July 1936. Jacques Penczyna, a political refugee, along with thirteen Jewish companions founded the first Thaelmann Centuria in Barcelona (not to be confused with the German Thaelmann Battalion formed subsequently in Madrid). According to a correspondent in a French Yiddish newspaper, they referred to themselves as the "Jewish Thaelmann group." There was an American group of athletes, headed by Alfred "Chick" Chakin, a physical training instructor at the City College of New York. Chakin, a Jew, returned to the United States that summer, but came back the following year to fight and die in Spain. He was one of two City College faculty and eleven alumni and students killed in Spain; eleven of the thirteen were Jews.

Throughout the months of August and September 1936, individuals and small groups made their way to Spain to offer their bodies and minds in the service of the Republic. Among those early volunteers was a group of Jews including a Leon Baum, who arrived in Spain on August 8, was immediately involved in the fighting, and was killed at Irun. Baum was the first Jewish hero of the Spanish civil war to be immortalized in articles, song, and poetry, including a poem by the famous Soviet Yiddish writer Itzik Feffer, entitled "A Song about Leon Baum." Accompanying Baum was Joseph Epstein, wounded shortly after his integration into a fighting unit. He returned to France, where he later served as a partisan leader. He was captured and shot by the Nazis.

Once the Brigades were formed, through the initiative of the Communist parties of several countries, men and women mainly from Europe hastened to join. For some—the French, Belgian, English, Swiss, Scandinavians, and exiles living in those countries—the journey presented no serious hazard. There were no obstacles in leaving their country and none, initially, in entering Spain. It was otherwise for those coming from Central and Eastern Europe, from countries already under the yoke of fascism or groaning under authoritarian reactionary regimes.

During the Inquisition in Spain Jews were maligned, persecuted, imprisoned, tortured, and murdered, and, toward the close of the fifteenth century, driven into exile. In this twentieth century, Jews facing incredible dangers were making their tortuous way to aid the Spanish people to defend their newly won democracy! [. . .]

The record of the Americans in Spain bears favorable comparison with that of any of the international groups. Their fighting ability received the highest praise from International Brigade leaders and from several military experts, including Colonel Stephen Fuqua, the U.S. military observer. Contained within that record is the valorous contribution of the large Jewish segment.

None of the battalion's historians recorded the exploits of the Jews; nor did they indicate that any of the Americans were Jews. In the two quasi-official histories of the Lincolns, both written by veterans (Edwin Wolfe and Arthur Landis) with some thirty years separating the two works, there is no mention of Jewish participation. The low level of Jewish consciousness has persisted as though Hitlerism and the Holocaust had never existed. The level of Jewish consciousness among much of the Left at the time was minimal. But now, so many years after the event, with hindsight readily available, and with a clearer political perspective, a historical accounting is due.

Yet of the many hundreds of American Jewish volunteers there were those who did identify as Jews. Among them were: David Miller—who was a Zionist when he went to Spain and remained one until his recent death; and Rubin Schecter, whose widow Rose commented to me that he had always been an ardent scholar of Jewish studies and had made it quite clear that his volunteering to fight in Spain derived largely from his determination, as a Jew, to fight back against Hitlerism. Wilfred Mendelson wrote to his father June 22, 1938: "Today Jews are returning welcomed by the entire Spanish people to fight the modern Inquisition, and in many cases the direct descendants of the ancient persecutions. . . . Yes, Pop, I am sure we are fighting in the best Maccabean tradition." Mendy was killed one month later. And William Harvey, replying to a question by a *Life* reporter, said, "I know what Hitler is doing to my people." Finally, a member of Local 16 of the United Office and Professional Workers of America wrote the following to his mother from a hospital in Spain, "I took up arms against the persecutors of my people—the Jews—and my class, the oppressed. I am fighting against those who establish an inquisition like that of their ideological ancestors several centuries ago, in Spain."

It is also illuminating to note that the highest ranking American, Lieutenant-Colonel John Gates (alias for Sol Regenstreif), is a Jew; that the last commander of the Lincolns was Major Milton Wolff; and that the last political commissar of the Canadian battalion was the American Jew Saul Wellman. There are the outstanding records of Captain Leonard Lamb, political commissars Dave Doran and George Watt, battalion commander David Reiss (under whose brief command I served as interpreter on battalion staff), company commanders Aaron Lopoff, Paul Block, Larry Lustgarten, Sidney Levine, Julius Deutsch, Irving Weissman, Yale Stuart, Manny Lancer, Lawrence Cane, Jack Cooper, Harold Smith, Harry Schonberg, Dave Smith—in fact a very high proportion of section (platoon) and company commanders and political commissars were Jews. Irv Goff was one of the three Americans who served with Spanish guerrillas fighting behind enemy lines in some of the most daring forays of the war. And, as held true for all the volunteers, one must pay tribute to the many unsung heroes among the privates and noncommissioned officers whose deeds did not receive the publicity earned by upper echelons of the military.

Leonard Lamb, a former teacher, was an unusual officer in an unusual army. He was assigned to brigade staff and was assigned a variety of responsible, hazardous duties. He guided companies into and out of front-line sectors; he commanded companies at strategic moments such as the movement of Company 1 in the historic crossing of the Ebro. He was wounded several times, the last during the first battles after the Ebro crossing.

Edwin Rolfe recorded what happened shortly after: "One day in mid-August, a familiar figure, neatly dressed in a light summer uniform, walked up to the tree under which Wolff and the other battalion officers lived and slept. Two of the older and tougher of the English battalion veterans gaped at him as he passed, paler than they had ever seen him and moving slowly. One of the Englishmen shook his head, breathed deeply, then blew his breath out in a half-whistle. Turning to his companion, he said, still shaking his head, 'Tough man, that Lamb, tough man.' Wolff and the others of the battalion greeted Lamb with mingled anger and relief; the battalion could well use the veteran officer, but Lamb was so evidently in need of further rest that officers and men alike shook their heads and told him he ought to 'get the hell back to the hospital where you belong.'

"Lamb's wound, covered with bandage, was still half-healed. He had left the hospital on a one-day leave to Barcelona and had continued to the front. If the hospital records are still preserved . . . he is still listed as a 'deserter.' " Lennie was one of the older Americans: he was twenty-six.

Wolff, veteran of almost all the campaigns from Brunete on, was one of the very few never wounded. He rose from machinegunner in the short-lived George Washington Battalion eventually to become a battalion commander of the Lincolns and respected by everyone as skilled, resourceful, and extremely courageous. Milt was twenty-three.

Nurse Fredericka Martin has supplied data to me about the many Jews among the medical personnel. Of the 124 under the aegis of the American Medical Bureau to Aid Spanish Democracy, 59 or an extraordinary 47.5 percent were Jews, distributed as follows: out of 29 surgeons and physicians 18 (or 19) were Jews; 3 of the 4 oral surgeons and dentists were Jews; 6 of the 16 medical technicians, physical therapists, assistants, etc.; 28 of the 48 nurses; 2 of the 22 ambulance drivers and chauffeurs; and 2 of the 5 engineers and clerks.

All the world knows of the exceptional skill and heroism of the late Dr. Edward K. Barsky, the outstanding medical figure of this group and perhaps outstanding among all the International Brigade medical personnel. (Fredericka Martin also notes that most of the Polish nurses and nurses' aides were Jews, as were most of the forty-plus Polish doctors. From Belgium a group of thirty women, some with husbands already in Spain, organized by the Jewish Bund, went to Spain led by the German Jewish refugee Doctor Blanc.)

One of the first Americans to volunteer was Ben Leider, a reporter with experience as a pilot. In the defense of Madrid in an air battle with fascist planes, overwhelmingly superior in numbers, Leider was killed.

The Americans came from a country rich in democratic tradi-
tions, quite different from the reactionary regimes typical of
Eastern European countries. The American Jews had not experienced the terror that prevailed, for example, in Poland. However, they were workers and intellectuals who had had rich
experiences fighting the dreadful consequences of the Great Depression.

Most of the Jewish volunteers came from major urban centers.
There, many had been involved for years in militant struggles
for welfare, for Negro rights, against family evictions, for jobs,
and for unemployment insurance. Three of the many active in
this arena were Sol Rose (killed in Spain), Sam Gonshak, and
Abe Osheroff (writer and producer-director of the prize-winning
Spanish Civil War documentary film in 1975, *Dreams and Nightmares*). From the Brownsville section of Brooklyn, where there
were so many Jewish activists, it is estimated that sixty-six went
to Spain. Only twenty-five returned.

Those not involved in community affairs were active members
of unions, mainly in light industry and in retail and distributive
trades. There were many teachers (coming mostly from the
Workers Projects Administration) along with other professionals
and a considerable number of students.

All of them had learned of fascism in Europe and saw obvious
signs in this country of our own brand(s) of fascism tied to an
old racism and bigotry. Nor was anti-Semitism a stranger
within the democracy we enjoyed. It was no historic accident
that so many Jews were members of, or sympathetic to, the
Communist Party and other Left organizations and that they
constituted such a large proportion of the volunteers.

Some were exceedingly young. When Eslanda Robeson, accompanying her husband Paul on a visit to the American volunteers in Spain, was struck by the extremely youthful appearance
of a few of the soldiers, she approached one (Maury Colow) and,
thrusting a finger at him, exclaimed, "How old are you?" Colow,
then eighteen, was one of several young Jews coming out of slum
areas of Brooklyn, the lower East Side, and other pockets of
working-class constituents and of poverty.

Students, factory workers, clerks, union organizers, teachers,
writers, Communists and Young Communists, Socialists, lead-

ers of the unemployment movement, people of diverse backgrounds and experiences, were fused into an effective fighting force, bound by the common hatred of fascism. Unlike most of their European comrades, with a few exceptions they had had no military training. From the outset their bravery was superlative. But it would take some time and many, many casualties before they became magnificent soldiers equalling their more experienced comrades-in-arms.

Approximately half of the American volunteers are buried in Spanish soil. Of those who survived, the vast majority were wounded, some two or more times, some very seriously.

The American volunteers returned to very warm but little applause. A few thousands adored and honored the returning soldiers, but the mass of the population was indifferent to or ignorant of the occasion. However, a very aware government did much to harass us, especially through the FBI and later the Subversive Activities Control Board.

Our problems did not compare with the more serious ones faced by our European comrades. For us there was some blacklisting, careers interrupted, in some instances never again to be resumed, and financial and psychological problems attending rehabilitation, especially for the seriously wounded.

Most of the veterans participated in the armed services and merchant marine during World War II. The Jewish component continued to maintain the same high standards of conduct set in Spain. Of the five Lincoln Brigade Veterans selected by Col. William J. Donovan to operate in the Office of Strategic Services behind the enemy lines, four were Jews: Irving Fajans, Milton Felsen, Irving Goff, and Milt Wolff (the fifth was Vincent Lossowski, a Polish American). Norman Berkowitz, Morris Breier, Larry Cane, Dan Groden, Herman Rosenstein, Bob Steck, Bill Susman, George Watt, Jesse Wallach, and so many others served with distinction. Sid Kurtz, Gerald Weinberg, and Sid Rosenblatt were killed in action in Europe. Cane and others were decorated for outstanding valor. A full roster of those who have served humanity remains to be compiled.

Was Luigi Longo in error when he wrote that "We, volunteers of liberty, owed an immense debt to the Jewish heroes who have written magnificent pages in all our Brigades"? Was he wrong in

urging that the story of the Jewish volunteers should be presented "for the admiration of the world"? And how is the story to
be presented "for the admiration of the world"?

Should not the full story be told of the heroism of the Jews of
the International Brigades, and especially of the extraordinarily
large numbers originating from Poland, the United States, and
France? Should not historians examine the ample evidence that
refutes the peculiar interpretations of the Arendts and Bet-
telheims? [. . .]

Let us herald the fact that more Jews, proportionately, fought
in Spain—where the organized armed resistance to fascism began (and in many resistance movements)—than any other minority or any other nationality in Europe!

ALBERT PRAGO was born in New York City in 1911, the son of
Latvian-Jewish immigrants. He taught social sciences in the
Works Project Administration adult-education project and was
a charter member of Local 453, American Federation of Teachers. He went to Spain in 1937. While there he was the Anglo-
American editor of the International Brigades' daily information bulletin, served on the Lincoln's Cultural Commission, and
acted as battalion interpreter. He was wounded at the second
battle of Belchite in March 1938. He returned to New York in
1938 and continued teaching and studying, earning his Ph.D. in
history in 1976. He has taught at the Jefferson School of Social
Science, at Cornell University's N.Y.S. School of Industrial and
Labor Relations, at Empire State College, and at the New
School for Social Research. He is the author of two books, *The
Revolutions in Spanish America: The Wars of Independence,
1808–1825* (1970) and *Strangers in Their Own Land: A History of
Mexican-Americans* (1973), as well as numerous articles. He is
now a member of the national executive of the VALB. This
piece is excerpted from *Jewish Currents* (February and March
1979) and is reprinted by permission.

The

FIRST BATTLES

The desperate military situation that the Spanish Republicans faced almost from the beginning of the war meant that the International Brigades, which were used principally as shock troops, as well as for boosting morale, were transferred to the front lines after all-too-brief periods of training. Whereas most of the European volunteers had a military background, very few of the Americans were so fortunate. Training took place in Madrigueras and Tarazona, both small towns in the La Mancha region, where the Americans had their first intimate contact with the Spanish peasantry.

The first, and costly, baptism of fire took place in the Jarama valley in February 1937, when the first large contingent of Americans, taking the name the Abraham Lincoln Battalion, took part in the defense of the besieged city of Madrid. Converging on the embattled Madrileños were four of Franco's columns. Within the city itself, Franco's generals boasted, a fifth column of fascist sympathizers was waiting to aid the

Foreign Legionnaires, army regulars, Moors, Germans, Italians, Carlists, and drafted peasants who together comprised Franco's army.

At Jarama, the fascists' aim was to cut Madrid's lifeline, the Madrid-Valencia highway. The Republican army thwarted the attempt and Madrid remained a partially encircled but unconquered city, while the enemy was compelled to concentrate its attention elsewhere.

In early July the Republicans began a major offensive, the first under a unified military command, to relieve the pressure on Madrid and divert the Franco forces from the far northern front. The attack is known as the battle of Brunete, baptism of fire for the recently trained American volunteers of the George Washington Battalion, the second American battalion to be formed. They were decimated, as were the troops of the Lincoln Battalion. The survivors were then merged to form the Lincoln-Washington Battalion. Eventually the hyphenated name was dropped and the military unit was thenceforth called the Abraham Lincoln Battalion.

The great majority of Americans who were engaged in battle before the fall of 1937 fought at Jarama and then at Brunete. A few fought on the southern fronts—some in the John Brown Artillery Battery and some in the Eighty-sixth Brigade, a truly "mixed" outfit of Americans, English, French, Austrian, German, Czech, and Polish volunteers. Not all battalion members were in the infantry, and the pieces included in this section describe some of the variety of war experiences on the ground, in the air, by nurses, members of medical units, and by truck and ambulance drivers.

—A.P.

· Marion Merriman Wachtel and Warren Lerude ·

Valor amid Slaughter

Bob shivered in the dawn of February 27, 1937. The leaden skies were swollen with clouds. Bob thought rain would again soak the Americans who huddled in the trenches carved from the rocky Spanish soil. The Abraham Lincoln Battalion was about to face its eleventh and most devastating day in the hills above the Jarama valley.

Bob wrote in his diary that captured fascist prisoners had told of lightly protected Pingarron Hill, the scrubby knob that rose above the road the Republicans wanted to control. General Gal, a somewhat mysterious figure with both Austrian and Russian army experience, designed an attack that he thought would drive the fascists off the highlands and back across the Jarama River.

At first, Bob thought the plan sounded good, based upon the information headquarters provided. He shared the news with his men. "Airplanes, tanks, armored cars, artillery, Cuban first aid men and main attack to be on our right," he told them. In his diary he later recalled: "24th Brigade and Americans to protect at the left flank after they had passed us 50 yards or more. Pivot movement to road and then our brigade to move forward. Plan good and sounded like good use of all arms."

But he was soon to learn, as the dawn spread, that the idea was poorly planned by General Gal and others in the headquarters, including Colonel Vladimir Copic, the newly appointed commander of the Fifteenth Brigade, which included the Lincoln Battalion.

Copic was a prima donna of a soldier. He strutted in high polished boots, wore a pistol on his hip, carried both map and binocular cases, and presented himself generally as superior to those around him. Then age forty-six, it was rumored that he was in Spain to rebuild a reputation tarnished elsewhere so that he could return to Yugoslavia a hero. A Marxist, he had been jailed in the struggle for his native Croatia's independence, then was drafted into the Austrian Army in World War I. He was captured and imprisoned in a tsarist camp, where he got a fuller taste of revolutionary thinking. In and out of jails in the tumultuous politics of Yugoslavia, he had tried his hand both as a propaganda editor and as a secretary of a labor party. When he arrived in Spain, he was appointed a political commissar. Then, when General Gal was promoted to a divisional assignment, Copic was named commander of the brigade.

Before the day was out, the opinionated, stubborn Copic would be responsible for the deaths of many Americans. Reports of the battle varied in their detail.

Bob wrote in his diary: "Early on Feb. 27, weather bad and attack put off until 10 A.M. At 9:50 artillery started and at 10 the 24th brigade started to go forward. We waited without promised machine gun support, without telephone, artillery going to the left and not helping us or the 24th brigade either. The armored cars were behind the hill, no tanks in evidence, no horses. 24th failed to move forward. Ceiling low. No planes."

As Rosenstone saw it: "Over the folds of earth, Captain Merriman could see the Spanish battalion leave its trenches, advance a short distance, and then pull quickly back as many men fell beneath enemy fire. Merriman was nervous. He knew that without the cover of artillery and the support of the Spanish battalion on his flank, it would be suicidal to ask his men to leave their positions. Transmission lines had just that morning been completed and Merriman picked up the phone to headquarters."

According to Arthur Landis: "Merriman spoke to the brigade commander, Copic, requesting immediate information. What was happening? Where were the tanks? Where were the planes?

Where was the artillery—artillery in sufficient quantity to make sense? The reply from Colonel Copic was vague, admitting only that there had been a delay. The tanks would be coming. They, the Lincolns must be ready to begin the fire-fight again. And did Merriman have an aviation signal out?"

Bob hadn't been told earlier about putting out an aviation signal, which he then was instructed to place on the nearby road. Underwear, white shirts, anything light-colored was gathered from the men in the trenches. Two volunteers, Joe Streisand and Robert Pick, dashed to the road with the bits of cloth, tied together to form a *T*. They immediately came under fire of machine guns.

Streisand and Pick worked to arrange the materials in the *T* formation. The enemy machine gun bullets danced around them. They struggled to point the long vertical line of the *T* toward the enemy, to give direction to the Republican aviators who were supposed to be on their way. Pick was cut down by the machine-gun fire, the bullets ripping through his stomach and chest. As Streisand went to his aid, the bullets hit him, too. The Americans, close by in the trenches, swallowed hard as they saw their comrades' bodies riddled by the relentless fire that followed.

Bob virtually pleaded, on his newly strung battle phone, with Copic. The attack could not go as planned. The support simply was not there. Bob repeated several times that the Spanish Twenty-fourth Battalion had not advanced, that machine-gun fire on the Americans was too heavy, that the plan of attack was falling apart all along the line. God, our boys are brave, he thought, grieving as he watched them go into the line of fire. Copic, on the other end of the phone, safely back at headquarters, bawled Bob out for not having the Americans advance as scheduled.

Bob told the commander again that the Spanish battalion had not advanced. But Copic insisted the Spanish had, in fact, moved out and that they were seven hundred yards ahead of the Americans. Where he got that information, no one knew. Bob, looking around through the din of fire, saw signals of the Spanish and noted they were, in fact seven hundred yards behind the Americans.

Bob shouted into the phone that the Spanish were not attacking, that the Americans would be slaughtered if they attacked without the support of airplanes, artillery, the flanking Spaniards. But Copic, sticking to his inaccurate view, ordered Bob to force the Americans to attack anyway. "At all costs," the Yugoslav colonel demanded, the hill must be taken by the Americans. Their attack could serve as an example to the Spanish and inspire them to join the effort, Copic said.

Three planes came over, instead of the promised twenty, and they didn't do much, Bob noted. The Americans, with virtually no other support, would have to move forward into the murderous fire from the enemy on the knoll because Copic, unable to see what was happening himself, was unwilling to accept Bob's battlefield report.

Landis wrote:

> Copic, angry at Merriman's defiance, and refusing to listen to any reasoning that questioned the orders he himself had received from Gal, sent the British captain (or commissar) D. F. Springhall to the American positions, together with Lieutenant George Wattis, to insure the order being carried out. . . . Springhall and Wattis (also English) headed for the lines on a motorcycle, Wattis driving. They made the two-kilometer trip in short order, entered the communications trenches, rounded the hill, and clambered along the Lincoln positions. . . . Springhill arrived just in time to accompany the American captain and his staff over the top.
>   . . . Robert Merriman, the newly appointed commander of a green battalion of unproved . . . troops, had dared to challenge the authority of the general of his division, and the commander of his brigade; he thereby risked the charge of *irresponsibility and cowardice*. Merriman had done all that he could, short of mutiny. And when he could do no more, he prepared his men for the attack and personally led them beneath the scanty covering fire.

So, against his will, after challenging his superior and losing, Bob gave the order for the Americans to attack. It was nearly noon. He decided that if he must send his men into the fire, he would lead them. He raised his left arm high, shouted for them to follow, and climbed from the trench directly into the line of fire.

Instantly, a bullet ripped into his shoulder, shattering the bone in five places. He stumbled and fell forward. Bullets zinged into the earth around him. Others reached out and grabbed him by the legs. They pulled him quickly out of the line of fire.

John Tisa described the Jarama action:

> The enemy machine guns began their ugly work. They pitted the sandbags all along the line in a constant staccato. Heavy firing came from both sides. Bullets sprayed in our direction like the heavy pounding of a riveting machine.
>
> Cross-fire from many machine guns made an impenetrable steel wall against advance. More groups and sections went over. Soon the calls for first aid came and then became insistent. Many got wounded just as they climbed the parapet to go over. Some comrades from among the recent arrivals, uninformed and inexperienced, went over the top with full packs on their backs and charged toward the fascists. Many wounded men crawled back to the trenches safely; many were killed in the attempt.

Another soldier, Joe Rehill, said he "never knew there were so many bullets in the world, and all of them seem to shoot around me. . . . The Spanish on the extreme right are scurrying for shelter. Then our boys go. I pass Jim, he smiles confidently and I give him a slap on the shoulder. The fire from the Fascists seems incessant. Rat, tat, tat, a tat! . . . I see another comrade who came across with me on the SS Paris. His gun was jammed, poor guy was actually crying. I can understand how he feels; *like myself, he never saw a rifle before.*"

Bob, wounded, immobilized in the trench, watched the slaughter. A first-aid man dressed his wound as he gave word to move some men into the American trench to back up his troops. They did so quickly.

Bob refused to be immediately evacuated. Instead, as his men continued to go over the top of the trench into almost certain death or severe wounding, he commanded others to take charge of the trench and what remained of the battalion. He thought his second in command, Douglas Seacord, would take up the lead, not knowing that Seacord himself had been killed moments earlier. The command fell to the hands of Lieutenant Philip Cooperman. Once Bob knew the British and Franco-Belge were positioned to hold the trench, he allowed the stretcher bearers to carry him toward safety and a battlefield hospital unit.

Even then, however, he demanded they make one crucial stop. He wanted to have it out with Copic, although his senior in military command and rank, for having ordered the Americans into the bloodbath. The stretcher bearers carried Bob to the commander's makeshift heaequarters. Copic, declaring Bob too weak for a conversation but probably knowing exactly what Bob had on his mind, refused to see him; the stretcher bearers carried Bob off to the medical unit.

Despite the confusion of the battle, word spread that Bob was wounded, that Seacord was dead, that the battalion was continuing to move up the rocky hillside. As Rosenstone recalled:

> Elsewhere on the rolling hills of the battlefield, in the dips of earth and through groves of trees, the men of the Lincoln Battalion were slowly and painfully moving upon Pingarron. They were going forward into a curtain of steel as the blue sky of Spain sang with death. As they went, hidden machine guns high on the right opened with a deadly crossfire. Still they blundered on, the enemy's guns piling up a heavy toll as man after man slumped to earth, some dead before they hit the ground, some almost sliced in two by the intense fire. Those with bodies shredded by machine gun bullets writhed on the ground and screamed for the first aid men who could not reach them through the barrage. Those who were still untouched deafened their ears to their comrades cries as they pressed forward, advancing in little rushes from mound to olive tree to fold of earth, moving toward the enemy with an audacity later called "insane." The bravest and luckiest of them even reached the naked approaches to the crest of Pingarron.

By about three o'clock, the clouds that had given way to sunshine gathered darkly and began to dump heavy rain on the highlands, turning the battleground into mud. The worsening weather, the overwhelming enemy defense, and the dead and wounded surrounding them combined to change the Americans' direction. With no formal order that anyone could recall, word moved among those still struggling up the hill that the attack was off, that they should fall back to the trenches and save what lives remained.

All through the rainy afternoon and increasingly cold evening and night there was turmoil at the battlefield medical units.

"Rushed there, even though I wanted to stop and have it out with Copic," Bob wrote later in his diary:

> It was a butcher shop. People died on stretchers in the yard. I had to sit up. Pick in front of me badly wounded and on stretcher. Heard that Springhall had gotten it at the same time. Went to operating room. Pulling bullets out of man who had become an animal. Several doctors operating on stomach exploring for bullets while others died. Question of taking those who had a chance at all. After doctor put my arm on a board and I wanted to eat, they took my revolver and glasses. Finally told that Springhall was waiting for me and we were going to American hospital in Romeral.
>
> Nightmare of a ride. Lost our way. Three and a half hours going but had to give up while I lay on the floor of the ambulance. Springhall could talk which surprised me since he was shot through the head and jaw. Finally arrived and heard English and saw fine, clean, new hospital. Immediately ate while on the stretcher and went to bed. During the night others came in and Morse was operated on. Coming along. Finally transferred to Alcazar de San Juan. Another bad trip.

Bob broke and cried when he was informed his runner, Pick, had died in the hospital. He knew the chances of survival in the field units were slim. The doctors and nurses worked valiantly, but the units were really first aid stations, not well-equipped battlefield hospitals. They lacked painkillers, so the miserably wounded reacted ferociously to the undressing of their wounds.

At the hospital, the battle still blazing in his mind, Bob settled back to rest as best he could. But rest would not come easily as he wondered who from his command had survived, who was wounded, who had been killed, why Copic had demanded the Americans take the hill, and why Copic had overruled him when he reported the attempt would lead to slaughter. It was there, in the hospital, that Bob dictated the cable he sent to me in Moscow: "Wounded. Come at once."

The postmortems that began even as the machine-gun and rifle fire blazed through the rainy afternoon of February 27 continued long after the clatter of arms fell silent. The Americans angrily demanded to know why the fighting had been so devastating on the hilly battlefields of Jarama, why their unit had been thrown into such an impossible situation.

The questioning continued in the hospitals and rest camps, where members of the Abraham Lincoln Battalion were sent to regain their strength. Bob and the others analyzed the first fighting the Americans had endured, the heroism they had shown, the pain they had suffered.

Typical of the American assessment of Jarama were the feelings of Mel Anderson, a volunteer from California. "Jarama was very destructive," he observed. "Half the guys I had come over with on the boat, young guys, were dead within two weeks of our arrival. Had barely arrived when they were on trucks headed for Jarama. We were promised air cover that didn't materialize." Anderson, a machine-gunner, crawled under fire to pull back bodies, the wounded and the dead, for treatment or eventual burial. "In two weeks' time, half of us were gone. What chances did we have of surviving this? But we went on to do a job."

An anonymous soldier, offering notes and observations for an official story of the battalion, asked troubling questions:

> Who in the Lincoln Battalion will not remember February 27th 'till the day of his death? Is there anyone in the battalion so calloused that he does not shudder when he thinks of the day when men cried in their desperation of whose faces were frozen into immobility by the horror of it? The day when men of the Lincoln Battalion learned that all values are relative to life, and when life is cheap all other values cease to exist. What of heroism can be said when all of the men of the battalion charged into the face of certain death—to escape it only by some freak whim of fate? Was it cowardice that made some men scream like stricken animals, after a bullet had plowed itself into their flesh; was it bravery that compelled others to keep their reason though their life blood was streaming from their bodies? To describe the brave deed of one who risked his life for the sake of a comrade is to forget or ignore those countless deeds of desperate courage that were not recorded on human minds befuddled by the horror that encompassed them.

Bob had mixed feelings about Jarama. He felt the holding of Madrid-Valencia road made the effort a success and he was, even at this early part of the war, soldier enough to know that losses must be suffered for gains achieved. But he was bitterly angry about the inadequate training time and the confusion in a headquarters that didn't know what was going on and wouldn't listen.

Bob hated Copic's arrogance. He could not believe, even weeks afterward, that a brigade commander could simply disregard a battlefield report and order the men into a rain of fire virtually certain of killing most of them.

Voros, who had interviewed Bob in great detail, analyzed the Jarama action this way:

> On February 27, a number of mistakes were made. Usually an attack is called off when certain key conditions don't materialize. The services did not participate in the attack in the coordinated manner as planned. It was also a mistake to inform the men in detail what support to expect in the attack because when the promised support failed to materialize they became reluctant to advance.
>
> The Americans were insufficiently trained. . . . The fascists showed their weakness in not counterattacking after the February 23 attack. Our attack on the 27th was the first counterattack against the fascist drive to cut the Madrid-Valencia road. The attack on the 27th had a strong positive feature. When the fascists saw so many new troops advance on such a narrow front they became scared of the unexpectedly strong forces opposing them. They eased their pressure and stopped their advance. The Madrid-Valencia road was saved.

This was the feeling of so many of the Americans—that despite the unbelievable losses, they had, in fact, held the road open for the Spanish Republic, the connection between the government in Madrid and the supplies in Valencia. "It would seem that the single most important fact to be learned from this attack," Landis observed,

> was that for the American Battalion it was a beginning of courage and not of failure. The Battalion would continue from this day to a point in the Spanish War where its name would be known and respected. When the opposing Fascist and Republican forces could be reckoned in army corps instead of brigades, . . . the press of Fascist Spain would still give the Lincolns special attention. Radio Burgos would tell of their annihilation, hysterically boast of their capture or destruction, and in this way attest to their fear of the

élan, of the courage, and of the fighting tenacity of the men of the Lincoln Brigade.

Only sixty to eighty Americans lived through the horror of Jarama without shedding their blood into the soil of Spain. One hundred and twenty-seven were killed and almost two hundred were wounded.

Enrique Lister, high in the Republican command, observed that "the combat behavior of American troops was excellent. They were very brave, very valiant. They came with a type of romantic idea to fight with the people against fascism. This was characteristic of the International Brigades. They were the ambassadors of many peoples of the world that brought these feelings. If we speak about Americans, they were people with democratic ideas. It was magnificient that they came to fight for us. It reminded me of the revolution in France, and, among great international happenings, this was one of them."

Ernest Hemingway, who arrived in March of 1937 and learned of the first American deaths in the Jarama battle from others, believed the orders to attack under such detrimental conditions were idiotic. His and other American correspondents' stories about the Abraham Lincoln Battalion moved America—for better and for worse. The list of correspondents who worked close to the American volunteers is as distinguished as any covering any war—Hemingway, Josephine Herbst, Martha Gellhorn, Herbert Matthews of the *New York Times,* and others. [. . .]

As they rested afterward, the Americans who survived memorialized the battle of Jarama in lyrics sung to the mournful tune of "The Red River Valley":

> There's a valley in Spain called Jarama
> It's a place that we all know too well
> For 'tis there that we gave of our manhood
> It was there that our first comrades fell

MARION MERRIMAN WACHTEL was one of two U. S. women members of the Lincoln Battalion (other women were medical personnel, a truck driver, and a social worker), serving at her husband's side as he commanded the U. S. volunteers. Since then she has served as a commander of the San Francisco Bay Area Post of the VALB. WARREN LERUDE, the coauthor, teaches at the University of Nevada. This piece is taken from their book *American Commander in Spain* (Reno: University of Nevada Press, 1986), and is reprinted with permission. Full references can be found there.

· Arthur H. Landis ·

American Fliers in Spanish Skies

Madrid Front, February 18, 1937. Allison, Dahl, Leider, and Tinker, flying in a squadron of eleven aircraft, ran into a fleet of Heinkels. There were four or five down beneath them for bait and some eighty others high in the clouds. Once again the fascists, thinking that the squadron was alone, were willing to fight. The Americans dived for the low flying Heinkels and brought them all down. Ben Leider got one (his second), James Allison and Harold (Whitey) Dahl, two more. Then, as the hidden Rebel fleet plunged down through the clouds, twenty-eight government Chatos spiraled out of the sun to reinforce the American squadron, while another twenty-eight Republican Moscas ripped into the enemy fighters from the north. The whirling kaleidoscope of battle continued. Seven additional Heinkels were shot down. Allison, wounded twice, had his tail assembly shot off and was forced down. He landed safely. Ben Leider was hit in both legs. Losing blood rapidly, he made for the landing field at Alcala. He overshot it and turned to try again. This time he made it but he came down hard. His limp body was crushed against the instrument panel."

The above is from an article by James Hawthorne, who interviewed American volunteers with the Lacale Squadron of the Spanish Republican air force in 1937. It depicts but a single day of battle by American fighter pilots in a war whose particulars were all too soon erased by the maelstroms of World War II, Korea, and Vietnam.

The loss of Leider was duly noted by the *New York Post*, for whom he had worked as a "flying reporter." The *New York Times* and other newspapers across the country eulogized his death, most printing the tribute to him broadcast on Radio Madrid's English hour. Little mention, however, was made of the fact that Leider was no mercenary. Indeed, his volunteering to defend the Spanish Republic was but a simple extension of his life pattern. A founder of the American Newspaper Guild, he had participated in its earliest battles for recognition. Using his flying ability, he had picketed by air with huge banners attached to his tail assembly. He had flown to Seattle to demonstrate against the *Post Intelligencer* of William Randolph Hearst. As Alvah Bessie, himself a veteran of the Spanish war and later, one of the famed Hollywood Ten of the McCarthy period, so succinctly put it: "Ben always knew that his ability to fly would be of use to his fellow men."

More than thirty Americans flew for the Spanish Republic; none for the fascist regime of Franco. Some were shot down. Others, taken prisoner, faced summary execution. For in that most sanguinary of wars—a million dead in the short space of two and one-half years—the cavalier spirit of the flying adversaries of World War I had simply ceased to exist. Volunteer Lieutenant Orrion D. Bell, who had flown in the U.S. and Canadian air forces, wrote of what happened when a pilot of the squadron in which he fought was forced to land in Franco territory: "The warning comes one night when our pilot is returned in a box dropped by parachute. His body is mutilated. The sight of it nearly shatters my reason. We turn out at dawn to give our answer."

The Spanish Civil War, in which the power elite of landed aristocracy, military, and church rose against the elected government of the Spanish people, with the aid of Nazi Germany and fascist Italy, has been described as the "last pure cause" and the "last crusade." That it was unlike any war before or since is certainly agreed upon. That the *air war* in Spain was singularly different from either of the two great wars is absolute fact.

Spelling it out for the aficionados of the quasi-myth and romance days of "Flying Circuses," "Lafayette Escadrilles," and Snoopy's "Red Baron," the air war in Spain was the finale to all that had been developed in the "Great War"—but honed to an absolute excellence. The aircraft flown were the last evolution of the colorful Fokkers and Spads. The Spanish Civil War was, in essence, the catalyst to the transition, the metamorphosis of air technology as it exists today. . . .

In *no* war have there been dogfights quite like those that took place in Iberian skies. For what with the slow speeds and limited armament of the times, a mixing of opposing squadrons over a battlefield was a sight to behold. At the peak of the Republic's strength—January 1937 through January 1938—as many as a hundred aircraft would slam it out in a kaleidoscope of barrel rolls, Immelmann turns, and protective pinwheels (Lufberry circles) over a section of front through which a jet of today would pass in a single second. Herbert Matthews of the *New York Times* wrote of a single engagement in Aragon: "September 3, 1937, witnessed the greatest Rebel air defeat of the campaign (Belchite). More than one hundred planes were involved in a tornado of screaming wings and raging guns. For the space of forty-eight hours the Condor Legion and the swarms of Fiats were driven from the skies."

That Spain was truly the omega of the romance period of fighter aircraft is solid fact.

The lines were precisely drawn. The Nazi Condor Legion served Franco, as did whole squadrons of Mussolini's air force. Soviet aid, at the request of the Republic, arrived belatedly some three critical months after that of the Axis powers. To oppose the Nazi and fascist air fleets, there was at first only the loyal air corps with its antiquated planes. After the swift destruction of these units—and for the first year—there was then the colorful combo of Spanish, Soviet, and International pilots—these last drawn from every country in Europe and the United States.

The first Internationals, arriving before the Russians, flew what can only be described as "waddling disasters," salvaged from Europe's junkyards, purchased at great cost, and literally smuggled across the Republic's borders. For the Popular Front government, from the first moment, had been denied its rights under international law to purchase arms *anywhere*. This, by the infamous London Committee of Non-Intervention. . . .

In the ranks of the International flyers were such notables as the writer André Malraux and the Italian Republican Randolfo Pacciardi. Malraux brought with him to beleaguered Madrid two ancient Potez bombers and a handful of pilots. Today he is France's minister of culture. Pacciardi flew briefly for the government and then commanded the famed Italian Twelfth International (Garibaldi) Brigade. He once had the audacity to leaflet Mussolini's Rome from a private plane, fleeing to France with Benito's air force in hot pursuit. Randolfo Pacciardi went on to become Italy's first post–World War II minister of war.

Stephen Daduk of New York was the first American to fly for the Republic. He arrived in the terrible days of November 1936, when Franco's Army of Africa, backed by masses of Italian tanks and German planes, was pounding against the living wall of militiamen holding shut the gates of Madrid. It has been verified that Daduk brought down a Heinkel 111 while acting as a gunner on a Breguet bomber. Days later he himself was shot down over Madrid's Cuatro Caminos district while flying a patched-up British Air-Speed bomber. Upon recuperation—he had sustained a broken thigh—he spent a short period training a company of the Abraham Lincoln Battalion for its first action. He then returned to the United States to raise funds for the Spanish Republic.

"Scotty" Nelson, Arthur Shapiro, and Albert Bauman were next in Spanish skies. *Current History* (January 1937) describes Nelson as "an almost legendary figure who bears many a scar in token of wars in Latin America, China and elsewhere." Albert Bauman, also a fighter pilot, was slated to command an all-Spanish squadron for a number of months on the Granada and Cordoba fronts.

Captain Bert Acosta, personal pilot to Admiral Byrd, famed Antarctic explorer, led the next group. Edwin L. Semons, a young New Yorker, after contacting Republican recruiting officers, approached Acosta, Lieutenant Eddie Schneider, Major Frederick I. Lord, and Captain Gordon Berry with an offer of $1,500 a month. They accepted. Joined by Lieutenant Edward

Lyons, they sailed for France on the *Normandie* on November 11, 1936.

Once in Spain most of the above separated from Acosta. He was then joined by men who can only be described as true mercenaries. With these he went directly to Madrid. Checked out in Potez and Breguet bombers, they flew for as long as a month over the Madrid and Somosierra fronts. A *New York Times* dispatch referred to them as "loading thirty-pound anti-personnel bombs for a Christmas Eve visit to Franco's Moors in the trenches at Carabanchel." The image of Acosta's group fared poorly with other American flyers. Lieutenant Frank G. Tinker, America's outstanding "ace" in Spain—he shot down eight planes—wrote of them that "they left an extremely unsavory reputation for the rest of the Americans to live down. They arrived in Spain drunk, were drunk practically all the time they were there, and were still drunk when they were poured aboard the homeward bound steamer."

Major Frederick I. Lord was also described as a "soldier of fortune." He was to tell *Life* magazine, however, that "the struggle of the Spanish people changed me from an adventurer to a zealous partisan." Born in Texas, Lord had had an outstanding career. He had enlisted in the Royal Air Corps in Canada in World War I to become one of England's top-ranking aces. By the war's end he had no less than twenty-two enemy aircraft to his credit. [. . .]

American pilots flew anything and everything. The required number of flying hours for eligibility, preferably military, was 2,500. How closely this was adhered to is a moot question. Instructors were either Spanish or Russian, most Americans having arrived in Spain after the Russians.

For the record, between fifty and a hundred Soviet pilots, together with their ground crews, served the Republic at one time. The fighter planes that accompanied them, the Polikarpovs 1-15 and 1-16, were superior to anything the Germans or Italians could put into the air—this, prior to the arrival of the Messerschmitt Bf109 in June 1937. The Polikarpov 1-15 was a biplane, called a Chato by the Spaniards—the name being an endearing term for a small snub-nosed boy. The 1-16 was a monoplane, affectionately called a Mosca, or fly. With the exception of the advanced SB-2, the Soviet bombers, the Katiuskas and Rasantes were far outclassed by the Axis Junkers, Capronis, and Savoias. The first squadron of Chatos to challenge the Condor Legion over Madrid shot down six Junker bombers from a flight of fifteen, and thereby earned the title of "La Gloriosa" from Madrid's embattled militiamen.

But, as stated, the Americans spent their first days in the "waddling disasters." And even with these they made their mark.

Lieutenant Orin D. Bell had, like Major Frederick I. Lord, flown in the Royal Canadian Air Force in World War I. His record too was exemplary. He had six kills to his credit. In Spain he shot down no less than seven Fiats and Heinkels on the Granada and Cordoba fronts. Flying with two other Americans, Charles Koch and James (Tex) Allison, in a Spanish squadron, he describes two of his victories: "We arrive at our objective, the trenches of Granada. Nine Heinkel fighters come out of the mists of the north. They slide in under our tails to attack our bombers several thousand feet below. Martínez signals and we break into a triangular combat pattern. Our engines are throttled way down. The next instant all of us are diving upon the enemy planes below.

"I brace myself. My mouth is open, my heart pounds wildly while I streak earthward. The wires of my plane hum an eerie note that is heard above the engine's drone. Down . . . Down. An enemy ship flashes in my sights and is gone. Another follows. I pull the trigger once, twice. The Heinkel hesitates, tumbles earthward.

"I pull up into a 'squirrel-cage' maneuver. At the top of it another Heinkel waits. I hesitate. One burst. Two. Flames burst around the enemy plane. By this time their flight is demoralized. They scamper quickly for home. Our group reforms and we head for our field."

Charles Koch, reputedly, shot down a plane in this same engagement.

American bomber pilots faired poorly. Major Lord, the only American to lead a bomber squadron—volunteers Sam Brennan, Sidney Holland, and Nolde and Finnick (first names unknown) flew with him—describes an air battle: "Poor old Sidney

Holland told me he had come to Spain to get another start in life. He went with me on a bombing raid early last winter, flying an old unarmed cabin job. A swarm of Heinkels—tracer and incendiary bullets. A burst of flame. He looked like a falling star as he plummeted to earth. We were surrounded by Heinkels then. My Spanish gunner—he was an orchestra leader a few months ago—had but one gun. Four of them were under my tail, so close I could see their goggles. But he disdainfully waved them to come closer. 'En Dios!' he informed me later, 'I had only a few bullets left.' " [. . .]

An example of close cooperation between Russian, Spanish, and American pilots is shown in Tinker's report of an aerial combat over the city of Teruel. The time was April 17, 1937. Lieutenant Tinker was acting commander of the mixed Spanish-American Lacalle Squadron.

"Then I saw the enemy. They were off to our right, in three echelons of seven planes each. Their lowest was at 10,000, their highest at 13,000 feet [. . .]

"Simultaneously with this I saw a patrol of ours close in on the lowest, while a second patrol headed for the middle echelon. Since the Katiuskas were now safe, I headed for the third and highest of the enemy echelons. We were eighteen to their twenty-two.

". . . Our first patrol (Spanish, under the command of a Captain Calvo) went into action against the first echelon. There was a fierce scramble for a few seconds, then two of the Heinkels came wavering down. They immediately went into their final spins and splattered against the terrain a couple of miles below. Then one of our planes came wavering out, caught itself for a moment, came around and up in a sharp left *chandell*, and collided head-on with an enemy plane. Even in the bright sunlight the explosion was blinding in its intensity.

"I waggle my wings—our break-up signal—and we closed on individual planes. There is a mad whirl of planes. Some slide across my sight—at first only gravish ones with black emblems—each getting a burst of machine-gun fire; and then, as the affair becomes more intimate, planes of both sides slide across so that caution becomes necessary to keep from firing on one's own planes. We have to be careful not to bank too violently or we 'black out'; that is, the centrifugal force draws the blood away from our heads and sight dims to complete blackness unless the pressure is eased. To black out completely in a dog-fight means almost certain death.

"I see a plane turning in toward me and I automatically pull over to meet it. I get in line first, and open fire, steadily this time. Although my adversary never succeeds in getting in line, I see his machine guns winking away and his tracers dripping blobs of smoke—as I suppose he sees mine—but he is just a trifle too late.

"Metal starts flying from the left side of his motor, followed by water and black smoke. Then a line of fabric tatters works down the sleek side of the plane. As he goes past he is in a sort of sliding roll, and is already headed for the ground trailing the unmistakable greasy black smoke. (I remember wishing at the time that someone was off in the distance taking motion pictures, so that I could see what a dogfight really looks like; you can't see an entire fight when you are in it.) We are still tangled up with a few Heinkels, so once more I start handing out short bursts. I get behind one of them and am just getting lined up for the kill when one of them gets behind me. Fortunately, out of the corner of my eye, I can see the familiar tracer streaks just off to the right and pull around in a violent vertical bank to the left. A close call! The Heinkel either can't follow or doesn't care to, and continues on down in his dive.

"I look around and note with relief that all my men are still intact and doing well. The Heinkels have got tired of playing, and are diving for the ground as fast as they can get clear. They can out dive us but we follow and fire until they are out of range.

"At this point more or less coherent thought started again. I saw that we had plenty of men below, so I pulled up and organized my formation again at 5000 feet. The only enemy planes in sight were two who were cornered in a little valley below by five of Kosakov's men. These two were polished off as I watched— they didn't have a chance. The valley had sides that were just high enough to eliminate any chance of the two unfortunate Heinkels being able to climb out, and our planes could out climb them; so all they could do was fly around in the little valley until they were shot down. You can't even surrender in an airplane; your opponents wouldn't know whether you were joking or not."

Tinker, Dahl, Baumler, Shapiro, Chang Selles, and a number of other American fighter pilots flew throughout the Italian debacle at Guadalajara—where a full four divisions of Mussolini's "Black-Shirts" ran for their very lives. Their Chatos, able to carry four twenty-five pound bombs in racks under the wings, were especially deadly to the ground troops—along with their incessant machine-gunning. [. . .]

Lieutenant Tinker writes of the Italian defeat at Guadalajara: "March 12, 1936: . . . we came down to 6,500 feet and accompanied the bombers across the lines. Even from that height we could see that a great battle was in progress below. The flashes of artillery from both sides were almost continuous. Three of our heavy bombers made a direct hit on the crossroad northwest of Brihuega and completely ruined it. They also wrecked fifteen or twenty trucks. One huge truck, actually whirling end-over-end, made a most impressive sight. As soon as our bombers were safely back in our territory we dove down on the poor devils ourselves and cut loose with bombs and machine guns. . . . I spotted one especially large group of Italians in wild retreat before a couple of tanks. At about 700 feet I opened fire with one upper and one lower machine gun. This was so I could see by the tracer bullets whether or not I was on target.

"By this time I could see the individuals plainly; they had also become aware of my presence. . . . I could see dead-white faces swivel around and, at sight of the plane, comprehension would turn them even whiter. I could see their lips drawing back from their teeth in stark terror. Some of them tried to run at right angles but it was too late; already they were falling like grain before the reaper. . . ." [. . .]

Whereas all Heinkels, and later the Messerschmitt Bf109s, were flown exclusively by Germans, the Fiat CR-32 was flown by Italian and Spanish pilots. Republican statistics—based upon enemy pilots captured—reveal that less than 15 percent of Franco's flyers were Spanish; 25 percent were German; the remainder, Italian.

Most Americans agree that Spanish pilots flying for Franco's fascist-military fought well. Also, if you pointed your plane at a Heinkel 51, the pilot, generally, would point it right back at you. This was not true of the Italians; though this fact is no reflection upon their courage. They simply had no desire to risk their lives for Mussolini, let alone the fat little *Caudillo*, Francisco Franco. Usually, if given a choice to engage or not engage, they chose the latter. Also, they had developed a healthy respect for the Chato and Mosca. Statistics, backed by Herbert Matthews and other American reporters, suggest that Franco's losses, as opposed to those of the Republic, were at a ratio of two to one. This with Russian aircraft as opposed to fascist aircraft, and not to the early "waddling disasters." [. . .]

Aboard the *Queen Mary* in the spring of 1937 were fifteen new volunteers for the Lincoln Battalion, plus two flyers, James Peck and Paul Williams, *both black!* This latter fact is singularly notable in that as of 1930 there were but *five licensed black pilots in the entire United States.* Both Williams and Peck had had considerable flying time in everything from Curtiss Fledgelings to Ford trimotors. Williams was an aviation engineer. They had no trouble at all at the air ministry, or with their Spanish and Russian instructors. Peck was checked out in an old deHavilland Moth, and then in the excellent French monoplane trainer, the Caudron. By the second week of training, in August 1937, he graduated to the Chato and was assigned to a squadron. Peck and Williams were to be two of the last Americans to fly for the Spanish Republic.

After Guadalajara the presence of International and Soviet pilots began to diminish. At the time of Brunete—the Republican offensive was to the west of Madrid—it is estimated that the Republican air force was already 80 percent Spanish. By the end of November 1937, it was *all* Spanish. James Allison, his wound still festering, was sent to France for treatment, and then home; Charles Koch and Major Lord, likewise Scotty Nelson, Lieutenant Orin D. Bell, Edward Scheider, Edward Lyons, and some of the bomber pilots had also completed their contracts and were on their way home. By the time of Brunete, only Albert Baumler, Arthur Shapiro, Frank Tinker, Whitey Dahl, Chang Selles, and the bomber pilots Nolde and Finnick, plus the transport pilots, still flew. These last were such men as

Derek Dickenson—he also flew fighter and observation planes—
a pilot by the name of Barney, and the very colorful Lieutenant
Rosmarin, who flew a Douglas transport for the government. [. . .]

Harold (Whitey) Dahl, still flying the Chato, though credited
with an additional Heinkel, was himself shot down and forced to
parachute into enemy territory. It was the second time he had
been forced to jump; the first, when his tail assembly had been
shot off over Teruel. His capture made headlines in every major
newspaper in the United States. He was sentenced to death by a
fascist tribunal for having fought for the "Red" forces of the
Spanish Republic. His wife—she had been living in Paris—made
personal contact with Franco. Her impassioned pleas sup-
posedly secured his release. Actually, the act was simply good
PR work for Spain's fascist-military in the halls of the U.S.
Congress. The "American firsters" of that day made the most of
it.

On July 29, 1937, Lieutenant Frank G. Tinker made his last
flight over the Madrid front. He writes laconically that "it was
uneventful." Baumler too left shortly after that.

The colorful period of International and Soviet participation
in the air war for the Spanish Republic was coming to an end.
Peck, Williams, and a few others still flew in Aragon. But that
was about it. Peck flew for just four months. In this short time he
brought down two Heinkel 51s and three Fiats, to become America's fourth "ace" in the Spanish Civil War. He was wounded in
one engagement, a bullet penetrating his seat pack to lodge in
his thigh. His last flight, for which he was decorated by the
government, was made against Italian air bases on the rebel-
held island of Majorca. Caproni and Savoia bombers had long
operated from these bases against Republican shipping and the
seaports of Barcelona, Valencia, and Cartagena.

James Peck's squadron of Chatos escorted several squadrons
of Soviet SB-2s, the world's fastest bomber at that time. Reputedly, the SB-2s wreaked destruction on aircraft and port
installations alike, while Peck's fighter group swept in low to
shoot up the fascist airdromes.

As stated, it was his last flight. Indeed, it seems to have been
the last flight of any International volunteer in the Spanish Civil

War. All left an enviable record; certainly the Americans. For during their period of combat they were accredited with upward of *forty-eight* Junkers, Capronis, Heinkels, Fiats, and the then new Messerschmitts. They produced four aces: Tinker with eight. Orrin D. Bell with seven. Albert Baumler with five. James Peck with five. [. . .]

In the skies above the ever mounting cauldron of flames and ear-splitting cadenzas, the young Spanish pilots continued to the end to go freely and courageously to that most unequal of all struggles. The little green Chatos and Moscas would dip their stubby wings, tipped with the red, yellow, and purple of the Republic, over the embattled trenches to give their men heart and courage. They would then rise in their coveys of threes and sixes to pit their diminishing strength against the swarms of Fiats, Heinkels, and Messerschmitts. Their prowess was such that they would win at the two-to-one ratio. But like their comrades on the ground, their victory would be hollow. For the Fiats and Heinkels were replaced on the morrow—the Chatos, never.

On April 1, 1939, the tragedy of Munich was compounded with the death of the Spanish Republic. Six months later World War II began.

The American volunteers returned to a country wherein the media of press and radio, *as if on cue,* ignored them, influenced then as now by the power and policy of government. Many of the flyers were subjected to a harassment akin to that given returning members of the Abraham Lincoln Brigade. Their passports were seized, their patriotism was questioned. Lieutenant Frank G. Tinker, for one, was denied his right of reenlistment into either the U.S. army, air force, or navy. *Within a year he had taken his own life.*

Major Frederick I. Lord, ill in a Paris hospital, received official notice from the army, informing him that his commission as a major in the United States Air Corps Reserve had been cancelled because he had served Spain's legitimate government. There simply was no precedent for such action in the long history of the United States. It was in contradistinction to all past policy. For Americans had volunteered—indeed, been honored by their government—for flying for France's Lafayette Escadrille, Canada's R.C.A.F., sundry Latin American armies, and, later, Claire

Chennault's famed "Flying Tigers." Why now, one would ask, were they not given similar respect, similar honors?

Shortly before his death, Major Lord wrote the following: "Why, why, I wondered, this sudden condemnation by the press, the army, and U.S. officialdom? I had believed Americans sympathetic to the ideals of democracy, but in Paris it seemed that America had sold out to fascism and Franco. I was puzzled but not disturbed. . . . For I had fought side-by-side with a nation of people who were not fighting a war of aggression, not fighting to conquer new territory or to enslave another race, but who were fighting that they themselves might live, and that their young Republic might not vanish from the earth. I think now that I understand what patriotism really is. I am proud to think that I have done my tiny bit."

An interesting addendum to Major Lord's record is that he fought for Denikin's White army in the Crimea in 1919, *against* the Soviets. This act had had no effect upon his air corps commission then. Indeed, and unfortunately, perhaps, it would seem that it helped to consolidate it.

One can only conclude that Ben Leider's thinking best epitomized that of the American volunteer fliers for the Spanish Republic. In a last letter to his brother on the eve of his death, he wrote: "And so it comes to pass, that I in the same cosmic mood in which my great grandfather mounted his immortal nag, *Rosinante*, centuries ago, and set forth to pit his single scrawny arm against the totality of world evil—I, a *Don Quixote* of space, now clamber into the cockpit of my trusty old crate, "The Mocking Bird," and take off into the blue to carry the battle for the good and the true . . .

"Your dauntless knight of the fallen arches."
Ben
Somewhere in Spain, February 1937

ARTHUR LANDIS went to Spain at the age of nineteen, and, after considerable battle experience, was appointed commissar of the Mac-Paps. On his return, he earned his living as a science-fiction writer but maintained his interest in Spain. The result was two books, *The Abraham Lincoln Brigade* (1967) and *Spain! Unfinished Revolution* (1972). He died in 1986. This is excerpted from a piece first published in *Air Combat* (March 1975).

· Paul Burns ·

Michael Kelly Reports

"Attention Irish Section!"

"Now, lads—"

It was Michael Kelly speaking. Michael Kelly of County Galway, otherwise Sergeant Mick Kelly, commander of the James Connolly Section, First Infantry Company of the Lincoln Battalion.

The place was Villanueva de la Jara, first training area for the Abraham Lincoln Battalion. The time—January 1937.

"Lads, this is the thing. When you hear the command Route Column March, Comrade McElroy's column will lead off to the right, McGrotty's column will follow moving to the left, and Wilson's men will bring up the rear, moving again to the right.

"Remember now, there's one Chau Chau gun to each column. Now lads, I don't want anyone of you to bollix it up. Atten-SHUN, Right . . . FACE! By the right . . . quick MARCH!"

The lean cheeks of the man tightened in a sardonic skull-like smile. Cold gray eyes permitted the indignity of pride, and seven hundred years of fighting men churned the red Spanish earth.

A song lifted to the cadence of marching feet. It was an old song, "Michael Kelly the Boy from Killan," having to do with another time, another place, another Kelly, another struggle.

"They're like another Citizens' Army," Sergeant Kelly murmured.

Days folded together like an accordion. Maneuvers gave way

to reality. Time found the Irish, the Cubans, and the Americans—the three sections comprising the first company—huddled in the wet February trenches of Jarama high above the Madrid-Valencia road.

"Here it is now," said Sergeant Kelly. "This is the real thing. We're to go over."

"When I give the command number one group will go first followed by number two and number three. 'Tis ourselves will go first.' Tis an honor lads, to go first. Now then look to your rifles. And remember, 'tis a mortal sin to cross your own fire."

"Up with you, lads."

It was up with you and over and down.

A snarl of machine-gun fire broke out of the fascist lines. Explosive bullets speckled the night.

"Good lads," Sergeant Kelley murmured, this time without fearing that the lads would hear the terrible admission. Then the clouds put on their swastikas and ordered rain.

Back through the rain came Sergeant Kelly, slowly, painfully crawling, pulling something. Lit by momentary shell flash the lean skull face leered back at a knot of men tending a Maxim, happy replacement for the French Chau Chau gun that was obsolete before World War I.

Lips flared back and the brogue played.

"Lads, 'tis one of the Cuban comrades. He's bad hit. Lads, he's a cool one. 'Don't bother about me,' he says. He wanted me to leave him there and bring in his friend.

"Now lads, I'll bring you the other one. The boys are doing great, they are."

He moved away running, crawling, flopping behind whatever cover there was. Then, soaked to the skin, his uniform torn and one puttee spiraling out behind him, he returned with "the other one."

Hands reached out to receive the wounded man and at that precise moment Kelly felt a great blow in the chest, toppled head-down into the machine gun pit, bucked up his back, pulled his knees up almost to his chin, then shot his legs straight out again and said, "A-a-ah."

In the hospital back of the lines, Sergeant Kelly looked up at the bearded French doctor and Spanish nurse bending over him.

He sorted out the words as they reached him, unsheathed his teeth in a death's-head grin. "Me name is Michael Kelly," he said very softly.

And the days passed by. New days brought sun and warmth, then heat along the Jarama river. Between the lines, theirs and ours, green small clusters of leaves struggled up from scarred vines.

Back from the dead came Sergeant Kelly, harbinger of spring, thinner, a little stooped, his brogue ricocheting off the rocks below the front line. "Me name is Michael Kelly," he remarked to a new battalion clerk. "The doctors wanted to keep me in the rear so I've come back on me own. Sure, what's a bullet in the side to keep a man in the rear? Here's me papers."

Unconvinced that "one little bullet in the side" did not really matter, Battalion Headquarters compromised with a man's pride as noted in the order of the day:

> Sergeant Michael Kelly, formerly in command of Section 1, 1st Infantry Co., is returned with partial disability resulting from wounds received in action February 27. Unfit for full-time active service, Sergeant Kelly is attached to Battalion Headquarters. His duties to be of a clerical nature.

On reading the posted order, the Kelly reaction was a thing of beauty plus sound effects. When his eyes lit on the words "unfit for full-time active service," even his best friends moved back. His mouth opened and his throat sent up a rocket of profanity—awe-inspiring, majestic, beautiful, which burst directly over Company Headquarters.

"Now lads," he said. "You all know better than that. Even the company commander knows better than that. Sure any one of you knows better than that. 'Unfit for active service,' am I? Ho, and myself just after having a good rest in the hospital. Not that I'm criticizing my superior officers. Indeed I'm not, I'm not one to go grumbling behind Captain Hourihan's back, lads. Tis himself is Battalion Commandant and what he says, goes. But, mind you, we all can make mistakes. Mind you, I'm not saying Captain Hourihan is making the mistakes. Sure he's not to blame at all."

"'Tis the doctors' mistake, it is. Not that they aren't good doctors. I wouldn't be the one to say they're not good doctors, lads, but—."

What was left of the James Connolly Section, the original "lads," welcomed him back to the line. Hugh Bonar, a quiet man from Donegal, wrung his hand nearly off. Paddy Stanley, from Dublin, who had been lured out from under the Kelly wing by the devious cajolery of the machine-gun commander, improvised some new verses to the immortal ballad "Biddy Mulligan":

> And where would you see
> A foine sergeant like me
> Michael Kelly, the boy from
> the Coombh?

Of course Kelly was *not* from the Coombh, but Paddy Stanley was not one to take too many liberties with Biddy's ballad.

And it came to pass that in the performance of "duties of a clerical nature" Michael Kelly managed to spend a good deal of his time in the front line while delivering mail to Battalion Headquarters or helping Doctor Pike and Doctor Simon in their campaign against dysentery by supervising the washing of mess kits after they had been scrubbed with clean sand.

And it did seem that the doctors had made a mistake, but you couldn't blame the doctors, for hadn't the entire British empire made the same mistake about the Kellys, from time immemorial?

No doubt the word went round in the fascist lines that Michael Kelly was back. Hearing which General O'Duffy and his blue-shirt Irish legion slunk ignominiously into the last pages of history and Generalissimo Franco frantically cabled Mussolini for another hundred thousand "Black Arrows—the kind you sent me for Guadalajara."

There came the day when Captain Martin Hourihan from "Philly" was promoted to the rank of line commander just before the Brunete offensive. Sergeant Michael Kelly was attached to his staff for special duties "definitely not of a clerical nature," said Kelly triumphantly. Definitely!

When Line Commander Hourihan got it bad at Vallanueva de la Cañada, Sergeant Kelly helped bring him in. Later that day the Lincolns crawled in a field of wheat overlooking the town. Fascist machine guns parked in church towers sprayed the field.

The flies were there ahead of time. Flies know about war.

Back of the infantry the Tom Mooney Machine-Gun Company gave covering fire for the men painfully advancing. Suddenly a brogue lifted above the din. "Don't shoot, lads, it's me Michael Kelly. There's a dispatch. General Miaja says the town is to be taken tonight." And through the wheat came Kelly.

He crawled over to the infantry commander to murmur in his ear, "and 'tis ourselves will take it." The town was taken that night. Among those who charged into the town that night was a thin little wraith of a man with a lean, dangerous face.

Others saw him fall, get up again, and pitch forward on his face. In the shell-streaked dark they turned him over. The little man was dead.

Someone took his papers and a militia book. Pasted in the book was his picture and below it his name was scrawled and the name was Michael Kelly.

PAUL BURNS was born in 1906 in Somerville, Massachusetts. After graduating from Middlebury College, he worked as a schoolteacher and social worker before becoming a journalist. He went to Spain with the second group of Lincoln volunteers, served at Jarama, and was invalided home after the first battle of Brunete. He served in the Eighth Air Force Heavy Bomber Group in World War II. He now lives in New York City.

· Jacques Grunblatt ·

Forever in Spain, I

October 1936. Even as a medical student in Marseilles I knew that the Spaniards had voted their king out of office and that Spain was a democratic republic, neither socialist nor communist. I regarded Franco as a traitor and, when the call came to save the Spanish Republic, I enrolled. I spent the next two and a half years in Spain. [. . .]

Strolling through the streets of Albacete I saw a new world. At the corner of a street I walked into a bar for a glass of wine. Inside it was shabbily furnished with rickety tables and chairs, but a victrola hoarsely played Spanish music. There weren't too many customers. Two Spaniards in old torn clothes, happiness radiating in their faces, were dancing around the little bar. I felt sure it was the first time Spanish peasants and workers such as they, who for centuries were exploited and downtrodden, felt free, happy, and uninhibited.

I do not know how long I stayed in Albacete. My first assignment was to be a doctor for a French group stationed in La Roda.

First Assignments. In La Roda I occupied the house of a doctor who ran away from the Republic. The house was spacious but not luxurious, and I used a big room in the middle of it for an infirmary. I had no beds, only mattresses. It was not long before my infirmary was full of sick soldiers.

137

Ironically, the first challenge I faced was an epidemic of mumps. Since there was no treatment for this disease, I had the men kept quiet and I treated them for their fevers and pain. One day Doctor Neuman, a highly placed medical officer, inspected my setup. He was very pleased and gave me my first pat on the shoulder.

A doctor from another French battalion visited me. He was clever. While I was concerned only with my patients, he looked in drawers and closets. He knew he would find something, and he did. In a medical jar he discovered a big pile of silver pesetas, which at that time were very valuable. He took them all, saying he would take them to headquarters.

After several weeks in La Roda, we were ordered to the front. That night we boarded open trucks and rode with the lights out for fear of attracting enemy planes. All night long we traveled over bumpy roads until we reached our destination, Morata de Tajuna on the Jarama river, part of the southern defenses of Madrid.

A range of hills formed the first line; a dirt road led to the hills, and a white barn stood on the right side of the road halfway to the trenches. Here I became the doctor of a cavalry squadron. By that time I was a lieutenant and wore an officer's uniform. The men and horses were stationed under trees behind the lines.

My squadron was composed of various nationalities: French, Belgians, Scandinavians, Italians. The only requirement was to be a horseman. We had about three to four hundred horses and men. Our captain was a young, dashing Italian with very little political preparation. With him was his young wife. His habits and way of running the squadron were those of the old European armies. The first night I was in the squadron, I was introduced at the officers' mess very formally and ritually, complete with a speech.

My medical team reflected the different nationalities of the squadron. There was Hans, a German, who was very efficient and very eager to maintain his position as head medic. I had a few Italian stretcher bearers, some of whom were mature men who played a big role in the Italian Communist Party. One Algerian appointed himself my personal aide because he expected some favors in return. I can still see his tall figure and round face as he very solicitously attended to my needs. Whenever I stirred and opened my eye in the morning, he was there at once with the best breakfast he could muster. Thanks to him I gained a tremendous amount of weight while we were held in reserve.

Some days he felt lazy and presented himself at the infirmary. He must have learned tricks from the Foreign Legionnaires. He would come to sick call complaining of a swollen, painful knee. I didn't know about the pain, but I did not see any swelling. Trying to be strict, I ordered him back to duty. He warned me that his knee was swollen, and if I did not believe him, I would see it in a short while. He returned half an hour later, and sure enough, he had a swollen knee. Since then I learned how the trick is done. He hit the knee lightly with a sandbag and the knee soon swelled.

My work consisted of holding sick call for my men and for men coming from the trenches. We treated injuries and all sorts of diseases. A few Spaniards were getting bismuth injections for syphilis.

From time to time my work and facility were inspected. General Gal, a military man who was not liked very much by anyone, inspected my post and cited me for an indelible stain on a sink, although everything else was spotless. I was glad when I had inspections by doctors like Doctor Michael, Doctor Langer, or Doctor Telge from the Albacete hospital. One time a soldier ran a fever for several days. I finally shipped him to the hospital in Albacete. Doctor Michael's first impression was that the man had typhoid. Doctor Michael censured me for keeping the soldier in sick bay so long. After testing and checking him closer, he decided it was not typhoid. Even though Doctor Michael made the wrong diagnosis at first and I was proved right, the citation against me remained on my record and did not help me as far as promotions were concerned.

The veterinarian attached to our squadron was a young Russian Jew who had just graduated from veterinary school. He was very dedicated to the animals and spent most of his time with the horses; he was a true *stakhanovist* (hard worker). Occasionally we had heart-to-heart talks. During the course of one conversation, he was critical of our captain saying that he did not mind that the captain lived with his wife in the squadron, but he expected the captain to be more efficient and more politically aware.

The cavalry was not called to duty on the front line often. In addition to the horses, we also had several motorcycles attached to our squadron. As long as the horses were not in use, our captain invented all kinds of exercises. One of his favorites was to have a horse compete with a motorcycle to show that a good motorcyclist can go everywhere a horse can go. It was interesting to see how a horse could keep up with a motorcycle on hills, through bushes and fields. One clever motorcyclist would win the game by driving his motorcycle between two closely growing trees.

To break up the boredom when our front line was calm, at night a few members of my team and I went on patrol between the lines. I was surprised to see my Algerian aide join us. This patrol was uneventful, but in the distance we heard noises and footsteps that could have come from an enemy patrol doing the same thing as we. During other lulls in the fighting, the opposing forces exchanged songs. A song that originated with the Republicans and was very popular with the enemy was "Ojos Verdes." Often they shouted to us, "Hey! Sing that again!" Unfortunately, the calm did not last.

Fierce fighting erupted along the Jarama front. The enemy was determined to break through our lines cost what it may. If we had given in, Madrid would have fallen. Many times our lines were close to collapse. One day the British batallion lost 50 percent of its contingent. The British doctor, Doctor Bradsworth, was so shaken by this defeat and having his post overrun that he was found wandering aimlessly until he came to my place. His thumb was injured; it became infected and had to be amputated later.

Even though horses at close range are easy targets for rifle fire, the situation was so desperate at one point that my squadron was called to boost the defenses. I followed close behind. Even before we reached the lines I had my first casualty. A stocky thirty- or forty-year-old rider fell limply from his horse. I was sure a bullet struck him because so many whistled in our ears.

In vain I searched for a wound. Instead he had suffered a heart attack in anticipation of the fight. He had no identification on him; all he carried was a thick pocket watch, which I gave to the political commissar of the unit. We held out, but at very high cost. The front line was stabilized and remained stable for the rest of the winter of 1937. We stayed at Morata de Tajuna until we were ordered to move to the battlefield at Brunete.

JACQUES GRUNBLATT was born in 1910 in Kolomyja, Poland. He studied medicine in France and volunteered for Spain in 1936. His first assignment was as a doctor in the cavalry squadron on the Jarama front, and his second with the Twenty-fourth Battalion of the Fifteenth Brigade. With the defeat of the Republican army, he returned to France, where he was interned in a camp in Gurs. He escaped and volunteered for the French army. After the defeat, he went to Mexico to practice medicine. He came to the United States in 1946, and, after acquiring the necessary qualifications, established a practice in North Creek, N.Y., where he still lives.

· Fredericka Martin ·

The American Hospital Unit

March 20, 1937

Anna dear:

I have heard just twice from the States and one note mentioning the fact that you were busy organizing a women's auxiliary to the Medical Bureau. So during this lull I'm going to try to write an appeal for you to transmit to your women associates to see if you can rally some support and aid for my girls.

Will you remember me to your nice Doctor Miller? I always think of him when I flit thru the store room and see the gauze and cotton stacked nearly to the ceiling in one corner and wonder what we'll do when it is gone and if none from the States will reach us. The lovely blanket you contributed is warming such a splendid young Spanish boy right now. We are all cowering in the present rainy damp weather inside those stone walls, even in bed with hot bottles and we have to pile blankets on our poor patients until they are nearly worn out by the weight alone. I am still clinging to the sweater you gave me. I have never been outside the hospital grounds since the day we arrived here and I see children only in the distance through the windows.

We have been here three weeks this afternoon. We started to unload our furniture about four o'clock. Two days later we received patients and worked madly day and night until a few days ago. Since then we have received only one or two patients a day. I wish I could convey my pride in my girls. They have been

142

superhuman. They have never lost their cheerful spirit or quarreled with each other or grumbled. Not *once* has a nurse been for a stroll. You see it is the nurse that oils the cogs of the hospital machinery. She prepares for the operations while the doctors sit and wait. And all the time she is caring for the patients. And except for one dreadful night when the floors were covered with wounded men on stretchers and borrowed mattresses, the patients here have had as good nursing care as any ward patient in New York City and better than many. We have thirteen Spanish girls whom we are trying to train but the results have been pretty hopeless up to now. Most of the actual work was done by our handful. When I tell you the girls had such swollen feet that some of them had to wear floppy patients' slippers in order to walk, it must sound unreal. But it is true.

I wish you would tell Jack Kahn how wonderful Sally has been. She has charge of our top floor with beds for fifty-four patients and space for extra mattresses. If you could have seen with your own eyes how neat and orderly those wards looked, the beds in orderly lines, the corners of the beds neat and trim, and the faces of the patients, smiling, contented, and happy. Our greatest reward is the grief that the patients display when they have to be moved on to the larger base hospital. And people come back from the front with stories that our fame has spread and all the boys want to be sent to Romeral if they are wounded.

The only trouble with Sally is that I cannot get her off duty at night. She is supposed to work from seven to seven in the day and Lini Fuhr has the three wards on the lower floor for the same hours. At night, Ray Harris works on both floors, with six Spanish girls to sit around and watch the patients and give them drinks and keep their hot water bottles filled. But every hour or so after seven I would spend a futile few minutes with Sally extracting a promise to go over to bed and then an hour later, I'd find her still on duty. And she would plead "But Freddie, I just had to do this for this patient. He's suffering so." And I would scold her like the devil and love her all the more for her devotion. At times there is no question of any nurse working less than sixteen hours a day or more. But these scenes took place when we were beginning to slow down a bit a few days ago. And yesterday Sally did collapse and is ill. All but one nurse has been ill in bed for two days and the cause was overwork. You can imagine how eagerly I am looking forward to the addition of more nurses to our group. I hope the committee has not forgotten our need in the excitement of preparing a new hospital outfit. If they cannot send us nurses, they could ship over six brawny women and assure our keeping on working. For if we get no reinforcements after six months all of us will be ready for the scrap heap. And four or six women, nurses, now, would mean we could manage the work and keep going for years.

I suppose you wonder what the rest of us are doing. I spoke of three nurses. Anna Taft and Helen Freeman work in the operating room—night and day. For there are tremendous technical preparations between periods of continuous operating. When poor Taft stands for ten to twelve hours in her gown and gloves, assisting first one doctor operating and then another, and Helen runs back and forth—real perpetual motion at last.

Our lab technician, Rose Freed, sandwiches in a great deal of nursing along with her laboratory work and is a peach. Myself— I don't know what I do or don't do really. I had to plan meals for the two kitchens, run the cleaning women, laundresses, two dreamy Don Juans who are supposed to be stretcher bearers and are just too elusive for words, always vanishing into thin air, buy some supplies in the village, give the nurses a helping hand everywhere and mother all the personnel. When I cracked up a few days ago, I had a record of three sleepless nights and a maximum four-hour nap one night. And the first day I spent in bed I was delirious at times and issuing orders in English and in Spanish for every sort of job. The strain has been terrible for it was just one million times more difficult to do since I had only a few words of Spanish and signs to see that most of the work was done. I didn't crack from the strain but a patient walking from the ambulance fainted and there was only another girl there and we had to get him to the house. And lifting him I strained myself but after two days in bed I'm hale and hearty again. Only once I was down, the nervous strain had a chance to express itself.

Now I could write stories for hours, if I had the hours, and I only wish I could so you could shout them aloud. But I do want to beg you, to show this to Mrs. Feltenstein and others of the committee and tell them about my girls and tell them I'm crying out for a few more nurses to help my girls before they are worn out.

If you want to help us or know individuals who would like to send supplies to us, here are suggestions, candy, fruitcake, crackers, cheese and fish pastes, cigarettes, of course, George Washington coffee. Small parcels are more apt to reach us than large. Whenever we are working at a headlong tempo, I am still able to fish down into my trunk and bring out a treat. You see on the boat we girls decided to save our boxes of candy for Spain and they were entrusted to me to dispense when I thought them most needed. I can still, as I said, provide another dozen treats, when work is terrific and goat meat or beans seem so difficult to swallow, I put two pieces of candy on a plate and put it in the center of the table and a cry of joy goes around and a yell that "Ma" is on the job again. It's very thrilling and I hope I can keep on contriving odd bits of surprises for them. They deserve so much, but it depends on the old United States and I am writing begging letters to a few people so that it can be kept up.

I had a small fruitcake and one day we had such a strain and a patient we all loved died and I made tea and called them into my room and fed each one a tablespoon of fruitcake. We had no knives at the time—hence the tablespoon. The result was dynamic. Anne stopped shivering, Sally's lips got a bit of color in them, etc. And I wished I had brought a trunkful of fruitcake for them.

Two things occurred to me without rereading this scrawl, which I am writing so hastily in an effort to utilize a free hour, never knowing when an ambulance will drive up and the mad rush begins again. One is that you may wonder why I write as if we had been here for years when we came here three weeks ago today. Well, a day seems ten weeks, sometimes a year. It seems as if we had been here for months and New York is a faint and unreal dream. All our lives we seem to have been running back and forth along these cold corridors, all our lives we have hated white moonlight because it means the birds of death are busy nearby, sometimes close to us and never did we consider moonlight beautiful or an aid to romance. All our lives we have been hating as we have learned to hate here, when we see the ravages of dum dum bullets in the flesh and bones of the best youth of all the world. The other thing I wanted to mention is the special strain of this nursing. There is nothing impersonal about it. Those patients are our comrades, are a part of us. When they suffer, we suffer and learn to hate them more. There is a terrific emotional drain always. If you have any voice in the committee, beg them to send us more nurses and doctors. Don't let them forget us. They can never fill the need here but they must never stop trying.

My best to you,
Freddie

FREDERICKA MARTIN went to Spain as head nurse of the American Hospital Unit. She graduated from the nursing school of Christ Hospital in Jersey City, New Jersey, and served on the staffs of Bellevue, Fordham, and Lying-In hospitals in New York City. She was a head nurse when she volunteered for duty in Spain and sailed with Dr. Barsky in January 1937. This letter is from Marcel Acier, ed., *From the Spanish Trenches* (1937).

· Lini de Vries ·

The Ebro Flows to the Thames

[. . .] Finally Doctor Barsky sent word that we were to begin leaving Valencia for Albacete. A building had been located that could be converted into a hospital. Within a few hours, four ambulances and six trucks carrying our goods and personnel slowly climbed up from sea level to the Plain of Castille. We were on our way to the Madrid front, but we did not know the exact location. Trucks passed us going the other direction, toward Valencia, with wounded, with women, but mostly filled with children and one or two adults watching over them. They shouted at us, "No pasarán!" (They shall not pass!) We answered, "No pasarán!"

Through fortified towns, around roadblocks, past cave dwellers and cliff dwellers, swerving for the many burros, we sped through the purple-pink sunset toward Albacete. Next we drove around huge bomb craters, as Albacete loomed ahead of us. As we entered the town, we saw walls half-standing, with bits of furniture hanging out defying gravity. Here there were more bomb craters that were fantastic and frightening. Soldiers everywhere spoke many languages. This was the supply depot of the International Brigades. No wonder the town was bombed often! I hoped we would not stay too long.

As we waited at headquarters to be assigned sleeping space, Doctor Bethune walked in, looking dusty, pallid, and sad. As I embraced him, welcoming him, I asked, "What is the matter? You look awful. You look sick."

147

"I feel sick, morally sick, that man can be so brutal as to fly low and deliberately machine-gun helpless women and children fleeing from a burning town. We were at Málaga delivering blood. The town was thoroughly bombed and captured by the fascists. We fled, and the people fled. We squeezed as many children as we could in our blood bank truck. The German and Italian flyers flew low, almost low enough for us to see the horrible grins on their faces, as they deliberately machine-gunned fleeing mothers and their children. I am lucky to be here," he answered me.

Believe me, I felt guilty to have been preoccupied about where I would sleep that night. When we were assigned space in the hospital X-ray room, I humbly looked for a spot on the floor to stretch my cramped bones. After the light was out, we opened the blackout curtains. The positions of the sleepers and the X-ray machines were weird as the soft moonlight filtered in on us. It was cold, as the windows were all shattered from the frequent bombings. But we were still alive!

We awoke stiff and cold. Our faces were dirty, our teeth unbrushed. We hoped we would get a little water. We did, and began what we later called a "whore's bath"—a bit of water for our teeth, then some to wash our faces and hands and under our arms. Finally we placed the basin on a chair and sat over the water to wash our genitalia. I don't know who named it a whore's bath, but I felt sorry for any poor prostitute who had to use cold water in such a bitterly cold room.

The bright sunlight of the day began warming our cold bones as we walked to headquarters to look for some bread and coffee. The streets were filled with men, old men and young men, in nondescript clothing that was supposed to pass for uniforms. The foreigners were more uniformed than the Spaniards. This was February 1937, when young and old had left fields, crops, and looms to go to the front. It was a people's army, as yet unorganized. The International Brigades had some organization. Many of them approached us and in their language asked what language we spoke. We smiled and answered, "American." Then came some who asked in halting English were we came from. I recognized their Dutch accent and replied in Dutch, "My parents are from Holland, but the rest are 100 percent Americans."

From then on, while in Albacete, the Dutch brigadiers became my escort. I was not too surprised when they told me that in relation to size and population of their country, the Dutch had more men in the International Brigades than did other countries. What Hollander had not studied of the long, hard fight for freedom against the persecution of the Spanish church, the Spanish royalty, and the Inquisition against the Hollanders? The same forces were the enemy today. I, too, had been influenced by Dutch history to go to Spain. It was the same church, the same aristocracy, the same family of the Duke of Alba, who were trying to prevent the Spaniards' transition from feudalism to democracy. We Hollanders marched down the streets singing the sixteenth-century songs of the fight against Spain. It was good to be with them here in Spain.

We are not born nationalistic, but we certainly acquire it. When I was with the Hollanders, I was all Dutch. When I was with the Americans, I was an American. Now I took sides with the Dutch soldiers. They disagreed with the judgment of the American Medical Unit, of which I was a member, about a German who had attached himself to the unit. We had met many Germans in Barcelona, some who had managed to escape Germany years ago when Hitler came to power, and some who were still escaping to "fight Hitler on Spanish soil," as they said. But this particular man, whose name was Rudolph, claimed to be an ardent anti-Nazi. We Dutch, who had little love for Hitler's Germany, smelled a rat. He was all "spit and apple polish" with the so-called important people, and arrogant and Prussian with the people who didn't count, especially women. It was true that he was extremely handsome and uniformed almost to perfection. Had Hitler equipped him? When he walked with us Dutch, he asked questions. When he was with the Americans, he asked questions. He gave up walking with us because we showed our suspicion of him. Stool pigeons always ask questions, I remembered from my mill days. Queer things, like slashed tires and motor troubles had been happening to our ambulances ever since we had been in France. I voiced my suspicions, but no one would believe me—perhaps because they thought I was a woman reacting to his misogyny—when I said, "There is something fishy about Rudolph. I don't trust him. Maybe he is a spy or one of Hitler's men in Spain." He was nothing like the refugee

Germans I had met in Holland in 1933, or like the many soldiers of the Thaelmann Battalion. He acted like a Nazi, filled with the superiority of a master race. My Dutch nationalism was stronger than my Americanism.

One night we were awakened and told to dress quickly, as we were going to the front lines. Walking through the cold, blacked-out town, avoiding bomb holes by the light of the moon, we wondered where we were headed. At the car pool we stood and listened to our instructions: "Drive without lights; soon it will be dawn. We hope the convoy is not known to the fascists. We hope there has not been a leak in information about the convoy. If you hear a plane or planes, jump, run, bury your face in the earth. Don't let the white blur of your face be a target for a machine-gunner in a plane." I had a fleeting wish to be sleeping in New York City, with my child in the next bed.

Our instructor continued, "Throw yourself into the nearest ditch when bombs drop. Keep the trucks a good distance apart in case one catches fire. Keep moving. Keep moving."

I hoped we would not be caught. We had a complete fifty-bed hospital ready to set up. Spain had no medical supplies. They came from other countries, and we were bringing ours. The Neutrality Act of the United States, England, and France prevented Spain from buying arms to defend herself, but at least medical supplies could get across the border. When I discovered I was riding in the ambulance that contained our highly flammable ether supply, I was more scared than ever, for myself and for our hospital unit.

As the drivers watched the road, we passengers watched the sky. I began suspecting stars as plane lights, until I caught myself—an enemy plane would not be using lights! At one alert, we jumped into the ditches, but we had not been spotted.

We were tired, hungry, and thirsty when we entered the small town of Lillo. We had been told that there was a big, new building in Lillo that we could use for a hospital. The only big building was a large, old church with beautiful gothic lines, but dank and dirty inside. The villagers told us the building we wanted was in the very next town, Romeral, but they insisted on giving us breakfast. First they brought us water to wash ourselves. While we waited for the goat to cook, they fed us peanuts and muscatel wine. Our medical chief had gone on to check about the building. We couldn't talk to one another, but there was really no need. The whole village, women and children and old men, surrounded us, beaming at us and embracing us. We no longer asked where the young men were.

Doctor Barsky sent word that we were to proceed to Romeral. The day was warm and sunny, and windmills turned against the incredibly blue sky flaked with white fleecy clouds, as we drove on. It was early February, and the olive trees were already garbed in their slate gray-green leaves. Only Don Quixote and his Sancho were missing from the scene as we entered the outskirts of the whitewashed village. To our right loomed a large building. It was not Don Quixote who stood there motioning us to stop, but Doctor Barsky.

It was obviously a new school building, and we watched children and teachers moving out desks, maps, and books. We walked into the building, weaving in between outgoing school furniture, and saw the huge rooms lighted by large glass windows. However, there was no heat, no plumbing facilities, no water, no electricity, no kitchen, no stove. It was just a new, two-story building, the first school Romeral had had, which they had recently finished building themselves. They offered it to us with great pride, to use as a hospital. It was late, and we took only the mattresses off the trucks.

We walked through the deep blue, star-studded night, past the silent windmills to a home where we were to be given our supper, which included the last eggs we were to see in many a month. We listened to speeches from the village authorities welcoming us to the Madrid front. Each speech was translated either by Mildred, our interpreter, or by Rudolph the German, who somehow was in Romeral ahead of us. Outside the door we heard women's voices arguing louder and louder. When we questioned our interpreter, she told us that the villagers were fighting as to who should be chosen, who had the right to work with us in the hospital. One voice, which later I was to know well, kept saying, "I have more right than Elvira. My father was killed, and my two brothers were killed defending Madrid. I am the only one left who can serve."

What people! The closer one got to the front, the stronger they appeared.

In the morning the villagers brought us water for washing, and coffee and bread to eat. Women and children kept arriving from far and near, milling around, all wanting to help us. We begged the village authorities to settle the argument, since we could not possibly use all of them. We needed a fixed number to be trained as nurse's aides, for the kitchen, for our ambulances, and for other jobs. Off they went to the mayor's office, and I felt sorry for the poor mayor, a dignified old man, being confronted by women who all insisted on their "right to serve Spain" by working with us.

We had exactly forty-eight hours, Doctor Barsky told us, to have the hospital set up and ready for patients. Thanks to the wonderful organization of the fifty-bed hospital materials from the States, our task was made easier. Boxes and crates of every size were painted with a broad stripe, one of five colors, each signifying whether it was to go to the kitchen, the operating room, supply room, and so forth. We nurses were accustomed to pitching in and not letting one another down. Our training had lasted three years, beginning with menial and often heavy work. We had learned through sheer necessity how to lift and move heavy patients and heavy objects without straining ourselves too much. We had waited on interns and doctors hand and foot, opening more doors for them than we wanted to remember. We had stood on our aching feet while they sat. So now we enjoyed the doctors' discomfort and grumbling as they pushed and hauled like anyone else. Some of them balked and complained that they had come to be doctors and not stevedores. Doctor Barsky, our chief, who was not well because of his gastric ulcer, was working harder than any of us.

The posters said, "Ahora todos somos iguales!" (Today we are all equal!) We gloried in this, but we recognized the physical differences between men and women. The doctors and ambulance drivers had to carry in the heavy crates and had to be carpenters to uncrate them. We helped the ones who cheerfully worked side by side with us by showing them tricks in leverage. Within forty-eight hours we were ready, but those hours will always remain a blur to me, since we hardly took time off to eat or sleep. Our group of seventeen was more than doubled by helpers from the village. Wires were strung for lights. Holes were dug for waste materials. Water was carried on women's heads and burros' backs. Food came in from nearby villages, and the stove was assembled. The dirt and rocks that flew out of the latrines were carried to the road and used to fill the chuckholes. When André Marty appeared, he gave us a pat on the back in praise.

Lillo, the nearby town where we had almost put up our hospital, had been bombed. We did not put a red cross on our roof because it would have meant annihilation, as had happened in Madrid, where hospitals had been bombed by German planes. I looked again with suspicion at Rudolph the German. He had known that we might set up in Lillo. And he could have conjectured that if we were bombed, though we could run to the fields, would we? Of course not; we would stay with our helpless wounded. I began worrying about bombings seriously.

Now it was February 1937, and we were to serve the Jarama, on the Madrid front. The men of the Abraham Lincoln Battalion there sang a song to the tune of "The Red River Valley":

There's a valley in Spain called Jarama
It's a place that we all know too well
It was there that we gave of our manhood
It was there that our first comrades fell

We are proud of the Lincoln Battalion
and the fight for Madrid that it made
For we fought like true sons of the soil,
as a part of the International Brigade

We who left part of our hearts in Spain, who left a job unfinished, will never forget this song. "A place where our best comrades fell"—the wounded were pouring in from the battle raging on the Jarama front. The Lincolns were bearing the brunt. Within four hours after the battle had begun, we had 93 wounded. Our hospital was equipped for 500. A little later, the same day, we had 200. I was on the first floor, where they came in. Those who had died enroute to us were left in the bitter cold courtyard. Occasionally from among the dead we heard a moan and found life.

The wounded lay on the floor, and two or three lay on each bed. First we fought to keep them alive. Later we got their names, in order to list them as wounded. When we had time, we went through clothing matted with blood on cold, stiff, dead men to see if they had letters on them or any identifying information. I cut through clothing of boys I had danced with on our way to Spain. My eyes were heavy with lack of sleep and unshed tears. This was no time to cry! The crying would have to come later.

Men coming out of anesthesia cowered, remembering the Moors on foot and horse at the Jarama front. Others shuddered when they heard planes overhead. Spain, a recognized, legally elected government with representation in the League of Nations, was being brutally attacked by Germans, Italians, Moors. We were outnumbered in everything, but the front still held. I, too, trembled with fear of the Moors. Thousands were dying, of which a small part were foreign volunteers, like the boys from the United States, here to hold the front, to hold Madrid.

Precious blood flowing from wounds was being exchanged for that from ampules brought to us by Doctor Bethune. I hated what I saw and the forces responsible for this suffering, anguish, and death. I hated the hand grenades, the shrapnel, the dumdum bullets, the machine guns, the mortar shells. I hated seeing the bleeding wounds, the living wounded, and the dead. A part of me died with every one who fell. The wounded became a part of me. I burned my living red cells trying to keep theirs alive. We had not slept in four days, other than in catnaps taken leaning against the wall. It was impossible to walk in shoes, so we put on the peasant *alpargatas* (espadrilles). We worked as one body, as a unit, to keep men alive. Day and night Doctor Barsky operated, by good light and by candlelight. He was our best surgeon for major surgery, and to this day I don't know how he did it. Despite his burning gastric ulcer, Doctor Barsky never lost his patience with or his kindness toward the many men from many lands with their many languages.

The wounded were given first aid at the front under fire. Those who could not survive the ambulance ride to our hospital at Romeral stayed at the hospital at Colmenar. As fast as we could we put the treated men who could travel on the ambulance train to lines further back. Our fifty-bed hospital was jammed with hundreds of wounded, but it was easing up. The front had been held fast at the cost of thousands of lives. Now we took turns to go off-duty to get a few hours of sleep. When it was my turn, I walked past the operating room and heard Doctor Barsky ask for me, so I stepped in. A pallid, fair young lad lay on the operating table. Doctor Barsky said, "He is Dutch. He does not understand English. Please tell him that we are going to operate. Tell him we are going to give him a spinal anesthesia; then help him get into position for the anesthesia."

The boy's eyes lit up as he heard my voice explain to him in his language what had to be done. His name was Peter. "Stay with me. Don't leave me. I am dying, I know. Don't leave me," he begged.

The doctor who was giving the spinal anesthesia said, "Okay, Lini, you can leave now and get some sleep. You need it badly."

Peter clasped my hand firmly as if he understood. "Don't leave me. Don't let me die alone," he whimpered.

I answered the doctor, "Later. I must stay with this wounded man now." Softly I spoke in Dutch to Peter about the streets of Amsterdam, about the beach at Scheveningen, as I watched his abdomen being opened, exposing a shattered spleen. I also knew it was hopeless now.

"Promise me before I die that you will keep on fighting for Spain and for what is right," he said. I promised him. "Sing me the cradle songs. Sing me the folk songs. Sing to me," he begged.

With a pinched throat and unshed tears, I sang to Peter as softly as I could. I thought again of Till Eulenspiegel's wife as she placed the ashes on the hearts of her sons and daughters: "As long as there is injustice in this world, you must fight against it." Peter had heard these words; he had read them in school. I was hearing them through the din of the bombers overhead trying to locate our hospital. Doctor Barsky finished operating by candle-light as our lights went out. Silent sobs caught in my throat as I felt Peter's pulse fading to nothingness, to death.

LINI DE VRIES was born in the United States of Dutch parents and grew up in conditions of extreme poverty. She went to Spain to serve as a nurse. After she returned, she was driven into exile by the McCarthy witch-hunts and moved to Mexico, where she became known as a brilliant practitioner and teacher of public health. She died in March 1982. The story is from her autobiography *Up from the Cellar* (1979), copies of which can be ordered from the Institute for Social Medicine and Community Health, 206 North 35th Street, Philadelphia, PA 19104, or the Passaic County Historical Society, Lambert Castle, Valley Road, Patterson, NJ 07503.

· Jacques Grunblatt ·

Forever in Spain, II

Brunete, July 1937. We were attacking at Brunete. My cavalry unit of three hundred men and horses were to hold the right flank at Quijorna. They left in the early morning.

My medical team and I were left on a little sandy spot next to some bushes outside Quijorna. It was a hot day and the battle raged around us. I became very thirsty and dug feverishly in the sand until I found water. After I drank it I discovered, only a few yards away, bodies and dead animals in various stages of decomposition.

My unit never returned. The only one who survived was Captain Alocca, who was court-martialed later.

I retreated a few miles to a house that was a kind of headquarters. There I witnessed the painful retreat of our forces. I took care of a Canadian journalist, Ted Allan, who injured his legs in the same car accident in which Gerda Taro was killed when their car collided with a tank.

The battle for Brunete was raging. One day Doctor Gorian, the medical chief of the division, asked me to go to the front lines to replace Doctor Grosfeld, who could not stand it anymore. His post was near Villanueva de la Cañada on the left side of the road to Brunete. He was the doctor of the Twenty-fourth Battalion, a Spanish battalion of the Fifteenth Brigade. Balcer was its captain. That was how I became permanently attached to the Fifteenth Brigade, the Abraham Lincoln Brigade.

157

Doctor Gorian gave me an ambulance and a Czechoslovak driver, and off we went to find the Twenty-fourth Battalion's field post on the front lines. Enemy planes were in the air almost constantly. We had to stop and hide several times. It became clear that if we hid, we would never get to our front post. I ordered him to drive despite the enemy planes. He refused. He was correct; tactically, one should never drive during a bombardment. Foolishly, I menaced him with my revolver. He was as white as a sheet, but he drove one-half mile. Only then did I realize there was no sense endangering him and the ambulance, and I went on foot.

Meanwhile, Spanish soldiers were retreating. Wounded, frightened, foaming from their mouths, eyes popping, they screamed as they retreated, "Don't go! The fascists are here!" Shells were exploding on every side, but I had to advance. I told myself, "You must find someone in authority before you turn."

I managed to find the field headquarters. Surprisingly, a flimsy line was still holding, communication lines still functioned, and I found my post. It had almost no cover, just a few trees and bushes through whose branches enemy bullets tore. The doctor had left the day before. The post was manned by medics and stretcher bearers who were doing the best they could under the circumstances. Many wounded lay on the ground; some were serious; others less so. There was no ambulance to evacuate them. We treated those we could.

I decided to go to field headquarters to ask for an ambulance to evacuate the severely wounded. I knew—or thought I knew—the terrain. In the distance I could see a little shack and knew that shack was the enemy line.

I began running through the bushes looking for headquarters. I did not know that the line was overrun. There was no headquarters, no ambulances. All the roads were under enemy small-arms fire. Then it happened.

Suddenly I saw the little shack. I realized I was lost behind enemy lines. A Moorish soldier in his typically baggy pants was ahead of me advancing toward our lines with his rifle in his hand. It was then that I must thank Doctor Robbins for my life.

A few days before this, when the Brunete front was still holding, I met Doctor Robbins on the road. He was supervising the quality and quantity of water going to the front lines. It was July, and I still wore my heavy officer's uniform, my high boots, and my cap with the insignia of my rank. I was sweating profusely. I asked Doctor Robbins if I could leave my uniform in his vehicle. He agreed and gave me a khaki shirt, a pair of pants, and a pair of Spanish espadrilles. After this change, I was indistinguishable from any private of ours or the enemy's.

That change of clothes saved my life as the Moor approached. But poor Doctor Robbins, he and his truck were pulverized by a bomb that day.

To this Moorish soldier, I looked like a Spaniard from his own lines. I yelled, "Adelante!" to him and passed him. Inside me was a voice saying over and over again, "This is the end!" I was sure he would let me pass, then take aim from a comfortable distance. He didn't. At the first bushes I reached, I made a detour. I got back to our lines and was almost taken prisoner. They also thought I came from enemy lines. I returned to my post. The situation looked desperate. At that moment, a herd of burros, the ones we used to carry ammunition to the lines, came running. We stopped them. Whoever was able to mount one did so. The more severely injured we put on stretchers and began our retreat under a hail of bullets.

The Twenty-fourth Battalion retreated to a small village in the hinterlands to rest. Some of the men, I among them, received permission to visit Madrid for a day. I bought a new uniform and boots, had a shoeshine and a haircut with my six hundred pesetas in back pay.

Even though the Twenty-fourth Battalion was held in reserve, I had to care for the ill and injured. One day a young Spanish nurse offered her services to our medical post. We had two doctors on call at that time. The other was my superior, only a rank higher than I.

Suddenly we received orders to move to the front at Aragon. My ambulance was put on a flatcar of the train while we occupied other cars. Oliva, the nurse, was asked by my superior to work with him in one part of the train. For some reason, or maybe out of love, she begged him to allow her to work with me in my section. She joined my medical team and remained my companion until the very end of the war.

· Don MacLeod ·

The Day the War Started

I stepped out of line when they asked for truck drivers. It was true drivers were needed, and I had driven a truck, now and again, between Santa Barbara and the flower market in Los Angeles for a relative who owned a flower shop. Besides, truck driving seemed to appeal more to my sense of adventure and the excitement of seeing new places.

So, after a few weeks in Albacete, Spain, I was dispatched to Madrid to join a transportation unit for the Fifth Army Corps. This unit was named by the French the "Regiment de Tren." Why the French were given the privilege of naming it I never learned. Anyway, French- and English-speaking together, we had about two hundred in the unit, including drivers, mechanics, cooks and some local people to help out when we were at any kind of a base that was not too close to the front. [. . .]

The orientation lectures we attended in Albacete were delivered by romantics with unbridled imaginations. They had us so loaded with wrong information about truck-driving in wartime that any reality would have seemed dull by comparison. I remember one "expert" advising us to zig-zag our trucks down the road if we were being strafed; another one was so melodramatic about our responsibilities that I had visions of myself leaping trenches with my truck while firing an automatic rifle with one hand and driving the truck with the other!

So, for two months before the Brunete offensive started we

had a chance to get used to each other—or try to. Although avowed antifascists, we were all pretty judgmental of each other with holier-than-thou attitudes based on "correct" understanding of Marx, Lenin, and Stalin surfacing every once in a while. At the other extreme, there was one guy from New Hampshire who said he heard the Republicans were in trouble so he came over to help them, he himself being a dyed-in-the-wool New England Republican! He was a good man anyway. But, in between extremes, there were many guys with good heads, a light-hearted sense of humor, a flair for fun and song, and certain characteristics inherited from our frontier background that we take for granted but that foreigners are quick to recognize and often find intriguing. [. . .]

Everyone was concerned with *when* the war was going to start and *where*. It seemed we all needed some time to come to terms with ourselves but didn't want to appear too anxious about it. Oblique questions were asked of officers; they didn't know anything either but had a stock answer ready anyway: "Look, Comrade, if we don't know when or where, the enemy doesn't know either, and there are a lot of spies and fifth columnists around who are trying to find out." A few political commissars (but not all) would add the "Trotskyites" to this grouping, but on the whole this was frowned upon. Spies and fifth columnists to be sure—reportedly there were many of those around, but they were so indigenously Spanish that we foreigners were categorically on the safe side of guilt. Trotskyism was another matter and to a prideful Bolshevik, as some boasted of being, even a mildly disgruntled member of the group might be suspected of being a "closet Trotskyite." One day the *cantine* humor of Bob English closed out the Trotsky business forever in our ranks when he laid a friendly hand on Arkansas John's shoulder and in his slow Kentucky drawl said, "Now take ole Arkansas here, he's not the kind of comrade who looks under his bed every night to see if there are any Trotskyites there. He doesn't have to look— he *knows* they're there!" Everyone laughed including Arkansas, who thought he had been paid a compliment. Arkansas John was a rural Depression sufferer whose plight was revealed to him like a flash from heaven when a pamphlet by Father Brown, a defrocked, excommunicated priest turned socialist, came into

his hand. The good priest's clarity of thought and simple style
explained it all to John's satisfaction. Now he was happy to be in
Spain where everything made sense, instead of in Arkansas
pondering his incomprehensible existence. But the griping,
which comes naturally to big-city dwellers, disturbed him and
he often expressed his fears that we were being corrupted by
Trotskyism. Bob's joke was so much appreciated because humor,
in a way, can be perspective, and in truth we . . . were watching
each other closely for some evidence of trustworthy leadership.
We had lots of guys who could organize a peace rally at home, or
take a crack at some obscure Marxist theory, but this war was a
whole new ball game with little expertise in evidence anywhere. [. . .]

The order to roll out from under our blankets, where we slept
on the ground beside our trucks, came at 3:00 A.M. the next day.
Lieutenant Saks Madigan was in charge. He was a man with the
right credentials, considering the kind of war it was. That is to
say, he looked and dressed like an officer, possessed a degree in
political science from an Eastern university, and was both a
peace activist and an organizer of a movement to outlaw
R.O.T.C. [. . .]

In the headlights of a truck we crowded around Madigan to
hear our instructions: The trucks were to travel thirty yards
apart. Just at the entrance to Brunete we would see a warehouse. Madigan's squad car would be waiting there to direct us.
What we were after was the sacked wheat that was stored at
Brunete. Spanish warehousemen would do the loading at the
three docks so it should go pretty fast, and it had better, because
Brunete, having fallen just yesterday, could expect a counterat-
tack sometime today. When our truck was loaded, our instructions were to pull out and park on the road facing back toward
Escorial. When all trucks were loaded. Madigan's squad car
would lead the convoy back. [. . .]

A word about the trucks: They were either French Fords,
called Matfords, or English Fords—Fordsons. All were painted a
uniform tan with Abe Lincoln's profile stenciled on the side. If
you could, you got your hands on a Fordson. They held up better
on rough roads, and the right-hand steering, where driving on
the right-hand side of the road was the rule, proved to be a big

advantage because one could watch the right-hand side of the road from the cab, so if you were passing, say, a tank on a mountain turn, you could look down and see how close your right wheel was to the dangerous edge of the dropoff.

Madigan finished his briefing. Now the real war was going to start. No doubt about it, this would be the biggest day of our lives so far. We started for Brunete just before dawn with Lou Ornitz driving the lead truck. I have a vivid recollection of him wearing a helmet, a five-day growth of beard, carrying a gas mask and wearing striped pajamas. Maybe he couldn't find his clothes in the dark, or maybe my mind after all this time is playing tricks on me. Probably the latter is the case, and yet the bizarre was almost commonplace in Spain at that time. Anyway, I never saw Lou again.

I was assigned to last place in line. Riding with me was our mechanic, Gilly, a very political youth with a dark five o'clock shadow and no conversation.

There was something ominously purposeful about him. [. . .]

The road sloped steadily downward until Valdemorillo, a village halfway to Brunete and leveled off to an arid plain of stubbled wheat. It was getting light. There must have been much fighting there the day before, because the forms of soldiers outlined in the early light, asleep under blankets, were discernible in groups along the roadside. A scent pervaded the air, which was neither pleasant nor unpleasant, but I could not identify it with anything in my experience. It seemed like the smell that might arise in the vapor if you poured a bucket of sugar water on hot ashes to put out a campfire. As the day grew hotter, the odor would become cloying and, at some point, shockingly recognizable as the smell of decomposing human flesh. *Death*. For the rest of your life you would remember the odor with loathing. The "sleeping" soldiers were, of course, the dead from yesterday's fighting, placed by the roadside to be disposed of when time permitted.

Lou Ornitz was already captured when our trucks reached the warehouse. He must have missed Madigan's squad car or inadvertently passed him on the road, because he and his truck sailed right on through Brunete and into the fascist lines.

The loading started. In the urgency to complete it before the day's battle heated up, teams of skilled Spanish warehousemen threw the heavy sacks on the trucks with the effortlessness of children throwing bean bags. It didn't take long for the first three trucks to be loaded and reparked.

The sun was coming up; it was going to be a hot day. Already one could hear the droning hum of Italian Savoias somewhere in the distant sky. Your bones told you that airplanes were the truck drivers' nemesis. My truck would be the last to be loaded, so there was nothing to do but wait around, mindful that my exposure here would be longer than any of the other drivers'. [. . .]

A lot of shouting and arm waving going on by the loaded trucks diverted my attention, but the competing sound of motors and cannonading made distinguishing the words impossible from where I stood, so I hurried over to see what the excitement was about. Madigan and Spike Steinbeck, the latter apparently speaking for himself and the drivers, were facing each other in high dudgeon. At some point in his life Spike had been a carnival barker, and although of slight build he was self-assured and his voice had the kind of authority that could turn a freight train up a side street. The drivers wanted to pull out immediately, and Madigan wanted them to obey orders and wait until all the trucks were loaded. I thought the drivers were right, but Madigan, having no experience to help him in a situation of this kind, decided to play it safe and hold on stubbornly, if irrationally, to his position. Meanwhile, the ever-lengthening line of loaded trucks kept growing into a bigger and more obvious target until the need to do something in the name of self-preservation began to win the argument for Steinbeck. The pressure on Madigan became too much finally, and with a feeble effort to salvage something from the argument, he said, "All right, if you leave you leave, but it's on your responsibility, not mine." That was enough for the drivers to hear. They flew to their trucks, started motors, and pulled out. Their action, of course, left Madigan in charge of practically nothing, so perhaps this could have been part of his reluctance to abandon the argument. There were still the trucks to be loaded, but nothing now could stop the drivers from taking off as soon as possible.

I felt a little sorry for Madigan and wanted to separate myself from his predicament. "Well," I said, "I've got to get back to my truck," and started off but stopped because Dave Thompson was approaching us. He raised his hand as a signal that I should wait, no doubt wanting me as a witness while explaining to Madigan about the Irishman and the missing truck. Madigan seemed to brighten up on seeing Dave. Dave had that effect on you. I guess he was my role model. [. . .] A concatenation of bomb explosions from a safe distance away triggered the comedian in Dave, who turned the visor of his hat crosswise on his head and, raising his arm for protection in the manner of W. C. Fields fending off a vase aimed at him by one of his tormentors, said, "Are you guys having any fun or do you want your money back?" It was a typical Thompson opening, which made us laugh, but before we had time to engage in any enjoyable repartee with him or discuss any real problem, two Englishmen, immaculate in shorts, approached us looking as though they had just walked off a movie set. "I say, Yanks," the taller one said, fingering his mustache, "Would you be good enough to help us out? We have two antitank guns over in a ditch. The bloody lorry that was transporting them ran off the road and now it won't start. Everything useless the way it is." "Very inconvenient," the shorter one said, "if the buggers decided to send some tanks down the road. Shouldn't take a half hour if we could hook a cable on one of your lorries."

Canonized by our movie scripts, it is hard for an American to refuse an Englishman who talks like that, and Madigan, with not much of anything significant to do now, obviously liked the idea of helping the Englishmen and had little difficulty in persuading Thompson to help, although Dave later said that something must have paralyzed his better judgement. So it was decided that these two guys would go off with Dave in the direction of Quijorna where the heavy fighting was in progress, and Madigan would follow with the squad car.

Meanwhile, Gilly was backing our truck to the loading dock, and before long I was behind the wheel heading up the road toward Escorial, having acquired a Spanish soldier from the Intendencia sitting on the loaded sacks with his rifle in hand. The sun was up and German Stukas and Italian Savoias were prowling around overhead shaking the sky as if they owned it.

Once in a while our pathetic anti-aircraft would put up a burst in their general direction, missing by a mile.

When we were close to Valdemorillo, a battery of our rapid-firing guns that were concealed and camouflaged opened up on a group of low-flying bombers and I thought we were being strafed, so I grabbed the hand brake and the three of us jumped out of the truck and fell face down in a little depression beside the road. It was an action dictated purely by instinct but, as it turned out, the right one. The bombers unloaded on the battery but we were so close they might as well have been after us. Their bombs screamed as they fell and the explosions made the earth jump. Our fingers tried to clutch the ground to keep us from bouncing. You thought you were going to be hit right in the middle of the back.

When this seeming eternity passed, we were covered with dust and dirt but unharmed, so we scrambled back to the truck while the bombers started to make a big loop. Maybe they were coming back for another shot at the guns because some were still firing. The truck appeared to be intact. I asked Gilly if he wanted to drive, because he looked so reliable, but he shook his head. "You're the driver," he said, "I'm only the mechanic." Our Intendencia man clutching his rifle climbed up on the wheat sacks and waited for the truck to start. The motor started, but I couldn't start. My left leg was jerking uncontrollably and I couldn't depress the clutch. Each time I tried, my leg went into a spasm. "Coño, vamos!" The Intendencia man hit the cab with his rifle butt for emphasis. From his view on the back he could watch the bombers making their circle and he wanted us out of there. I shot a pleading look at Gilly, but he just sat there looking reliable, as usual. Again and again I tried to make my spasmatic leg behave, but the disastrous quivering that seized it would not let go. My mortification was so great I started to cry.

The planes had come back and were almost overhead again. Gilly and the soldier leaped out of the truck and headed for the ditch; I just sat there crying, hoping, I guess, to be blown up with my truck. But this time the bombers ignored us. No more bombs were dropped and the planes headed down toward Brunete. In my desperation I frantically grabbed my knee and pulled it up to my eyes. In this position, my knee hiding my tears, I continued weeping. Maybe it was only for minutes or seconds, I don't know, but when I released my knee the spasm was gone. Managing a weak grin, I waved my two somewhat reluctant passengers aboard. They came, I suppose, because they hadn't much choice—it was either that or walk. I put the truck through its chain of gears and we were on our way again.

The dead lay still unburied, so the stench of death stalked us beyond Valdemorillo. An old man driving an oxcart on which was slung a gigantic barrel of wine was just entering the outskirts of Escorial. We had seen him in the headlights on the way down, waving his stick to attract attention and shouting admonitions that he was transporting wine for the soldiers of the Republic. He and his plodding ox had traveled, perhaps, two miles since the beginning of that day, the biggest day of my life.

It took a while to unload, but afterward we had only to park the truck under the trees by the monastery wall; following that, there was an easy stroll to the warm showers and a good breakfast with chilled white wine at the Miranda y Suiza hotel. During this happy interval I was blessed with the sweetest sensation of my life. Nothing like it had ever happened before, nor has it happened since, although I have yearned for it like a Ronald Colman seeking the reentrance to Shangri-la. Apparently my small private triumph after the tension of the morning's events was rewarding me with a little peek at the mystery of self. The benefits of learning anything about one's personal mystery must be great indeed because I felt at perfect peace, unneedful of any approbation but my own. Everything I watched, all that my senses recorded, seemed more important than anything I had ever experienced before. In those Depression years, awareness of life's accidentalness weighed on the promise of youth like a burden, yet as I made my way to the hotel on that unforgettable morning I felt liberated, *significant*, walking in a bright spot of light.

When Dave Thompson finally drove in, we all deserted whatever relaxed position we were in and stood up, recognizing as we did so that the arrival of Dave and Madigan was what we were waiting for. Dave's truck was covered with yellow dust and so was he, except for masklike ovals around his eyes where he had rubbed the dust off. "Madigan's gone!" he said as he opened the door and unwound his long legs to get out of the cab, "strafed, burned to a frazzle. I saw what was left of him afterward. Christ! I hope those bastards got him before the car burned up." We gathered closer, eager to hear more, but Dave was intent on making his report to the Estado Mayor. "I better go," he said, "I'll tell you later." But we wouldn't let him go. The shock was too great. The drivers crowded around him, making him the center of a tight anxious ring. "Well," he said, "did Mac, here, tell you about the Englishmen?" There were nods of assent. "We got them out of the ditch finally, but it took a while. Then we started back and I picked up an old man trying to get to Valdemorillo. I wanted him to get in the cab, but he insisted on climbing on the back where he could watch for planes. 'Mucho ojo,'" Dave said, using the old man's gesture by pointing to his eye. "When we got near Brunete, I couldn't see anything there but a cloud of dust, and then the old man started pounding on my cab. I stopped and heard the plane just as his guns opened up. I could see the shells hitting the road ahead, so he overshot us and went on straight down the road. That's probably when he got Madigan, who must've been a good target with the speed of his car helping that bastard to keep him in his sights. When I got there his car was in the ditch burning like crazy. I stopped and tried to look in . . . there was no use . . . I gotta go," he said, and pushed his way out of the group.

So that's how it went on the day the war started. [. . .]

Don MacLeod was born in 1913 in Fish Creek, Wisconsin, and attended Santa Barbara State College and the University of California at Berkeley, where he was attracted to politics by the Upton-Sinclair-for-Governor campaign of the 1930s. After fighting in Spain, he worked for the International Longshoremen's and Warehousemen's Union until his retirement. He now lives in Berkeley, California.

· James Neugass ·

Give Us This Day

Deep in the olive groves at sunset
longer than the memory of police chiefs
grow the shadows of headstone olive trees
Deadmen's shoes march on other feet
long after laces and soles are gone:
rifle straps fell away and string broke
Worn by the sweat of many a comrade's back:
fondly shells still slide into the chamber
the breechlocks of the antitank batteries
Have turned to museums of fingerprints
but their beloved muzzles will throw
explosives so long as there is night.
how are the lines holding? where are the lines?
bring up cannon before sunrise, ammo, water

How could Spain have been rich?
     nowhere were fat Swiss landscapes
     or comfortable parklike rural scenes
No mellow pastures or dreaming spires
     the streaked shoulders of the hills
     always a proving-ground for sunsets
For mobile brigades of battle clouds,
     hands of the wind fast scene-shifters
     preparing stagelike landscapes always for tragedy:

169

Thorn bushes burned toward evening
    like liquid flame: what wealth was there
    but in the skies and the hard empty hands?

Where was the glamor of historians?
    were they here? what did they see?
    who was rich? where was the wealth
Long deserts with oases of olive trees
    mirages of wheatfields and vines
    exhausted salt plains of Castile
Monotonous one-well towns of Aragon
    mud walls rising from mud ridge-strung
    like cascades of standing reddish dust

kitchens should be underground, dig schools deep
take the children to the deepest end of the refugio, dig.

The church towers were pretty
    the walls of monastery gardens strong
    churchwalls were strong as fortresses
The hermitage where the bishop
    summered was as pretty as a calendar also
    his cedars were firewood for Alcoisa
Monotonously the people cooked
    in one dish and ate from one plate
    there were stoves only in the convents
Monotonously we used the half-built
    Republican schoolhouses for hospitals
    these were the only white walls in Aragon
Where was the glamor of that
    luminescent past of gilt and gold
    silver brass and flea-ridden satins?
Of banners pennants flags as red as blood
    and yellow as gold? none but belfry saints
    had seen the past: they looked down on us
With stone eyes full of grandeur
    as we marched out of the rising sunlight
    leaving our dead but taking their guns

because of the sky there was no rearguard
no rear every nursery and fireplace a trench

[. . .]

Sleep had the smell of flowers
        in a funeral parlor there were flowers
        but no sleep: we longed for the perfume of
Woodsmoke, cooking and of home
        there were the tropical spring airs
        and nothing clean but children's eyes
We smoked dry olive leaves and straw
        go-lousies antitanks and pillow-slips
        we ate raw pork fat with wild onions
Pulled olives off the moonlit trees
        feasted the smearing of Moorish cavalry
        with beefsteak cut from their machine-gunned mounts
We slept in the olive groves of Quinto
        the plains of Aragon are scored with
        the foxholes our bayonets and mess tins dug
We curled into the frozen mud at Celadas
        stood sleeping against walls at Monte Rosario
        slept waist-deep in Escorial's irrigation ditches
Sucked moist mud in barrancas near Brunete
        came blinking out of the cellars of Teruel
        marched singing into sun-baked anthills at Valverde
But it was always a question of the lines:
        where were the trenches? were the men advancing?
        had we hauled the artillery closer each night?
yellow and red were their banners:
blood and gold
their program: blood and more blood
silver and gold

Plucked clean as a tooth from the bomb-rotten
        village street then dumped on the road the Captain's
        laundry was lost the laundress her father mother:
Sunset bleeds woodsmoke down the fuming streets

fire warms engines and coffee, in a smashing
    of icicles we move off, too sleepy to curse:
Headlights raised partridges which flew
    blind ahead of us up the road to the front
    hungry, we carried guns fit only to kill men:
We blew up the trapped ambulances
    We lowered the bandaged nurse
    to the cleanest part of the ditch:
There never was such an afternoon
    such keen Alpine evening air no such silence
    but for the single rifle shot over the hills:
They want war   Their stomachs can eat
    only war the droning of planes soothes them
    the sound of planes is morphine for their sleep:
Armed with pawnshop rifles and a knowledge
    of why we had come, with memories that
    went back through centuries the men advanced
Still in the clothes in which
    we had left our jobs, singing the
    same song in many languages we advance

    [. . .]

The I.B.'s were the most ragged
    filthy hungry red eyed bastards
    that ever went under the name of troops
But they could fight and they fought
    they cursed their officers, groused and squawked
    but they held their lines and the lines held
Every man was his own general but they
    could obey; The Internationals never broke
    never was "some day comrade" said with such longing
Some day: no soldier has ever oiled
    or used or hated his rifle so well
    no troops ever loved peace like them

they wanted nothing for themselves not for themselves
every grove is a sanctuary each hilltop a shrine

Forget the bronze tablets and
    hand-illumined scrolls leave out
    medals citation bars and stripes
Some day their history will
    be carved ineradicably across
    the earth by tractor-drawn plows
Mercifully let a last kind bomb
    save the informal cemetery
    of the International Brigades
From him who could not take our trenches
    let the fist never come unclenched the calloused right
        forefingers never grow soft
Unknown soldiers? They were all
    unknown: International as sunrise
    misty etchings of their olive grove tombs
Will never hang reverently draped
    in lace and immortelles in chapel-like
    parlors of Back Bay and Park Avenue

Whitehall Arlington and the Etoile
    will not pay bronze and marble to them
    every milestone is their cenotaph
Do not look for their metal names
    shaded by village memorial trees
    the horizon is their triumphal arch

write "paid up and in good standing"
save the helmets save the shoes

When in the evening secret service men
    lock vaults of cross-indexed fingerprints
    and the morgues of passport photographs
Where the faces of the Brigades
    fade and bleach but do not die
    longer than the memory of police chiefs
Grow the shadows of footstone olive trees
    deep in battlefield orchards at sunset
    thrushes the men had cursed for airplanes

Sleepily find places for the night
      secure among boughs grafted by peace
      to the seared and war-torn trunks
Only that the lines shall hold!
      nothing else matters there is no
      hardship no anguish no other pain
Dig the trenches deep and crooked
      send shells and tanks and planes
      fuel and the best guns to the Front
Let civilians feed wells of supply
      guard crossroads keep the highways healthy
      pulsing hot as the blood in our foreheads
Let the lines hold hard then advance
      let those camions wind over mountaintops
      let the color of the flags never fade
Hold them high as they flow above the
      roaring camions: let the memory of the songs
      the volunteers sang never die from our throats.

JAMES NEUGASS was an ambulance driver in the medical corps.
This poem is excerpted from a longer piece published in *Story
Magazine* (August 1938).

· Evelyn Hutchins ·

A Woman Truck Driver

[. . .] I was much more aware of what was going on generally in the world and in Spain, and more concerned and interested than my brother. However, my brother and I have always been very close and when he discovered that I was trying, I was interested in and trying to go to Spain, he actually got there first. There were friends of mine, other friends, close friends of mine who went to Spain. I was married, I wasn't living with my husband, I wasn't living with my husband because I didn't wanta live out in the suburbs and he worked and lived out in the suburbs. And I had asked him if he would head up the garage for the American Hospital and he said he would, so he had gone and then uh a couple of my very close friends wanted to go and that left my brother and he decided to go and then that left me. And it was a little more difficult for me to go because I didn't, I didn't fall into any kind of slot. If I was going to be a soldier it would've been easy. But since I was not a nurse and not a doctor and not a . . . X-ray technician, lab technician or something like that, they found it very difficult to send me there as a driver. They couldn't accept the fact, here, the people who were responsible for paying your fare or whatever, they couldn't accept the fact that a woman would go over there as a driver. [. . .]

The driving there wasn't that much different from driving some of the back roads or some of the smaller roads any place in the States. If at that time you were to take a trip let's say from

175

New York to California, you'd have to go through some pretty winding old roads. So, the added problem that they had there, they already had problems in keeping the roads repaired. So you had, like you have here, potholes after a bad rain or something like that. While you had potholes that were there for quite a little while and got to be deeper and deeper and deeper, so sometimes you had to go very slowly, particularly if you had any wounded in your ambulance, because you had to ease yourself down to a very deep pothole and the ambulance would be crooked, one tire would be going in one while the other would be going in another one [pothole] and sometimes there is nothing that you can do that is going to ease it for anybody. And it was a very rough ride, there is no question about it. The Spaniards tried very hard to keep them filled, but all they could fill them with for the most part was gravel. And gravel doesn't stay very long, they didn't have the asphalt to put in on top of the gravel. So some of the roads were really pretty bad. [. . .] Some of them were dirt roads that had been used a long time by these little carts that had metal wheels and they were narrower. They had very deep grooves in the wrong places—etched in, dug in at some rainy season or something like that. But some of the roads were passable and you could go fast enough. But that wasn't the main problem. The main problem was the fact that very often you had to drive at night and you couldn't drive with any lights on. And that can be a little hairy—that can be a little difficult. Because if you know anything about Spain, the roads will come up and go up to a hill and just beyond the crest of the hill it will turn sharp right, or it will turn sharp left without necessarily much of a warning. So if you go too fast, you're liable to fly out over the edge and go down into ten feet or twenty feet into a kind of rubbly rocky field. [. . .]

I was put on an ambulance and I went back and forth to a small town near the hospital. And then I went from one American hospital to the other American hospital. I didn't go any-place—any distance, to bring back the wounded. I just went small distances. There were jobs in between something like that. There were some very strange jobs. Like for instance, my am-bulance was used at one time to take a whole big load of pig manure from the hospital out to the cooperative, out to the peasants, because they needed it. And I had about a three-hour job after that to clean up—you have never smelled anything more horrible in your life than pig manure—it is violently awful. So, as I was sent to all these various jobs, little by little they took me off of bringing in wounded from one hospital to the other. And more and more I was put on a trucking type of work. [. . .]

Okay. If you're involved in a war, nothing is romantic. The people who think it's romantic are those people who aren't involved in it. War is hard work, it's dirty, it's sweaty, it's uncomfortable, you do it when you're tired, you do it when you're hungry, you do it when you need a bath. You don't get anything usually on time. You don't, can't choose the kind of food that you want. You can't lie down when you feel like lying down. There's nothing you can do when you want to do it. You have to do what has to be done then and there. There are long periods in which you can be bored, because nothing is happening. On the one hand you're glad that nothing is happening, but on the other hand, you're not doing anything else that you want to do either. So it's very boring, and you know that something is going to be happening and you get tired, nervous about it, impatient about it, and you want to get it over with, something like that. So you can't win. The main thing that you have to recognize, if you think about it at all is that it's a hard job. You have to work hard, long hours, and there's nothing romantic about that. And anybody just doesn't know what they're talking about if they think it's romantic. If they think it's romantic to be in a situation that might even be very dangerous, that's not romantic. If you think it's an adventure, it's really not an adventure. [. . .] Because there is nothing adventurous about killing anybody or being in that situation, or being killed or being hurt, there's nothing like that at all.

EVELYN HUTCHINS was born in Sohamish, Washington, in 1910. She was, at various times, an artist, dancer, union organizer, and machinist. She went to Spain as one of two women members of the Abraham Lincoln Battalion, other than those attached to medical units. After her return she was several times elected secretary and commander of the Los Angeles post of the VALB. This interview has been edited from a taped interview done for *The Good Fight*, a documentary film produced and directed by Mary Dore, Neil Bruckner, and Samuel Sills.

The
ARAGON OFFENSIVE
and the
RETREATS

The Lincolns, along with the MacKenzie-Papineau Battalion (known as the Mac-Paps and made up primarily of Canadians, as well as a large component from the United States), fought their next major battles in the mountainous Aragon region—at Quinto, Fuentes de Ebro, and Belchite. During this phase of the fighting the American soldiers "matured," so

that journalists such as Herbert L. Matthews described them as becoming seasoned veterans.

As the fierce Spanish winter was closing in, the Republicans captured the strategic city of Teruel. But just as in the experience at Brunete—one often repeated—the Republicans were tragically hampered by a lack of adequate supplies. Soviet military aid, paid for by the Spanish government, never equalled the aid provided the insurgents by Hitler and Mussolini; and the Republic was not able to purchase oil from Texas Oil Co., or trucks from Studebaker, Ford, and General Motors, all of which had supplied Franco, on credit, since the beginning of the war.

With fresh matériel and military personnel pouring in from Germany and Italy, Franco's forces were able to recover Teruel in February 1938. Its recapture turned out to be the beginning of the end, although the war was not terminated for another thirteen months. The Republicans still hoped they would be able to turn the tide, but this could only have happened if the Western democracies had come to their aid. Despite strong popular pressure, none did. The disastrous retreats began on March 10 and continued through part of May, when the Franco forces reached the east coast and physically divided Catalonia from the rest of Republican Spain. The Lincolns and the Mac-Paps suffered great losses in this period—in wounded, killed, and captured. Many—probably most— of those captured were killed.

The pieces in this section, more than in any other, describe the realities of the war, the heat of battle, the fears and comradeship of the men and women volunteers.

—A.P.

· Al Amery ·

Fuentes de Ebro

[. . .] For a while there was a lull in fire, with none of the artillery and *avion* that was supposed to help us. Then as some tanks appeared in the valley below our trenches, coming from the right, the rifle and machine-gun fire grew hot. But so obsessed were we with our purpose, and working up our determination to spring over the top when the time came, that we were oblivious to the fire growing hotter, deaf to the absence of a shot from our own artillery, blind to the fact that no planes had appeared, and dumb as to what to do after getting over the top.

The vague suspense that had started to wind up our nerves months ago now reached the height of its tension. The main objective we had lived for solely, up till now in Spain, appeared with sudden and dramatic effect. The parapet itself became the dividing line between the past and the future, its coarse soil impressing us with mystic importance. Over the top we could charge and either win or die. Two alternatives, no more; and the war was still mystery, the enemy still impersonal—as if they were actually fiends from hell instead of normal human beings like ourselves. We still felt more like spectators than participants. We could hear only a hurricane of sound that seemed like some manifestation of nature gone crazy. We could feel nothing but suspense, stretching our nerves until we felt numb—inside and out. (So this was what we had come to Spain for! To go over this parapet—and then what?) We could see no enemy trenches as we raised our heads now to look; nothing but our own tanks, twenty or thirty, coming, not over us according to plan, but from our right in the valley, running parallel to our own trenches, which were halfway up the hill. Then, as each of us looked blankly around him, seeing the tense, puzzled faces of his comrades, he could only feel more bewildered than ever. (If only one man knew what to do—one man, at least, to a section!)

The tanks moved right along, every once in a while one of them pausing to fire with its light artillery gun. Then one of them turned up to our sector of the trench, clattering like some prehistoric monster up to where Bill Neure stood. It pointed its gun at Bill, who stood waist high above the parapet to face it. Some Spanish riflemen riding the outside of the tank jumped off, and, crouching, came at us with rifles poised to shoot.

Guts shrank to aching void. What the hell! Are they the enemy? Are we the enemy? Who is the enemy? I was tempted to shoot, yet felt sure they were Loyalists. (You certainly couldn't tell by the uniform!) My hands craved the feel of a rifle, and I became acutely aware of the fact that I had none. The best shot in the section without a rifle! But as a section leader I was supposed to direct other men with rifles, not use one myself. I saw a small shovel on the parapet and grabbed that convulsively.

Bill Neure faced the tank with its gun aimed at his chest and raised his fist in the Popular Front salute. At this, the riflemen beckoned us to follow them and leaped back on the sides of the tank as it careened away.

There were six or eight men riding the sides of each tank, and later we heard that this was the first time men had ever ridden tanks that way in battle. We also heard that somebody in the leadership had seen it in a movie and decided to try it in action. It could work in some cases but it looked crazy there.

Bill sprang out of the trench then, his young man's feet spurning the ground.

"Come on, comrades!" he shouted.

Never before had I felt so eager to follow a man and a command. There was everything good in Bill Neure: youth, enthusiasm, modesty, courage, and the kind of leadership Debs spoke of,

that rises with the people, not over them. *My God! Bill Neure!*
The symbol of all we were fighting for—a symbol without knowing it—and his words just like him: a yell to encourage us, not an
order to command us.

"Come on, comrades!"

Bill must have hesitated a few minutes while we were all
staring at the tanks, perhaps because he could see that nothing
was transpiring according to plan. But when he yelled "Come
on, comrades!" he must have decided that there was nothing else
to do. He started running, bending low, and while I watched him
he never looked back. I never saw Bill Neure again.

I called out, "One at a time, boys!" and yelled foolishly in the
excitement: "If I get killed some one else take the *avion*-signals.
I'll carry them till then." (But a lot of good the *avion*-signals
did!) Then, turning to Tommy: "I'm going now. You go last. See
that everyone goes before you do."

Gripping the shovel that I had picked up, I took a deep breath
as if for an icy plunge and climbed over the parapet stiffly. I was
amazed to see how stiff I was. My muscles seemed to have
withered in seconds to the vanishing point of strength. I moved
as if in a nightmare, with a wild beast chasing me and my legs
without sensation of movement. I was a spark of willpower
represented by *I*, and nothing else as far as my actual strength
went. Yet every atom of my flesh tingled as if with electric shock,
as though the bullets, like a swarm of some super-deadly hor-
nets, would infallibly hunt me out. I noticed them sizzling with
sparks off the barbed wire in front of us, and without thinking
turned to run alongside the wire to get around the end of it, a
hundred yards away. *A hundred yards—oh Christ! A hundred
yards before I could even start toward the fascist lines!* The air
seemed alive, a-roar like a mighty conflagration, crackling,
snapping, whining, louder than anything I had ever heard before. My skin seemed highly conscious of this; but between my
skin and this little central spark that was *I* there seemed to be
nothing, no bone, power of muscle, or feeling of courage. Just
this little spark within a skin of fear. Minutes passed like hours. I
fell automatically, as I had been trained—but not in cover, because there was no cover. Somehow, I could move, like a ma-

chine. The great objective had vanished. No enemy trenches—nothing but this inferno of sound around me. The sole reality: this immense but invisible conflagration, as impersonal as the idea of God, as ruthless as the idea of hell.

Gradually, I acclimated myself and discovered a little feeling. Without a rifle I felt incomplete, and thought: Good Christ! Why don't they let section leaders have rifles? Then I was surprised that I could think of such a thing when each minute might be my last. I clung to the shovel as a substitute, remembering what I had read in *All Quiet on the Western Front*, that the Germans had used shovels for hand-to-hand fighting. (Huh! Hand-to-hand, at about a mile distance?)

Then I saw Mac, who had been drunk the night before, lying nearby, stiff, shrinking, blank as a mummy in expression—and became aware of the presence of others in the attack besides myself. Actually, I had been minutes without remembering my section, or my mission—without knowing anything except that this little spark received messages of terror from every pore of his skin.

"Follow the tanks!" I yelled. "Follow the tanks!" and got up to run again. (Falling down every five or ten yards confuses the enemy: he thinks you may be hit, so he thinks his range is right.)

A glance showed me the whole section streaming out behind, not well spread out because the barbed wire hemmed them in, some running, some lying prone. In another moment that seemed an hour of running, with less than a puppet's sensation of movement, I saw that we were simply moving parallel with the tanks and our own trenches and getting nowhere. At this, an idea popped into my head so quickly it surprised me—surprised me to discover I could still think, I guess.

"For Christ sake let's get back in the trench!" I shouted. "We can follow the tanks that way as far as it goes."

This was surely one of the most brilliant ideas I ever had in my life, and may well have saved some lives. If we had reached the end of the barbed wire we would have run into more accurate fire that would have slaughtered us. And if the tanks had not done as they were planned to do—break down the barbed wire in front of us—why should we make useless targets of ourselves?

Apparently, the tanks just intended to run parallel with our trenches—which didn't make any sense to me.

Nobody could hear me, but I pointed back to the trench and many followed me. We rushed into the trench; and as we ran through it, the few Spaniards we saw from some other battalion crouched underfoot and gazed up at us resentfully as if they blamed us for all this excitement.

Through the trench we scrambled about three hundred yards in safety, still in line with the tanks, and then came to an end of our hill where the trench curved to a stop like the end of a snake's tail. A gully sloped down and up to another hill on our left, occupied by men unknown to me. The valley through which the tanks rolled continued in front of our line of trenches. There, I paused in bewilderment. The end of the trench seemed the end of the world.

But the Spaniards from the other battalion had a machine gun nest there; and one of them, evidently an officer—though hatless, uniformless, stripeless, and weaponless—gave an enthusiastic sweep of his arm to motion us over the top.

"Al asalto!"

At moments, a haze of dust hung over that parapet, raised by the slashing hail of lead. And there I discovered—as though abruptly only then—the full danger of that mystery which resembled the snapping of hundreds of bullwhips, of that vicious discord I hadn't yet seen draw blood. We crouched way down below the danger point now. The trench was heaven, the outside, hell; the feel of the earth, homelike; the air above, mad.

The Spanish officer motioned us over. Bewildered, we looked to one another, awed by death within arm's reach, haunted by thoughts of the terror of a man's last breath. One strong man's face caricatured its former self—no artist could have done as well. An ashamed smile plastered one corner of his mouth up in a sneer, a stubborn frown creased his brow, and his cheeks looked shrunken as if death had already gripped him. His eyes gazed blankly, unfocused, void of all but a grasping instinct for self-preservation. Yet to him we looked for leadership. He had been in the world war.

The Spanish officer cursed.

"Me cago en Dios!" he cried—*I shit on god*—and shouting, "Vengan!" he sprang over the top to run like a hare down through the gully to the next hill.

Immediately, Andy, a big Swede, jumped awkwardly up and ran like a galloping ox. Next, it seemed that memory would haunt me to death if I didn't prove as good as the rest. Still with the shovel, I leaped out; and becoming more aware of whip-snapping lead than ever, dove, as if the ground ten feet down were water, landed on my side, and rolled like a drunkard.

I ended up too dizzy to rise in a slight depression in ground that gave temporary protection; and another man, a Ukrainian, lay below me with the fear of the devils and gods in his face. (For any extreme fear puts you back to your childhood, and if you believed in god then you are apt to feel something similar while the fear lasts. They used to like to say that there are no atheists in foxholes—as if that proved something! And how many true Christians are there on a battlefield?) The two of us lay head to head, taking one haunted look at each other's eyes and then lowering our heads.

I remembered then what Merriman had said—if the fire is too hot, do not advance—and shouted, though I realized the next instant I probably could not be heard:

"Don't come over! The fire's too hot! Don't any more come over!"

Still another one came—Paddy, an Irishman. To fool the enemy he tried my trick of rolling, but his face went slack with amazement, then tight with fear. He let go his rifle and rolled past me as if he couldn't stop.

"Jesus Christ! Are you hit, Paddy?"

Paddy held one arm with his other hand, and it seemed to me he nodded while rolling. He ended in the same depression in the ground below the Ukrainian and myself, gripping the wounded arm bent over the top of his head with his face jammed in the dirt.

It never occurred to me to try to pick him. up. I was no hero; and if I had tried we would have almost certainly both have been hit. He was heavier than I was—almost everybody but the Spaniards was heavier than I was.

I said to the Ukrainian, "I'm going"; and with my back needled and pin-cushioned with dread, got up to run awkwardly—legs so stiff and breath in such gasps I couldn't run far. I dropped once in the gully, wholly exposed to fire but so exhausted I had to stop; then rose and tried to sprint again until I reached cover on the next hill.

Three weeks later I discovered I had yellow jaundice. Maybe it was affecting me then without my knowing it. Anyway, for whatever reason, my lack of energy kept on surprising me.

Seeing Andy, the big Swede, walking ahead up the hill, and no fire coming from the men on top, who stood watching us, I realized only then that the men on top must be Loyalists, and stopped to look back to see the man who had lain near me come running; and still another, Jerry, come over the top and run and fall, run and fall again until he got across to safety. Poor Paddy lay near the bottom of the gully. From my position he looked exposed to fire.

"Jesus Christ!" I groaned. "Poor Paddy. He must be dead."

I could look back along the valley from where I stood in safety now, and I wondered where the tanks had gone. All I could see was here and there a dim figure lying seemingly lifeless on the hillside in front of our trenches, and others on a small rise in ground along the middle of the valley; and away down, some ant-sized figures clustering about what appeared to be a trench on the opposite side of the valley, jumping into it and skulking ferociously in front of it.

My heart jumped, thrilled for the first time that day. Had we captured something? And if so, what the hell was I supposed to do? The tanks hadn't gone that way. Maybe some other company had had that objective. But where the hell were the tanks? What was I supposed to do?

I started toward the others on top of the hill, feeling only half a man without a rifle. My hands ached for a rifle as surely as they have ached when they were freezing. Then as I neared the top, the Spaniards yelled, "Abajo!" and I realized I was exposed. Crouching low, I ran to safety.

They had a nice place: trenches on the forepeak of a jutting hill with the top scooped out like a bowl, making a sheltered spot where they could relax in the sun. I admired it as I would some fine house—even a palace—this little spot of safety in the sun. A few shells came over but not to menace us on the hill; and there I found Andy, sitting with a cup of water in his hand, as steady as the rock under him, his rifle on his knees.

"Well, what'll we do?" Andy asked, grinning. "Where do we go now?"

"Follow the tanks," I parroted. "But where the hell are they? Did they go by?"

"I don't know. Let's go out in the trench and see."

We went through the trench, passing the Spanish officer who had led us over the top, talking in such rapid-fire Spanish I couldn't understand a word. The officer nodded with a grin as we passed.

On the peak of the hill a Spanish machine-gunner showed us the enemy trenches—our first sight of them—nearly a mile away, and the mystery cleared slightly in my mind. I saw the greyish mounds of dirt that must be enemy parapets, and I knew what lay behind them—fascist fiends. I had a concrete objective for the first time that day—something to see and attack if possible, but not yet to hate. I had learned to hate years ago—learned to hate my father, learned to hate a rival in a love affair, and all conceited bullies. But such hatreds now were blurred and my emotions stupefied. I was like a man coming out from under ether; and as the Spaniard let me try the machine gun—inviting me with a casual wave of his hand—for a moment I peppered away at the enemy parapets like a boy shooting at a tin can. I thought I ought to feel some kind of hatred as I shot, but I couldn't feel anything.

"Christ sake!" Andy was amazed. "There's no tanks out there. What the hell is this? What the hell we gonna do? And look—it's a mile, anyhow. Tell me how the hell we're gonna run that far." He laughed boyishly, adding: "I could do it because I don't smoke. But you guys smoke too much."

I shrugged my shoulders, and we decided to go back and see what the others were doing.

Back of the trenches we found the Spaniards laughing at Jerry. They explained that they had yelled, "Abajo!" to Jerry at the danger spot we had all crossed, and he had been lying there ever since. I called out for him to come quickly, running low.

Then the three of us sat together, smoking and giving cigarettes to the Spaniards.

"I guess Paddy's got it bad," said Jerry.

"Who, Paddy?" Andy's face looked like a tomb. "Jesus Christ! Are you sure? Where is he?" He jumped up, dropping his rifle.

Jerry stood up and pointed to the figure in the gully.

Andy stared, trying not to believe. "I'm going down and see."

"No, don't!" I pleaded. "It'd be suicide to go back and bend over him. They must have two machine guns that just cover that gully."

Andy lowered himself abstractly to the ground—as if he weren't sure the ground was there, or he living, or the sky overhead. "But Paddy," he muttered slowly, like a child, "Paddy was such a good guy."

"But the thing is—what are we going to do now?" asked Jerry.

Jerry didn't like to hear about Paddy. None of us liked to hear or think about it. Paddy was one of those people who never complain, who never spare efforts to cheer up their friends, and are rarely at a loss for a good suggestion in time of need.

I suggested we stay where we were. Andy didn't say anything. Jerry looked thoughtful.

I didn't feel capable of leadership any more. I couldn't say: "Come on, guys. Let's go get those bastards." The bastards were too far away for one thing, and I was beginning to realize how little I had in common with Napoleon. I didn't think I could walk a mile, then, let alone run. Still, if someone else had said "come on," I would have followed him.

One of the Spaniards, a kid about seventeen, came back with his arm bandaged, and I jumped up eagerly to ask for his rifle. He looked very happy as he gave it to me. "I'm going to the hospital," the kid said. "Good luck!"

Hours late, the *avión* came, bombing and strafing the fascist trenches. But it couldn't have done any good. At that point it was about as useless as a schoolteacher slapping a bad boy's wrist. If we had been within three hundred yards of the fascist trenches and started running just as the planes appeared, it would have been one military tactic worth a try. As it was, none of the battalion was less than a half a mile away, and those of us still able to stand up had no enthusiasm left for running.

My sad excuse for a brain was too dull to start linking things up so soon. I just thought it had been one hell of a mess, and I, myself, had proved neither the hero nor the genius I had hoped I might come somewhere near being. I suppose I had some vague idea that a Lenin would have found some way to snatch victory from the jaws of defeat and have us all singing the International in triumph before the day was over.

(But how could a plan be so violated as that one was? We never knew. They told us later, there wasn't much to the plan. It was just to take Fuentes de Ebro and then continue on the road to Zaragosa. Yeah, but why didn't the tanks go over our trenches and break down the barbed wire? and why didn't the artillery fire? and the planes come on time? As far as we knew, we had no artillery there at all. Perhaps right there could be seen the beginning of the end of Spain. It was either the most colossal stupidity or the most brazen sabotage! You can't run a mile through heavy machine-gun fire with no support and then tackle the enemy hand-to-hand.)

As the planes went away a man came running up from the gully, speaking in broken English.

"Jesus Christ! I go out there to scout, and all them fascist machine-gunners turn on me. All them! Look!" He showed several holes in his clothes, ragged and hanging by shreds. A dozen or more bullets must have come within a half an inch of his flesh. His face was ashen, his eyes starting out of his head. "Look! I lay down for an hour and they fire all around me but never hit me.

"Water! Give me water! Agua!" he cried, and gasped with relief as a young Spaniard handed him a tin cup full.

Andy laughed. He was beginning to get the war psychology. "You'd think he had a baby," he jeered. Then he jumped up, pointing to the trench on the other side of the gully.

"It's Paddy!" he cried. "He's running! He's alive! He's going back to the trench."

Andy stood pointing with his face like a picture of a saint's head.

A dead weight left our hearts, seeing Paddy run with full strength back to the trench. [. . .]

We dug trenches about five hundred yards closer to the fascists and stayed there two weeks. Our morale hit bottom and stayed pretty low until our next battle at Teruel, where intelligence prevailed and we did a great job. This boomed our morale up again. Any time we did a great job, no matter what the difficulties, our morale boomed.

"I didn't know what the hell to do," Jerry said. "Honest! I didn't know what to do or where to go."

"Nobody did."

AL AMERY was born in 1906. A high-school dropout, he joined the navy and the army. He went to Spain in 1937, where he served in the Mac-Paps until he was wounded in 1938. After he returned to the United States he ran a ski-tow in New Hampshire and then worked as a millwright.

· Joe Gordon and Leo Gordon ·

Seven Letters from Spain

August 26, 1937

Dear Gus,

I suppose I did leave kinda abruptly. There's just one defense I have. It was necessary. As a matter of fact, it was the only way. Some time ago I informed Agnes that I wanted to go. She nearly passed out. She refused to discuss the question at all. Had I persisted, it would have broken us up eventually. It was then I knew that if I were to go at all it would have to be done on the q.t. If you think I could have done otherwise you just don't know Agnes. I'm sorry I hurt her. It's the toughest part of being out here. But look at it this way. On all sides of me in camp, the same problem confronts hundreds of the boys. I talked to them. One tells of how he managed to circumvent his mother. He told her he was going out west as a salesman. Thru some arrangement, she gets his letters postmarked from California. Then there's a Canadian who's all busted up cause he learned that his wife and kids are penniless. There are many other cases. What's your solution? Stay home and fight fascism in the United States while the fascists take over Spain? That wasn't the way the fighting Lincoln Battalion was built. Sentiment didn't stop the fascists at the Jarama River or at Brunete.

In the book *It Can't Happen Here* Doremus Jessup comes to this conclusion. Although at first deterred from fighting the powers-that-be because of his family, position and responsibilities, he later decides that these are age-old excuses that men have used to keep them from the struggle. After all, it's only a matter of time before there will be very little choice as to what sector one will be able to handle a rifle. Before long, Spain may be the quietest spot on the globe.

I hope Agnes snaps out of it. I've already sent two letters. My staying at home wouldn't have altered her financial status. On relief, one can live as cheaply as two. Thanks a lot for wanting to give her a hand. I wish she'd take advantage of your offer.

Chosie is going home. It may be a matter of weeks or months however. These things aren't done instantaneously. I met him about two weeks ago in a hospital in Albacete. He had picked up a piece of shrappel in his leg at Brunete. Chosie has established a reputation in Spain that will live as long as the Republic exists. A hard-bitten soldier who never knew the meaning of fear, he participated in every major engagement. In moments of crisis, of swift battle and instant death, when some of the stoutest hearts cracked (names that would astonish you), he never deserted his post. They talk of his exploits, stories that never got back to the States. Others got the publicity, but Chosie did the job. The history of the Americans in Spain is yet to be written. If it's in any way accurate the name Joe Gordon will be plastered all over its pages. You may think that I'm melodramatic in my description. Actually I've been understating the facts.

I've been palling around here with a guy from my neighborhood, Hy Stone. Another tradition. Back home, he was sort of a quiet, retiring kind of egg. Out here he went thru hell and spat in the devil's eye. Here's the story. Near Brunete his company underwent a terrific bombardment. His entire command was killed (commanders don't live very long). Hy was appointed adjutant (second-in-command). Actually he ran the show. At about that time he received news that both his brothers had been killed. They watched him closely, fearing that he would break. Hy compressed his lips—and went into action. The rest is on the books. 'Cause Hy Stone was cited for bravery shortly after. To give you an index of his character: he spent a coupla hours telling me the most important part of the war was ducking into cover and digging in at every available opportunity. A friend of his cut in and casually remarked that he thought Hy was a damn fool for running along a ridge once in order to draw enemy fire so that he could discover their positions. That happens to be the closest substitute to suicide yet known to science.

There's a Negro section leader in my company who is very popular. Very intelligent, good at sports (yes, we have them occasionally), and a born leader. Once while marching down a road we passed a vineyard. All the fellows looked at the grapes longingly but in vain. There are certain restrictions about picking fruit. Sort of protect property if you know what I mean. Coming back we walked thru the same field. Suddenly Milt blew his whistle—an airplane signal! The entire mob dived into the bushes out of sight. Presently we heard the recall signal. Everybody emerged grinning widely—with peculiar bumps protruding out of their shirts. I got into a talk with him one day and learned that he was Milton Herndon, brother of the famous Angelo.

I can't tell you anything about the war that you don't know. In fact you're in a better position to get this information than I am. Right now, I'm in a machine-gun company learning the various operations that go with that phase of the work. You can tell Agnes that that is a very safe job cause the guns are always behind the infantry which means that they are far removed from the front lines. We are getting a lot of intensive training, which has thus far removed a lot of excess poundage from yours truly. Living conditions are fair—which means that you eat adequately and sleep adequately but that you can't exactly dissipate on luxuries.

We always have a flock of notable visitors. Last one was Ralph Bates—who is a regular guy.

There's another Negro comrade here who knows Yank. He used to work with him in the Workers Alliance. His name is Charlie Lewis.

I kinda miss Staten Island. Not the Island so much as the water. Here we've got to tramp seven or eight miles to get to a swimming hole. So don't forget to appreciate the place a little more for my sake. When you write, let me know what Agnes is doing, etc. I hope to get a letter from her soon since yours was able to get here. Give my regards to all.

Leo

The correct address is: Leo Mendelowitz-274, S.R.I., Plaza de Altazano, Albacete, Spain

December 6, 1937

Dear Gus,

Why doesn't Agnes write? I haven't heard from her for a coupla months. Is there something wrong? Hasn't she received my letters?

It took more than a month for your letter to reach me. But I can't kick cause at least I got it—which is something.

I would have written sooner—but honest I lost your address along with practically everything else I had some time ago.

Also I've been sorta busy. I bounced out of the trenches a while back—somewhat pale and shopworn but otherwise in good condition. I'd feel pretty good about it except for the fact that we left some good men behind. For keeps.

About Chosie. I just got word from him that he's stuck in Paris. Trying to get home but it's tough titty. He's working on a committee. Write to him at the following address: Joe Gordon, c/o Bill Ellis, Hotel Minerva, 20 Bis Rue Louis Blanc, Paris, France.

I wrote to Agnes in care of the W.P.A. Teachers Union.

I've just returned from a leave in Madrid. It was swell. I wandered around looking at tall buildings and bumping into all kinds of people. I guess I'm just a city guy at heart. Besides I took a warm bath—which is news. But it's no use—I'm lousy all over again.

Thanks in advance for the package. Spain is kinda short on those little things which we're accustomed to at home. So I'm keeping my fingers crossed.

Magazines are right up my alley. All kinds of literature.

Bumped into Sam Wiseman a week ago. He drove up to our quarters in the midst of his sight-seeing tour. We talked about home news. Ask him about it when he gets home. He might remember me—modest little me.

Have you seen those films taken lately in Spain? Antifascists on the march, etc. Look for the machine guns. I'm wearing a black jacket.

I haven't run into the people that you mention.

In answer to your question as to when I'll be back. If it weren't for [my wife] Puny, my answer would be simple. I'm a volunteer. I joined the colors to fight fascism—in general. Now that I'm here I've developed a personal grudge. Remember, I always was a stickler for paying my debts. When I dragged in Milton Herndon and a coupla other stiffs, I promised 'em I'd do my damndest to ruin a few fascists. So I'd like to stay and see this thing thru. But as I said before, there's Puny—

I suppose you'd like to know how things are going out here. As far as general news is concerned you're probably better informed than I am.

But there's other things—things you've got to see in order to know. The inconquerable spirit of the Spanish people, for instance. While I was in Madrid, never once did I hear anyone even doubt the eventual outcome of the war. It's inspiring to witness how the people put up with the lack of bread, tobacco, milk, etc., etc., without a word of complaint. Everything for the front! All for "la victoria"!

Other things—

Milt Herndon's grand charge thru a hail of fire up a slope in front of the enemy trenches where his whole gun crew was wiped out. They must have known they were doomed. But the order came to advance and not a man faltered. Let the fascists produce such an evidence of indomitable courage!

And little José Juárez, who crawled up a while later with the ammunition. We had to point out the bodies of Milt and his comrades before we could take the ammunition away from him.

And Jack Schiffman who, mortally wounded, kinda smiled and gave the Red Front salute before he collapsed.

Likewise Otto Reeve, Negro Y.C.L.er from L.A. who rode atop our tanks up to the enemy lines. With a bullet thru his arm, he managed to drag a wounded comrade two kilometers back to a first aid station.

I gotta mention Tom Malone, our political commissar, big, lumbering Mick from South Brooklyn, who took every conceivable risk to bring up food, water, cognac, blankets. He never slept. Day in and day out he carried on until he collapsed. He's good material so we recruited him for the party.

And many, many, many others. We can't lose this war—cause
the guys just don't know how to lose.

Incidentally, you've got a lieutenant in your family. At present,
I'm holding down a job as adjutant of a machine-gun company.
But you can still call me.

Leo

P.S. Tell Puny, I love her.

February 18, 1938

Dear Gus,

Was unable to write to you for awhile cause I lost your address
along with everything else I had, some time ago. Getting your
New Year's card, however, solved that problem. At that, it traveled around a coupla months before it reached me. Partly due to
the fact that I was on the move all the time. Also my number has
changed from S.R.I. 274 to S.R.I. 250.

I still haven't received your package of Tauhma's letter.

Don't wait for me to answer your letters before writing again.
There's too great an interval between the posting and receipt of
mail. I intend to do the same.

Got a letter from Puny. Says she's drifting around. What's it all
about?

As to my present circumstances. Spent a month in hospital on
account of being wounded up around Teruel. A slight shrapnel
wound near the temple. Nothing serious—since as I have
pointed out time and time again us Mendelowitzes are a very
tough breed. I'll be rejoining my battalion in a coupla days.

Its quite a story—the defense of Teruel, I mean. Do you want
to hear all the gory details?

As you probably know, hard-hitting Spanish troops led by the
famous Lister and Twenty-fifth divisions smashed thru the city
of Teruel and drove the fascists back into the hills that surround
the town like a necklace. They were then relieved and the International Brigades called in to hold the line. A desperate series of
counterattacks were immediately initiated by the enemy. The
Thaelmann Battalion bore the brunt of the initial advances. The

phlegmatic Dutchmen held their fire until the fascists were within a coupla hundred meters—then methodically moved 'em down. When my outfit took their positions over a few days later, the terrain in front of our trenches was covered with dead and decaying Moors.

In the next few days, the fascists attempted an encircling movement on our right. Our observers reported huge concentrations of troops, artillery, and munitions being moved in.

On January 19, an exceptionally heavy artillery barrage on our right flank confirmed my decision to take a look at a coupla guns we had stationed on a strategic hill. When I got there, the shells were landing close enough to make a guy feel kind of uncomfortable. In awhile, direct hits made the place look like a shambles. A shell landed on one of our gun crews and wiped 'em out. Others tore down the walls of the trenches. Under this effective cover fire, they attacked. Came over in droves, shoulder to shoulder. A quick checkup disclosed just a handful holding the hill. No time to bandage the wounded. No time to mourn for the dead. The Maxim had to be shifted. Willing hands tossed the gun up to the top of the parapet. One burst—then another. But still they advanced. Our rifles popped away—but it looked hopeless. Then a guy yelled "They're down." Sure enough they had hit the dirt. Was fixing a jam when a terrific concussion bowled me over. Got up with my head spinning, the air full of dust, more guys pawing the ground. Clapped my hand to the side of my head, warm liquid trickled thru my fingers. Wondered if that one had my name written on it. But it was spelled wrong.

Sequel. In a hospital train on the way down, I spotted Lee, Brigade scout, arm in a sling.

"Yeh. Mashed my arm. They're gonna take it off."

"The hell with your arm. What's the dope?"

"The British came up and so did the Carbineros. We held the line." Lay back smoking a cigarette. Felt pretty good.

It's a good thing I'm thru writing 'cause I hear the dinner bell.

Yours in haste,
Leo

June 27, 1938

Dear Gussie,

I've got a little time on my hands now, so I'll try to write a letter. I won't go into the past, it's too long a story, but one thing. I made my mind up that I don't intend to see the United States for a mighty long time.

Spain has changed a great deal since I left. The Spanish Army is slowly but surely developing into a real modern army. Plenty of headaches to be sure, continue to pursue us, but that too we are slowly but surely overcoming. Somehow or other I just can't get this picture out of my mind, a beautiful apartment, with a radio, all modern conveniences, a group of comrades, reading and discussing the struggles going on in different countries. But let me tell you something, it's a wonderful time reading about the hardships that people go through, about the mistakes that were made, etc. But when you go through the experiences yourself, baby, it's a bitch. It's terribly hot now, which made all movements difficult and makes your own life miserable. The boys keep kidding themselves about ice-cream sodas, smokes, etc. They're wondering if there's any left in the United States. And then the women through the world, pictures and stories, play a neat little role here. There's quite a shortage of foods, etc., nobody's putting on weight in this country. Sometimes we don't smoke for a week or more. I don't know what this country does, but do you know that the most hardest thing to do is write. Funny, but you just can't think of anything to write about.

Well I guess you might as well stop writing to Leo, tough break, he was really outstanding, he fought to the very end, and took plenty of fascists with him as he went.

There isn't much more to say, the war is still going on, and will keep going on until we have final and complete victory.

Yours, regards to all
Joe Gordon
Lincoln Battalion

August 25, 1938

Dear Gussie,

I received your letter two days ago, [but] because of the terrific battles that are taking place, I have just been able to read your letter. It's taken me four hours to get this pencil, paper, and envelope. Franco's forces are now attempting to push us back across the river. They are using tremendous amounts of planes, artillery, trench mortars, etc. We as usual have plenty of morale, faith, etc.; the main thing is, that we are holding 'em. Negrin said, "Resist is to advance"; that suits me. We are now in high mountainous terrain; Cousin, there's a million and one difficulties. For an example, we haven't had a drink of water in days, it takes eight to ten hours to get water. All told we have been in action thirty-three days. Lots will help the soil of Spain grow richer, the rest go on and on.

We hoped to get pulled out for a rest and reorganization soon. It might take a day or five months—no one knows. Our main reading matter is the Spanish press. We keep time with the news, particularly international news. You got boys here that will make Harry Gannes look sick.

Lou Secundy was wounded very slightly, a scratch; he's fooling around somewhere in the rear.

Heavy shelling is now taking place all over these hills—what explosions, a million pieces of rocks and shrapnel flying all over. Their (fascist) planes are in the air continually. They're dropping leaflets, what a laugh, leaflets and bombs. I thought that was our tactics. Feel like an outsider about family matters, don't know what to say.

Will be waiting for an answer and packages.

Comradely yours,
Joe Gordon

P.S. Regards to all.

P.S. Will try to get last pictures of Leo (if I ever get a chance to—hot stuff here).

P.S. Will write again soon. Pretty hard writing now. One of

these goddamn bombs from the planes just dropped so close, I swear I caught a cold just now. Any how I'm just about deaf.

P.S. Leo's name is not listed dead, wounded, or anything, which means he's marked as missing. There's channels through which you might try to find out—try.

Can't seem to write to the folks. Just doing all my talking and writing with a gun and got a half a dozen notches already.

September 19, 1938

Dear Tauhma and Gussie,

I received your package. I don't know how to write flowery words of thanks, but I'm sure you know how I feel. Got it in the night, went through a mad scramble over mountain tops, but I held on to it, as tight as my gun. No need sending clothes outside of a warm shirt and socks, goddamn, maybe you ought to throw in some heavy underwear, *pero nada mas.* Haven't the slightest worry about getting killed, "honestly" just don't enter my mind. You know we sing a song around here, don't know the title, and can't give you the tune—it goes like this, "Old soldiers never die, never die, never die, old soldiers never die, they simply fade away."

The fighting is very hard; we're holding 'em down; the sky is black with their planes bombing and strafing every minute. Their artillery never lets up, while we have rifles and machine guns. We're tired, almost out, we're looking for rest, but the fascists are not. (They change their men every ten days.) We'll fight to the very end, and sometimes that looks like it's not too far off. However I'm not worried (not supposed to be, I'm a party organizer). My favorite dream is taking a bath. I'm getting plenty of mail, and fan mail too, it's entertaining. Though it's difficult, I'm learning quite a bit of Spanish, which I expect to use later.

There's a guy you know, Tauhma, he's from your union, he told me about you. His name's Irving Mitchel. He's pushing daisies around. Don't know how much he charges.

Wanna do me a favor, slip a bottle of American whiskey in a

package to me. This cognac is vile. Got to have that here, cold etc. You understand. Give my regards to your mother, sister, brothers, and husbands.

Comradely yours,
Cousin Joe Gordon

September 26, 1938

Dear Gussie,

I'm taking time out to write you a letter while I'm still sober. We are now in a small town celebrating and, Cousin, what a celebration. By now I guess you know why. The International Brigade is leaving Spain. What a surprise! At first we didn't believe the rumors, then when they took us out of the lines, they told us officially. These last three days of action were the toughest in the entire war. I won't go into details but I'm looking for grey hairs. So now everyone is stamping their feet, looking at clocks, etc. The route is Barcelona, Paris, and New York. Won't mind Paris, You know, I know that town better than I do New York. It's a beautiful joint, in short I'm mad about it, and then cold, starchy "London." But the beer is swell and the women are so "comradely cold" from there.

And dying to get a bath and a good meal under my belt, gee—good food. Well nothing more at least in this letter except thanks for the package. Everybody is kicking the gong; think they're going to break it soon. So long.

Hasta La Vista

JOE AND LEO GORDON grew up in Brooklyn in the depths of the Depression. In 1932 they joined the Civilian Conservation Corps, and by 1933 both were active in the labor movement. In 1935 Joe went to work in a cannery in California, where he helped organized the workers into a union. He was one in the first group to sail to Spain, leaving on December 26, 1936. Leo went in 1937 and joined the Mac-Paps. Both were wounded and returned to action. Leo was reported missing in March 1938. After returning to the United States, Joe joined the merchant marine. During World War II, his ship was torpedoed in the North Atlantic, and all hands were lost. These letters first appeared in *Massachusetts Review* (Spring 1955), and are reprinted with permission.

· Milt Wolff ·

Teruel: Another Hill

It was clear and cold, visibility was good. He had no trouble picking out the black decals on the planes that circled above the hill. The red and gold standards of the cavalry and infantry massing at the foot of the winter-grey hill flowered in the morning sun.

The lead plane peeled off, banked, and dived, screaming toward the crest of the hill. Mitch saw the bomb separate from the plane [and] wobble its way down to the crest of the hill. The plane flattened out and roared up to join the circus above. Then the plane next in the ring, and the one after that one, one after another—in shrieking dives—plastered the hill. The bomb bursts flashed a dull red, the explosions rolled like summer thunder barreling down some rock-rimmed canyon.

A black cloud reached up to meet the diving planes. All bombs away, they streaked into the cloud, machine guns rattling, and out again, to turn and repeat, one after another, blindly strafing the positions on the hill. Below, the fascist troops defiled for the attack. Mounted officers trotted along the ranks, standard bearers held their breeze-blown pennants high to mark unit flanks. For a brief moment a quietness set in as the last plane tailed off to the west. A few bars of music reached past the hill, coursed over the field of blackened vines to where he leaned against the tank. Then the Italian mountain guns and the German 88s opened up. The cloud of smoke and blasted earth, blistered, bubbled, and burst in shades of grey, green, and orange. The sharp snapping of the big guns slapped against the skin, all nerve ends now. The rumble of the exploding shells up around the top of the hill hollowed his insides.

The formations of fascist troops moved out. The cavalry taking the easy slope, the slope facing Teruel; the foot soldiers moving up like a breaking wave, turbulent with the ranks clawing for footholds on the steep southern side of the hill. The 88s and the mountain guns fired a last salvo and let up as the cavalry approached the ring of fire and smoke. Machine-gun and rifle fire rattled furiously. It intensified as the foot soldiers approached the defenders' positions. Grenade explosions mingled with the crackle of small-arms fire. The cavalry fell back. The foot soldiers broke and followed them down the hill.

Mitch Castle turned away from El Muletón, to see how the others were reacting to what was going on up there. They were all standing, facing the hill, on the paved road where the kilometer marker read "19." Nineteen kilometers from Teruel, taken by Lister's Spaniards in December, held by the Fifteenth Brigade through January, now lost to the enemy. El Muletón was the last piece of ground held by the Loyalists on the Teruel front. The members of the brigade staff stood, each apart from his fellows, spaced and strung out like misshapen beads on the cold, grey road. The Soviet tank, a lopsided lavalier, its cannon dumbly sighting the hill. Copic, his sheepskin collar drawn up around his neck, his face a clenched fist, stood at the head, the commander. Dunbar, the Englishman, bundled up in a greatcoat, his profile sharp and chalk-white, stood two paces behind. Then came the others, Commissar Doran, his fists deep in the pockets of his trench coat, straining against an invisible wall. Merriman, second in command, scanned the action through binoculars, the knuckles of his large hands ruddily reflecting the glare of the winter sun. And the others who were somehow on the brigade staff. He did not know what their titles or duties were, anymore than he knew what his were. Mitch had been acting commander of the battalion and when the battalion commander had returned, they had dumped him on brigade instead of returning him to command of his company. Policy, they told him: you can't go from Bn command to CO. Not done.

Units of the Thaelmann Battalion held the hill. They are Germans, Austrians, and other antifascists from the heartland of fascism; exiles from their homeland, escapees from concentration camps, each one marked for death in his country. There is one on that hill that Mitch knows, Rhienhard, a Communist. Rhienhard had been at Benicasinn with him. He was a short, slight man. Thin, white hair barely covered a battered and scarred skull, in which lively blue eyes stood out in sharp contrast to the patches of dead skin that covered his face. Rhienhard had been in the hands of the Gestapo for eight months, tortured, beaten, and almost broken, but not broken. Now on this hill with the others, pounded by dive bombers, 88s, mountain guns, holding, not breaking, not yet.

Mitch watched the fascist officers regrouping their units. Ambulances came up to the foot of the hill. Behind them columns of lorries brought up replacements. A low-lying cloud of dust farther back concealed the arrival of other convoys resupplying the artillery positions. The sun was well up, now; everything stood out in clear detail. Though the breeze had died, the stink of hot brake linings and exhaust fumes carried to kilometer 19.

Mitch moved over to stand beside Dunbar. Jesus Christ, he said, they're getting the shit kicked out of them up there, Dunbar. Isn't there something somebody can do something? Dunbar shook his head. Anything? Mitch insisted. Dunbar turned away from the hill to face Mitch. Nothing. The Englishman mocked Mitch's Brooklyn accent. There ain't nothing to do something about anything. And then he went on in precise, well-formed British tones. All functioning units are committed elsewhere, and there are very few of those. The rest aren't fit. Then Jesus Christ, why don't we—they—take them off the hill, for Christ sake? They won't, won't be taken off.

The shelling let up and in the sudden stillness Dunbar turned to face the hill. Then the racket of a machine-gun fire and exploding grenades began once again, a small sharp clatter seeming almost harmless following the stormy uproar of dive bombing and artillery barrages.

They're still turning them back. Dunbar turned to face Mitch. You know, he said, they've sworn to hold the hill, *"cuesta lo que cuesta,"* as the Spaniards say—to the last man, if necessary.

What? Mitch shouted over the din of the dive bombers and artillery, which had begun again. It seemed to Mitch that they were determined to flatten the hill, wipe it off the map, and the Thaelmanns with it. What kind of bullshit is that . . . Dunbar turned to Mitch. They are Germans, after all, you know—as though explaining something basic to a child. They've probably decided that this is where the battle ends, for them at least. Dunbar's smooth white face, flat and finely defined as in a drawing of an Egyptian pharaoh, froze in resistance against the anguish in his voice. Only his large, elliptical eyes, the cool grey watering over betrayed what he felt. He turned away to look toward the hill. They've been at it an awful long time, he whispered. One might say since 1930, six, seven years. A long time to be fighting fascism. A long time to be fighting at all. What about this chunk of iron here, he turned Dunbar to face the tank. Can't we at least get the cannon going . . . There's four rounds left, a litre or two of petrol, Dunbar pulled away from him. We need it here, for all the bloody good it'll do us. Up there it won't last more than five minutes. Looking toward the hill, now almost completely concealed in clouds of dust and smoke, I wonder how long they will . . .

He sat on one of the fenders of the tank. The metal was warm from the sun that had shone on it all through the day of standing there; it had not moved. He was alone in the dark. He sipped cool *vino de campo* from a tin mug and munched on a chunk of white bread. The hill seemed larger in the night, its lines softer and more peaceful looking. The fascist *camiones* wound down the road from Teruel, lights blazing, into the saddle before El Muletón. They slowed to take the rising road that went halfway up the hill. They drove with their bright lights on, one after another, in a long snaking column in the night. He could hear the racing motors, the grinding of gears. They moved up the hill and down again, their lights on, all through the night, each truck with its bold, unafraid headlights glaring on the way up, red tail lights dancing erratically as the empty trucks raced down the hill.

He pictured all the *soldados* along the thinly held line, seeing, as he saw, the unimpeded, unconcealed build-up of fascist forces. The remnants of the Brigade, Lincolns, Mac-Paps, the British, Spaniards of the Twenty-fourth watching, feeling in their guts, as he did, the weight of fascist *camiones* rolling up the tons of shit to hurl against them in the morning. The bright lights mocking their helplessness, while they, like himself, without even the comfort of a smoke, fearful that the spark of a *mechero* or the dim glow of a butt would betray their positions.

Not that there were that many cigarettes around. Mitch was reduced to stuffing his pipe with a brand of wartime tobacco he called dehydrated horseshit, when he could get it. *No hay tobaco, ni canones, ni aviones.* They had fuck-all, as the British put it. The grand alliance of the Western world sat on their collective asses watching Il Duce and Der Führer pound the shit out of the Republic, and did nothing to help.

Somewhere, up there on El Muletón, in some pitiful little hole in the ground, Rheinhard had squeezed off his last round of nine millimeter ammo, fixed the three-sided bayonet to the muzzle of his 1905 Remington Rifle, scrambled out of his hole, came to his feet—it is better to die on one's feet than to live on one's knees, Dolores—faced the cold, white sun sinking in the west behind the ruins of Teruel, and was cut down. The Thaelmanns had held the hill all day. Now they were all dead. The ululating dirge of the Moorish mercenaries howled in the sudden night.

The wine in the tin cup had soured, the crust of bread rock-hard now. The steel hulk of the tank, cooled in the blackness of the Aragon night, clattered icily among the bones in his spare frame. Mitch stood away from the tank. He dumped the wine on the marker that read 19 kilometers. He hurled the hardened bread in the general direction of El Muletón, at the Moors singing there. He turned to the *chabola* where the men of the Estado Mayor were poring over maps, planning the next move, finding another hill that somehow was important, that somehow they would take and hold, waiting, hoping. . . . somewhere in the night someone was softly singing "Freiheit." [. . .]

MILT WOLFF was born in Brooklyn and went to Spain in 1937. There he rose in rank from private to major, and he was the last commander of the Abraham Lincoln Battalion. He went on to serve in the U.S. army in Burma and with the OSS in Italy. He is now national adjutant of the VALB. This selection is taken from an as-yet-unpublished novel.

· Albert Prago ·

I Will Never Forget

On a side road between Madrid and Tarazona (our training base) somewhere in the La Mancha region, the driver brought our truck to an unexpected halt. Out of gas? No, just a damned, bloody flat.

One of us was assigned to assist in replacing the tire. The remaining seven split up into two groups to scour the nearby *pueblo*, about three hundred yards distant, for eggs. We had some soap; a swap would be easy, if there were eggs to swap. The Spanish Civil War was about eighteen months old and everything was scarce. Our diet could be called monotonous: three days of chick-peas alternated with three days of lentils, a poorly refined olive oil, an occasional piece of burro meat, one loaf of bread daily, perhaps one potato a week, and occasional tidbits rounded out army fare. So eggs were a delicacy much sought after, and we knew we had a reasonable chance of success in getting them. Especially if one had soap to exchange.

In my group were Bob, Ed, and a Cuban comrade named Pedro. Given the briskness of that January morning and given the purpose of our going to town, we covered the three hundred yards quickly.

The *pueblo* was small. Very small. One main street and one paralleling it with two or three narrow alleys crossing them. This *pueblo* didn't even boast a square, at least not one worthy of the name. Baking in the sun were the usual whitewashed houses, all rather similar. They were all shuttered! We did not see a living thing—save a few miserable, skinny, flea-ravaged curs; some were one-eyed, and some hobbled with one leg dangling or dragging, and all looked sad. They didn't even yelp at us. Our venture didn't seem very promising.

We stopped in front of the door of one cottage, and by prior agreement our Cuban comrade assumed command. He knocked gently but firmly. Almost immediately the door opened—a bare dozen inches—and we could see a señora's frightened countenance. "Buenos días!" she said, smiling bravely.

What could she have thought? She saw four smiling, unshaven faces below which were oddly clothed figures we called soldiers. If uniforms are a distinguishing feature of soldiers, then we were something else. True, we all wore the same kind of baggy pants. After that, diversity was the norm. Even our berets were of different styles. . . . Who could we possibly be? And what were we doing here? For what evil or strange purpose? What troubles were about to descent upon this isolated hamlet and its citizens? We were unarmed—did that make things seem less ominous?

After exchanging brief salutations and after informing the señora that we were *norteamericanos*, volunteers in the International Brigades, her frightened look was happily transformed. The Cuban had uttered the magic words. I don't know which aroused the greater interest or curiosity: *norteamericanos* or *Brigadas Internacionales*. In any case the fear was gone. The Cuban now made known our desires. Could the señora exchange some eggs for some soap . . . *Huevos por jabón. Jabón sí, jabón* . . . SOAP . . . Ah! . . . SOOAP!

"How many are you?" she asked. We replied that we were four plus five more: two comrades were fixing our truck and three others were at the other end of the street . . . also hunting for eggs. She invited us into the two-room hut, whose rather dark interior normally received a little light from the now shuttered window. Señora introduced us to her embarassed ten-year-old daughter, whom she sent off at once after whispering we knew not what into her ear.

Señora bade us sit on some stools and straw mats in a semicircle around the hearth. The fireplace in a peasant's hut is a major center around which important matters, such as cooking and eating, take place daily.

The señora stirred embers and added a few pieces of wood. She had wasted no time, and we silently congratulated ourselves on our good fortune. Our hostess broke some eggs into a large bowl, then stirred briskly. Oil was poured into a huge pan, nicely heated to receive the well-beaten eggs, and a large omelette—six eggs—was on its way.

In rushed the ten-year-old—what timing!—breathless, glowing, and thrust eggs into her mother's hands. The purpose of her errand now was quite clear. After stealing a quick glance at us, out dashed the daughter again. The señora smiled at us, and returned to her cooking preparations.

Crack, crack, crack . . . another six eggs, some firm beating, another pan, oil, judicious pouring of the beaten eggs, and another large omelette was on its way. Slabs of bread materialized and two wine decanters were passed around. Back came the daughter loaded with bread; with her was a friend bearing a flagon of wine . . . the señora's neighbors had been generous. Both girls were accompanied by several elderly *campesinos*. More greetings and introductions, which were happily interrupted by señora serving the first omelette.

We set to. A three-egg omelet each! Fresh, home-baked, mouth-watering bread! Home-made wine! *Maravilloso!* Perfection! I never ate better. I have never eaten better since.

Elderly citizens crowded into the cottage. Nut-brown seamed faces, some smooth-shaven and a couple of grey beards, for all of whom our presence was an amazing occurrence. While they had heard about the International Brigades—that foreigners, volunteers from several countries were fighting for the Republic—they had never seen any before. They had never seen any Americans before. They had never even seen, close up, any *extranjeros* before. Tourists had no reason to stop in this *pueblo*. What a curiosity we must have been to thus break up the dreary routine of an insignificant, tiny peasant village, far from any major urban community. A village that had been emptied of young men and many of the young women; the men were in the army and the women were working in factories or in hospitals. Sud-

denly nine young American men, soldiers, appear out of nowhere. I don't think nine Martians could have produced a more
astonishing effect.

One old *paisano*, wearing a beret as did all the others, at first
refused to accept that we were Americans. Said he, we spoke
Spanish with strange accents and intonation (he was referring
to the Cuban's fluent tongue and my barely adequate Spanish),
but, he continued, it was Spanish and therefore we must be
Spaniards coming from who knows what province. I don't remember what finally convinced him. It might have been something trivial, like the way we handled our forks—that had been
commented on—or the intensity of Cubano's explanation, or
Bob's midwestern twang, or Eddie's graphic gesticulations, or
. . . something said or done lead the old man to conclude that we
were indeed *extranjeros, americanos. . . . "Válgame Dios y me
cago en . . ."* He excused himself, dashed out, and returned with
two cronies to whom he could introduce the *americanos*, including one Cuban—whatever that was—but, *claro*, he spoke a
strange yet fluent Spanish.

Dried grapes were distributed all around, and some nuts; and
we drank more wine. Of course our drinking from the common
purrón was the cause of comment and much good-natured rib-
bing. You can't imagine how awkward we were at this ancient
art of drinking from a *purrón*. One may not touch lips to the
spout, which is held some distance from the face while a grace-
ful arc of full-bodied wine is aimed for one's mouth. With mouth
open, one swallows and gulps and swallows the uninterrupted
flow, and it is expected that not one drop will touch one's chin or
neck or shirt. After many experiences we had learned, but not
one of us was 100 percent perfect. Or even 80 percent.

It had not taken too long to change tires, but there had been
time enough for all of us to have enjoyed a remarkable meal, in
such warm surroundings, among such generous, such wonderful, *simpático* people—circumstances we could not have possibly anticipated. But the time had arrived to say farewells. Tears
rolled down the cheeks of our hostess while her daughter was
inordinately quiet. There were rounds of *abrazos* and *abrazos*
and more *abrazos*. We gathered our forces and started back to
the truck, accompanied by a dozen men and about twenty kids.

A grizzly grey peasant—one who asked us many questions—took me by the arm and whispered, "Come with me!" I protested; I had to get back to the truck with the others, but he persuaded me that what he had in mind was important and that it would not take long. I told Bob, our *jefe* of operations in the cultural commission, what I was about and he said, "Okay! But make it snappy!"

My friend guided me around a corner, then thirty or so dusty yards to a shack that served as the storehouse for all rationed goods for the villagers. Almost everything, especially foodstuffs, was rationed—strictly rationed. The commissary was set up by the *pueblo's* Popular Front Committee, a universal procedure throughout the area. My friend introduced me to the *campesino* in charge.

I was no end embarrassed to be introduced as "an American hero who came 3,000 miles to fight at our side." I said that the real heroes were the Spanish people so valiantly resisting the armed might of the fascist invaders. Handshakes were firm and warm. My friend now revealed his reason for bringing me to the *comisariado.*

Said he, "I should like you to give this comrade, as a token of our gratitude—just as a token mind you, one kilo of sugar."

"Of course I would like this comrade to have this sugar," was the response. "Even much more. But I have no right to dispense in this way what belongs to the people. And besides you have no right to make such a request." A somewhat heated but still amicable dialogue followed. Much of it was beyond my Spanish but the gist of it was apparent.

One kilo of sugar! That would be some bargaining item in sugarless Tarazona. I ventured, badly, very badly, most ungraciously, "I'm willing to pay for the sugar, comrades."

My intentions were good so that the two *ancianos* did not take offense at my gaucherie. They looked at me askance but with compassion and understanding. And dignity. Always, dignity—a unique Spanish trait common to all social classes. "We are sorry, but such a purchase is illegal. Nor can it be considered. But we understand, amigo." They returned to their argument, which was settled suddenly with an extraordinary compromise.

One-half a kilo. To be taken out of my friend's personal ration!

That meant that his family would be without sugar for at least several weeks! I could not accept it.

Could not? The two *paisanos* managed to overcome my embarrassment and weak resistance. An old newspaper was expertly folded to hold the one pound or so of sugar, and it was turned over to me without further ceremony. I stammered, "Muchísimas gracias, camaradas!"

"It is nothing! Go with God!"

We exchanged hurried *"Adiós!"* . . . upraised clenched fists and *"Salud!"* and then my friend guided me to the truck. On the way he said, "You know, you look very much like my son. He is not as tall as you, but you have similar appearances."

"Where is your son?"

"At the front. He is *miliciano*. I don't know which front, I think near Madrid. He has been gone for just over a year. We miss him . . . very much. You know, *amigo americano*, I'm sure my son would have wanted you to have this sugar."

I gulped. I could say nothing. We embraced . . . *Adiós y Saludi!*

Clutching the makeshift bag of sugar, I piled into the waiting *camión* whose motor was already roaring. We all waved vigorous goodbyes to the people and a score of children who lined the road. The elders smiled bravely, the children were ecstatic. A sudden turn of the road, and that was the end.

I shall never forget our hostess and the Spanish peasants of that tiny *pueblo* somewhere in la Mancha. I will never forget.

· Sam Carsman ·

Memoir

We spent the whole winter in those positions, never once being sent to the rear, and never seeing a woman's face or being able to relax in a hot bath or a comfortable bed. But we amused ourselves in many ways, and I for one enjoyed the life quite well. At night, in the cabin, we would huddle together beside the fire, and the bull would fly and tall tales would heat the air above us. Now and then we would be able to get an extra barrel of wine, and we would sing revolutionary songs, and other songs of a more jovial character—all through the night.

I will remember one occasion—I forget just now whether it was Christmas or some other holiday—when we received a most unusual visitor. He was a captain in the Spanish infantry who had come down from the lines to pay the *americanos* a visit. He was a very picturesque fellow mounted on a splendid white horse, which he rode at the head of a column of ragged infantrymen, organized into a washboard band. They tailed after him playing on their makeshift instruments, and doing a pretty good job of it. The captain himself rode in the grand manner—proud carriage, chest inflated, and a rakish smile on his lips. His clothes were, if anything, more ragged than those of his followers, and his face was unshaven.

He dismounted in front of our shack, made a gesture, and four of his men who had brought up the rear of this unusual cavalcade came forward, carrying on their shoulders a large keg of wine. Without saying a word to us, he pushed open the door, and the men entered and deposited the wine on the table. When we had all gathered round, attracted by the curious event, he made a little speech in which he expressed, in the name of the infantry, his appreciation of what we were doing for his country. He felt that it was a tremendous thing to have crossed the great ocean all the way from America to fight for Spain. He tapped the barrel and drank a toast to us. After that we settled down to the typical Spanish custom of repeated speeches and toasts, drinking, and singing of songs.

That night was really a corker. Maybe the wine was stronger than usual, or maybe we just blew off the cork, but anyhow, every man-jack of us got polluted. Timpson—the commanding officer—was set up at the observation post, and Jack Waters, who was the lieutenant in command of the gun positions, was there in charge. Jack was always one of the boys and understood the need of letting off steam once in a while. He got lit up too. It had snowed again during the night, and about three o'clock in the morning Jack looked out at the snow and suddenly got the bright idea that it was time the battery had a midnight drill. After blowing his whistle, he bawled out: "Action station on the double quick!" All of us piled out into the snow exactly as we were. None of us stopped for coats or hats. In fact, damn few of us even had pants on. I, for one, was out there in my underwear, completely barefoot. Jack, in order to maintain his dignity, had on his pants, but little else. Around his bare chest was strapped his Mauser pistol. We lined up in front of him, and there in the snow we began to execute close-order drill, marching up and down the fields, singing revolutionary songs lustily.

When you're drunk, it is said, one can get away with murder, and so it was with us. None of us showed any ill effects from that night. In fact, it lifted our spirits for a time. The Spaniards went away next morning, thinking that the stories and pictures about American gangsters and clowns were actually understatements, compared to the way we Americans had acted.

SAM CARSMAN was born in Wilkes Barre, Pennsylvania. Shortly after graduating from high school he joined the army and served in Panama. He then returned to Wilkes Barre, where he was active in the unemployed movement and helped to found the Young Workers' League of Pennsylvania. He volunteered to fight in Spain in 1937 and was one of the few Americans assigned to the John Brown Artillery Battery.

· Ben Iceland ·

The Big Retreat

When the fascists retook Teruel, we came down out of the mountains and took up positions in an orange grove near Sagunto. It was a lovely spot after the cold and snow of Teruel, and a very welcome respite. There were ripe oranges to hand, no planes overhead, the grub was hot, and there was even a view of the sparkling blue sea. We were also given a day's leave in Valencia for hot baths and delousing. There was time too for a whiff of the *putas* in the cafés.

We remained in the olive groves for about a week, listening to rumors about a coming fascist offensive in Aragon, or perhaps even one of our own. Then the order came to move, and late one afternoon we headed up the road to Catalonia. We thought at first that we might be going to Barcelona, which was beginning to be bombed heavily by the fascists. But that was not to be. Near Tarragona we turned off toward Lérida, and all night we tried to get some sleep in our overloaded autocars as we headed northeast. When the sun came up, it was a strange, wild and empty countryside we saw.

Sixty kilometers to the north were the Pyrenees, snow on their lofty peaks, and beyond was France. It seemed so long ago that I had climbed those mountains into Spain. We set up our guns on a wide, lonely plain near Huesca, and the hot sun glared down in early spring. There were eight Americans, one Australian, and an Englishman in the Czech (Klement Gottwald) anti-aircraft battery. We were all observers, except for M. Hawkins who had been assigned to the Oerlikon gun, which was used to protect the battery from strafing aircraft. During the day there were always two observers scanning the skies with their glasses, while the others lolled in the dugouts, or when it was hot, as it was then, took it easy in the shade of some large, jagged rocks.

Charlie Bartelli, a lean and laughing Canadian, who had just turned twenty, was writing a letter to his sweetheart. M. Hawkins was telling about his life on the San Francisco waterfront. He used to refer to himself in a humorous, self-deprecating way as B.I. (Basic Industry) Hawkins. He explained that he had taken that nickname because the political people he had known at home, and also here in Spain, were always "yapping" about, and glorifying, men from the waterfront factories. The nickname stuck. Irving Peters was griping about the many fronts he had been at, and how he should have been repatriated, and the many guys who had been sent home—most of them undeservedly, in his opinion.

"At Brunete, when I was in the machine-gun company," he started to say, when Eliot, a tall, grim-looking Australian, growled at him: "Aw, keep your bloody mouth shut for a spell." Eliot despised Peters for his griping and for his disinclination to work. "I can't figure out how so many good guys get bumped off, and a *coño* like you is still around. You'll probably go home and tell everybody what a hero you've been in Spain." "Nuts to you," Peters lamely answered. He was scared of Eliot.

Louie Roberts, a New Yorker, was telling Crosby about all his love affairs in Valencia. He had had many of them, and took them all seriously. He knew practically all the whores who frequented the Café Vodka in Valencia, and there was a table in a dark corner of the café where he would sit with his back to the wall, and from where he could eye everyone who entered the place. Before settling down to business, the whores would sidle up to him and greet him effusively. He would engage many of them in what seemed to be very serious talk, sitting there with his tight beret covering his right eye. Louie spoke Spanish well, but it was not his conversation that attracted the ladies of the Café Vodka. Louie was an "organizer"—somehow he always seemed to have things—scarves, silk stockings, soap (not the

Spanish kind), and real white bread and butter that he had obtained from ships in the Valencia harbor. It was a priceless gift he had, in those days after our hospital train had been bombed and the fascists had cut through to the sea. But that was later.

Crosby was an avid listener. He responded to the amatory exploits Louie was regaling him with in a high-pitched laugh, or with the one word in his vocabulary he used most, "Wowie," and then he took a slug of wine from his canteen.

Crosby sometimes had as many as three canteens—one or two always hanging from his shoulder, and one usually in his pack. His constant concern was to see that they were always filled with the bitter red wine, which at that time was issued every day. Crosby didn't smoke and he didn't like sweets; so he would exchange his ration of those commodities for wine; or if we happened to be going through a town, he would always manage to find the local tavern and fill up his canteens—sometimes with anise. He came from Oklahoma and had worked as a truck driver for an oil company. I first met him on the boat from New York to France. All of his time on board was spent at the bar. Crosby hadn't the slightest idea of what was happening in Spain. On board, I once asked him why he was going to Spain, and he told me that a friend of his had told him he was going, and had sent him to someone called "Jim," who had advised him to get a passport and then sent him to someone called Bob in New York, who sent him to see a doctor for a physical, and a few days later he found himself on board a ship bound for Europe. Crosby was a Catholic, and I remember once in Tarazona how he expressed wonderment to me that he couldn't go to mass in the church in town. It was hard for him to understand why most churches in Loyalist Spain were closed down. He was a real political innocent—always friendly and smiling, always cheerful, and almost always a little drunk.

One morning, on a high hill near Teruel, a lone fascist plane was strafing our battery. Crosby and I were in a shallow ditch some distance from the guns, and we decided to make a dash for the deeper trenches surrounding our battery. When the plane zoomed past us and disappeared over the next hill, with the tracers from Hawkin's Oerlikon streaming after it, we started to run. But in no time the plane flew back, and very low this time. We flopped to the ground and could hear the rattle of the plane's machine guns, and, almost simultaneously, the bullets were ricocheting around us. Then it swooped past, and before we could decide whether to get up and make another run, it was back. But this time, it seemed, the pilot had decided to have some fun with us. He didn't strafe, but released some small hand bombs or grenades which exploded some distance from us. I was hugging the ground, arms around my head, but Crosby was looking up, and he swore he saw the pilot leaning out of the plane and throwing the bombs. The plane didn't return, and when we got back to the battery Crosby was in a state of high exhilaration, laughing and shouting, "Wowie, wowie, wait till I tell the folks back home about me being chased by a plane. Bet they ain't never heard one like that before."

The alarm rang—a clang of metal against a hollow shell, and then the whistle. The battery sprang into life; swiftly the men ran to their posts and the long green muzzles of the guns were swiveled upward. The shells were in a dozen hands ready to be plunged into the breeches. We braced for the first concussion. It was a false alarm. Peters had spotted a bird through his glasses that he mistook for a plane and had yelled "avión." Everyone laughed, relieved. The guns were lowered and camouflaged. Stillness again steeled over the brown, parched fields.

It was a strange front. There was not another unit near us. For four days there was absolute quiet—not even the usual tuning of the machine guns in the morning. We knew that there were the lines in front of us, but we never saw a man, an animal, or a vehicle. It was most welcome, and we wished it might never end. The grub was coming up regularly, and we were getting rid of some of our lice, and there was not the sight or sound of a plane in the sky, and not far to the north were the majestic peaks of the mountains.

We knew it couldn't last. One morning, while it was still dark and we were all asleep, we were awakened with the not-unexpected yet dreaded words: "Marchar, hombres—pronto." In thirty minutes the guns were mounted, attached to the trucks, and we were on the move. As usual, we observers were crammed into the truck containing the gasoline drums—and if you've ever been in a steel autocar crammed with drums of gasoline, still sleepy-eyed, and with the freezing night wind going through your threadbare jacket, you can understand why we were grouchy and sore. And as usual, Irving Peters managed to get the softest and most comfortable spot, and made it more uncomfortable for all of us. Louie, who was particularly put out, started to threaten Peters and call him names: "You lazy son-of-a-bitch, *coño*, why don't you get yourself shot and become a hero. One of these days you'll wake up dead, and it'll be a good thing for everybody." Peters just smiled foolishly to himself, wrapped a blanket around himself a bit more closely, and closed his eyes. It did no good talking or yelling at him, and even if we could get him to move, in a little while he was always back in the best spot. We kept getting colder and colder, and we huddled close to one another in a frozen stupor, pitying ourselves and thinking of home and warmth. We sped through the deserted countryside, and when we passed through the whitewashed medieval towns where people were sleeping warm behind walls, we felt even more miserable.

In the morning we reached a small bridge where a dirt road led south to Belchite, and the main road continued east to the coast. We stayed there for a few hours, speculating about where we were going. Schutz, a German-American seaman, was sure we were going to take up positions in Barcelona, where there had recently been many heavy air raids. "I can just see myself walking along the Ramblas with all the pretty girls and flowers," he mused. "What a swell place to fight a war." And then he started teasing Louie. "Hey Louie, think of all the putas you'll be able to screw there." Louie, not even deigning to reply, just arched an eyebrow and looked at Schutz with a slightly condescending air. Schutz was always teasing Louie. Basic Industry Hawkins volunteered his opinion: "If I know this outfit, we'll be going to the asshole of creation, with no putas, no flowers, and a sky full of *aviones*." Tall and calm, Eliot listened to all the talk and then settled the question: "Why don't you fellows stop yapping and daydreaming? We are going wherever they send us, and if I know this bloody war, it is not going to be to the blue

Mediterranean, least of all Barcelona. So pipe down, and lets make up our minds we're here for the duration, and most likely, not that long." Eliot was right. We took the dirt road south.

We didn't see any planes, but from afar we heard the throbbing of planes in the sky, and then the faint thud of the bombs as they hit the ground. In the afternoon we passed through Caspe. It had been bombed. Many of the homes were demolished and the streets were cratered. Most of the people had fled to the hills and the neighboring olive groves. "We're in it again," I said to myself. "Will it ever end, my new world of bombs and blood and noise and fear?" Far away across the hills could be heard the familiar sound of heavy artillery—very faint. When it grew dark we got to the little town of Azaila, only a few kilometers from Belchite. We were creeping along at a slow pace—without lights. The Spanish drivers, who, it always seemed to us, judged a truck by the noise they could get out of it, were grinding their gears, using their brakes, cursing one another, and making a horrible din. Some black, menacing tanks crunched their steely way past us. On both sides of the road was a long file of men, grim-faced under helmets, with rifles and packs. Some men were bent over with the burden of the squat Russian machine guns; others, first aid men, were carrying rolled-up stretchers on long poles. When our trucks stopped we heard snatches of talk in Spanish, French, and what seemed to me a Slavic language—Polish I thought. Then we heard English spoken, American English. We started to yell, and we were yelled back at. It was too dark to recognize any faces, and we couldn't get off the trucks for closer contact. "You call yourselves soldiers?" one of the Americans gibed: "Why don't you get off those trucks and fight with the infantry like men?" Another wit added: "Boys, it looks like we're going to get plenty of shit from the *avión* today; the anti-air is here, and you know what happens when they're around; we never saw you shoot down a plane, or if you did, it was probably one of ours." Someone else said: "How'd you get those piecard jobs, through W.P.A?" We took the kidding good-naturedly and did some taunting of our own. Someone struck a match to light a cigarette, and a shout went up: "Apaga la luz!—put out the light!" and curses in every language. Some cavalrymen galloped by, looking huge and formidable in the darkness.

A few hundred meters from the town, we left the road and started crawling and bumping across the fields. It was very dark, and some of the men had to go ahead and guide the trucks with flashlights. We huddled together in the trucks, talking in low tones. Louie muttered: "My God! Another front—If I get out of this alive, I'm going to ask to be repatriated. How much can a man take? If I'd only get a leave when this is over."

"Two to one we get a position out in the open, and no more wine and cognac," remarked Crosby. "By the way, has anyone got anything to drink? I've got some dirty old cigarettes and a bar of chocolate for exchange." No one took him up.

Schutz, who was a good mimic with a queer sense of humor, started to imitate the whistle of falling bombs and the ping ping of bullets overhead. B.I. Hawkins growled at him: "Why don't you cut that out, you *coño*? We'll be hearing the real stuff soon enough." B.I. was always very nervous and shaky before any pending action, and when it was over he was visibly atremble. But it was amazing how calm and cool he seemed to be while firing the Oerlikon at low-flying planes.

The trucks stopped and we all piled out. We could only see a few yards around us, and after helping unload the instruments and setting up the guns, we started to dig shelter for ourselves. Louie, Irving Peters, and I set to work digging a foxhole for the three of us. We only had one shovel and one pick, so one guy could sleep while the others worked. Louie wrapped a thin blanket and poncho around him and was immediately asleep on the cold, rocky ground. The ground was so hard, and our tools so dull, that we accomplished very little, and after a short while our backs and arms ached. All around us the men were digging, and nothing could be heard but the grunting and the thud of picks in the rocky soil. Our section leader, John, a Czech-American, came to exhort us to work harder. John was our liaison man with the Czechs, who spoke and understood little English. When we had any requests or gripes they had to go through him to the Czech command. We sometimes had the feeling that our messages, or the replies, were slightly garbled in transit. John came from Cleveland, where he had worked in a steel mill. He was a pleasant guy and a hard worker. We continued to dig out pitiful little handfuls of earth in the darkness, our bodies aching from weariness and lack of sleep, all the while cursing the war, and the thought of daylight weighing heavily upon us. Thus we passed the night.

When the first light appeared over the bleak Aragon plains, we saw we were in a flat field with no vegetation but a few dwarfed olive trees. The foxholes we had dug were pitifully shallow—no more than two or three feet deep. Louie started yelling at Irving Peters for not having done his share of digging, and threatening to throw him out if he dared to duck into any part of the foxhole when the time came to take cover. Peters said nothing, just smiled. He was used to being a scapegoat for everybody's wrath and frustration. There was hardly any protection for the guns, and a half-hearted attempt at camouflage had been made with some branches of the olive trees. For breakfast we had a lump of congealed, sticky rice, stale bread, and the lukewarm stuff that passed for coffee. Hawkins, his hands trembling, remarked: "Things sure do not look promising this morning in sunny Spain."

The air began to throb with the old familiar hum—"Messerschmidts," yelled Eliot, and there in the western sky, first one black speck and then another and then a third appeared, growing larger, and the air filling with noise. We were ready, and when they came within range, our guns opened up; volley after volley thundered into the sky, and as the shells left the gun barrels, we could hear them whistle in the air for a few seconds, and since it was not yet completely light, we could see them explode in the sky, way up, like dim streaks of lightning. The planes floated serenely around and under the bursts of shrapnel, and the white puffs of smoke disappeared into the atmosphere. Then from the south came the hum of more and heavier motors—Heinkels and Capronis came into view, and then more Heinkels and Capronis, and the silver Messerschmidts above them, and our guns were firing in all directions; the air was thick with the smoke of our guns and the smell of burnt gun powder made our mouths dry.

From our left the French battery was also firing; but still they came on, circled over us disdainfully, and then they headed for the ridge beyond which lay the town of Belchite and the Loyalist troops. They dropped their bombs, and the whole west was filled with smoke, and through it all could be heard the thud of the fascist rapid-fire artillery and the rattle of machine guns. Then the fighter planes started to form a maddening circle, and one after another they power-dived with a roar, and strafed beyond the ridge, and came up out of the dive, and then circled and dived again, with no letup.

"Where are our fucking planes?" we cursed. "Why the hell aren't they around when we need them?" "Those poor bastards in the line—they're getting hell," Eliot said. "By God, I don't envy them—if they hold it will be a miracle—I saw them throw stuff at Brunete, and Teruel was bad enough, but this beats it all—and the lousy French keep the border closed."

Then suddenly the air was cleared of planes, and although the artillery was still pounding and the machine guns firing, it seemed unnaturally quiet. Our guns were leveled, and we sat down utterly exhausted; yet the day had hardly begun. The food truck came up again and dished out some more of the same cold, sticky rice we had had some hours before. Maybe they had a premonition that it would be difficult to feed us in the immediate future. They also handed out a can of bully beef to each man, and a ration of cigarettes—those utterly unspeakable, unsmokable Spanish "pillowslips"—fat stubby cigarettes wrapped in paper that was always coming loose—grainy stuff that always mixed in our pockets with bread crumbs, lint, and cotton threads, and which we rolled, hoping to get a puff of smoke, but usually in vain.

Like the rush of an invisible express train, with a whistle and swish, a shell hurtled toward us. Startled, we flopped to the ground, and the shell exploded a little beyond the battery. Then three more shells in rapid succession—one of them a dud. We were under fire from German 88s, a gun that was first introduced in Spain and used both as AA artillery and against troops on the ground. The order was given to find cover. So long as we were under fire, our guns were useless. Sure enough, Peters was first in the foxhole we had dug, and Louie and I cursed and pummeled him to make some room for us. He did not listen, and lay at the bottom of the trench, and we could feel his body trembling, and he said: "What are you guys so scared about?" and continued shivering. Every few minutes the shells came.

Then the planes came back, but our guns were silent, and we huddled in the earth. From over the ridge to the west the noise of battle continued, and we three lay fearfully in our shallow trench, expecting the artillery to blast us out of our hole. Now we were all trembling, and my mouth was dry, with not a drop of spittle. I thought to myself: "What the hell are we hanging around here for? Why don't we move? Why isn't headquarters ordering a change in position?"

A strange dog, long and horribly skinny, with every rib showing and with his tail between his legs, crowded into our dugout, trying to nuzzle his way between us. Louie grabbed him and threw him out bodily, cursing: "Stay out, you lousy mongrel; it's crowded enough in this hole." But the dog was mortally afraid. He no sooner hit the ground, than he crawled like a streak back again, whimpering and trembling all over. Louie threw him out again, but it was useless. He came back and tried to inch his way to the bottom of the dugout, crying softly in the back of his throat, and we did not have the heart to throw him out again. I thought: "The poor dog is even more miserable than we are, not understanding why men should be hurling death at one another, making the ground quake, and sending bombs down from the blue Spanish sky."

The artillery was no longer firing at us, and we all rose up out of the ground, and the guns were readied for action. Our commander, a young, soft-spoken Czech, went around to each gun crew, speaking words of encouragement. John, our section leader, spoke to him, and then he told us that we were waiting orders to move. Our position was too open and unprotected, and the enemy had us under observation. Obviously things were not going well for us in the lines.

The sun was overhead and burning when soldiers, fear graven on their pale faces, started to run across our position from over the ridge to the west. Some had rifles; others did not. Our commander went out to meet a group. He was carrying his long Luger pistol and stopped one group of retreating men.

"Get back, you cowards, or I'll shoot," he shouted in poor Spanish.

The soldiers stopped, for the moment more terrified by the pistol in front of them than the enemy. The youngest of the group, a boy of about eighteen, started to cry. But the groups coming from the ridge were increasing in number, and one brave man could not stop it. He put his pistol back in his holster, swore, and went back to his dugout. The soldiers scampered away, and we all felt a little contemptuous, and yet sorry for them.

"After all, they're only kids," Louie said. "They don't know what it's all about. We would like to get out of this place too."

Finally the order came from headquarters to retreat. Reluctantly we got up from our dugouts. One of the Czechs, a member of the communication squad, had been killed, his head mangled by shrapnel. We covered him with some earth and stones. Three or four others also had slight wounds from shrapnel. None of the Americans were hurt.

When we started to load the trucks, we were under fire again. First the instruments and then the boxes of shells were hoisted onto the trucks, and then our personal belongings. The fascists were firing shells with overhead shrapnel, and often while we worked, we would have to drop everything and duck back into our holes. While we worked we were unafraid. Terrified soldiers were streaming past us, with nobody seemingly in command, all headed east. Some of the retreating soldiers had blood-soaked bandages wound about their heads. Men retreating are contagious, and in times like that when every instinct tells you "run, run with the rest and save yourself," it is not bravery that keeps men from breaking; rather it is shame—shame at the thought of acting like a coward in front of your comrades—shame at being the first to give way—shame at the thought that you, who had come thousands of miles to fight, could not take it. So men act nonchalantly, when inwardly they are consumed by fear.

When the trucks were all loaded, and even before some of us had a chance to get on them, they were off. We started to yell for them to stop and started to dash after them, but it was too late. Of the Americans, Eliot, Louie, Crosby, and myself were left behind. We had no arms—just our packs and a couple of blankets. There was nothing to do but walk and hope to meet up with our outfit in some new position they would undoubtedly set up. We joined the helter-skelter mobs of men, all going in the same direction, away from the front. But it was impossible to escape the front. The fascists, knowing that the men were in retreat and the front broken, continued shelling us with over-head shrapnel—shells that exploded up in the air and rained down. Squadrons of planes would dive and strafe, and we spent much time that day hugging the good Spanish earth.

The wide plain was full of retreating men. Many of the Spanish soldiers were carrying suitcases. We met some men of the French battery. They told us they had been forced to blow up their guns, not having the time to pull them out. They seemed utterly demoralized and said they were heading for the coast. They slyly hinted that we accompany them to Valencia. The thought of that sunny Mediterranean city, surrounded by its orange groves and gleaming near the blue sea, was tempting. Eliot, who could speak some French, gently told them to fuck-off, and dead tired, we kept going ahead. Eliot was a union organizer in one of the Australian port cities. He was a Communist and one of the bravest, most dedicated men I have ever met. He had no small talk, no sense of humor, but he was a good man to be with in time of trouble. When I thought I could hardly lift my legs any longer, he gruffly offered to carry part of my pack.

It was growing dark when we reached Azaila. The town had been bombed about a half hour ago, and a thick cloud of smoke still hung over it. We hurried through the crowded, narrow streets, anxious not to be caught in another raid. Everybody else in town had the same thought. Carts were being piled with pitiful household belongings, and black-tunicked, bent peasant men were leading their burros, with women and children sitting on the heaped-up carts, and sheep and goats following behind. Soldiers, peasants, burros, sheep, all living things fleeing the fascists and their thunderous death from the skies. Many of the women were weeping, leaving loved ones buried in the debris of their homes. Most of these peasants of Aragon had never passed beyond the fields of their village, and were almost more terrified to flee to the unknown east than to stay at home and wait for the fascists. But the tide was to the Mediterranean, and the black sorrowful mass choked the roads, looking fearfully up at the sky.

Some distance from the edge of the town we found a small barn filled with straw. Other soldiers were already there and the place smelled of unwashed bodies. We burrowed deep in the straw and fell asleep immediately. At dawn we awoke and shook the straw from our clothes and hair. We had some bread, and I also had a tin of sardines that I had saved from a package my wife had sent me many weeks ago. We tore the bread apart and were dipping it in the olive oil in which the sardines had been packed. The smell of the sardines and the oil was strong, and the soldiers around us eyed us hungrily and enviously. When we had eaten, one of the soldiers asked us for the can. He dipped a tiny piece of bread in it and asked: "Sardinas americanas?" "Sí," I replied, "sardinas americanas."

"There is much food in America, is there not?"

"Yes," I said in my poor Spanish, "much food."

"Then why did you come to Spain, the land of war and hunger?"

"To fight the fascists," I said.

He looked at us with bewilderment, and shaking his head muttered something to one of his buddies.

It was with an effort that we left the barn. Our muscles were stiff, and it was difficult for our swollen feet to fit into our shoes. Although it was very early, the road was as crowded as the day before. Rumors were circulating that the fascists were here, there, everywhere. An Italian Savoia appeared in the sky, and panic spread among the crowd. There was a rush for the fields at the side of the road; women were screaming and children were crying. A two-wheeled cart, with the braying, terrified burro still in the traces, had overturned in the ditch. Dogs were barking and snapping at the frightened people. However, the plane neither bombed nor strafed; it just circled overhead once, way up, and flew away.

The road ran straight across the plain. There was no shade on that road, and even though it was March the sun was burning. In the distance, the whitewashed houses of a town were shimmering. Louie and Crosby sat down to rest. Louie was carrying an enormous pack, filled with the many articles he had accumulated in Spain—stuff he meant to take home with him, he had explained to us, when he had been kidded about the size and contents of his pack. He had a special attachment to a heavy steel German helmet, which had a bullet hole in it. He never wore it, but carried it with him everywhere. It was his good luck charm, and he felt that as long as he had it, he would come home safe. Crosby was quite drunk, since he had been sipping wine from his canteen all day. Eliot and I, who were not so heavily loaded, both actually and figuratively, decided to keep on moving. That was the last I ever saw of Crosby.

We felt uncomfortable on the road and decided to cut across the fields and low hills where it would be less dangerous, even though more arduous. Many other soldiers had the same idea. So hour after hour we trudged across the fields, cursing the Spanish sun and the lack of shade. For miles around there was not a piece of shrubbery or a tree. When night fell, we lay down in the field and huddled closely together, covered by our ponchos and one thin blanket. We fell asleep immediately.

Early next morning we continued east across the fields. The sun rose and it became hot again. We were hungry and we were lucky we had some very stale pieces of bread and a couple of cans of bully beef to eat. But we had no water, and the soldiers we met had no water, or said they hadn't. We were so tired we could barely move, yet we dared not stop, fearing that once we felt the luxury of resting, it would be difficult to move again. The planes were active that day too, and the throb of their motors filled the air, and bombs distantly exploding.

We were wondering what had happened to our battery. We were pretty sure that by this time they would have set up new positions, and when we saw planes we expected to hear the familiar explosions and see the white puffs in the sky.

Two soldiers were passing close to us, one of whom was bandaged around the head. They were ragged and covered with dirt, and on both their faces was that gaunt and yellow look of men who had just come from the front. They both were carrying rifles, and nothing else. They were tall and did not look Spanish. Then one of them, with an unmistakable English accent, asked us in halting Spanish if we had any water.

"Are you guys from the Lincolns?" we both burst out, overjoyed. Yes, they were from the Lincolns, or "what was left of them," they bitterly exclaimed. "The Fifteenth Brigade was wiped out—nobody fucking-well left." They said brigade headquarters had received a direct hit, and many officers and men had been killed. They listed casualty after casualty. We had no way of knowing how much truth was in their statements, but it did seem pretty bad. And they cursed as they told us how their right flank had broken.

"We could have still been holding the lines if not for those bastards in the Eighth Brigade—anarchists or marineros I heard," and then he rambled on: "And what did they do for six months after we took Belchite and gave it to them? Did they build a trench? Not even a foxhole, the lazy bastards, and then they expect us to hold the lines with peashooters against all-hell-breaking-loose."

The soldier with the bandaged head did not say anything. He was leaning for support upon his more voluble comrade, and looked deathly pale. He needed water badly, and his wound needed dressing. We kept walking, glad to be with these men from the Lincolns. The soldier with the bandaged head stopped.

"I must stop," he said. "I can't keep up with you. I'll stay here and rest." His buddy also urged us to go on without them. We said we would stay with them for awhile, secretly glad to rest our weary swollen feet. I had my emergency first aid kit. We took off his bloody bandage and applied a fresh one. The wound was not a serious one—just an open cut on the scalp, matted with blood and hair. But he had lost plenty of blood and was faint and needed water. We all needed water.

Two Spanish soldiers were passing us, and Eliot, taking hold of one of the rifles, approached them.

"Comrades," he said in broken Spanish. "We need water for a wounded soldier."

"We have no water," one of them replied.

Eliot lifted the rifle, a bit menacingly, and approached nearer. He did not have to say anything more. One of the soldiers gave him his well-filled canteen, and the wounded Lincoln drank as much as he could. We also took some hefty swallows, feeling like thieves. The canteen, almost empty now, was returned to the soldier, and Eliot apologized: "I'm sorry, comrade, but we needed it. You can probably get some further on." The soldiers left, muttering under their breaths. Eliot, I know, would never have used the rifle—and besides, it was not loaded.

"Coños," exclaimed one of the Lincolns. "They're probably cursing us now; you come thousands of miles to fight in this fucking war, and you'd think they would give you a little water when you need it."

"Aw, lay off of them," said the wounded one. "They're probably conscripts; they don't understand the situation as we do, and they've been through hell too." His buddy could only shake his head wonderingly and say: "Look at the guy—a hole in his head and still PD'd [politically developed] up to the asshole."

I was thinking of how the brigade had been broken up, and how at this very moment the newspapers back home were probably headlining the rout, and of my wife and family reading about it and worrying themselves sick about me. And here I was, walking next to an Australian who came from the other side of the world, and walking in utter fatigue over strange fields and hills through strange medieval towns, and avoiding death that other strange men were hurling at me with their planes and cannon. I felt homesick and the tears struggled to my eyes.

Late in the afternoon we came to the town of Híjar. It was deserted. Never before had I seen such fearful wreckage. Hardly a house was standing. Large bomb craters were in the streets. The railroad tracks along the station were twisted grotesquely. A café in the town square was filled with soldiers drinking wine from huge barrels; other soldiers were filling their canteens with wine. The proprietor had fled. Eliot and I were welcomed into the drunken crowd. When they found out we were Internationals, they surrounded us admiringly and began to drink to the *"extranjeros"* and to the "Lincoln *Brigada*," and pressed some wine upon us. We did not need much urging and were soon a bit drunk.

We staggered when we left the café, but we were thankful, for the wine made us feel happy and free, for a time, of the tension and fear we had had for the last couple of days. For the first time I heard Eliot express an irreverent political sentiment:

"Christ, will this bloody war ever end? I haven't been near a woman for a year, and I've forgotten what they look and smell like, and if I ever again get near one, I wouldn't know what to do." But then in an afterthought—"First though, we've got to lick these bloody fascists."

As we neared the edge of town, our ears caught the drone of planes cutting the clear air, and all of a sudden we were drunk

no longer. We looked at each other knowingly, and I began to feel
that weight in my stomach. When we could see the gleaming
specks getting larger and flying in our direction, we jumped into
an irrigation ditch at the side of the road. We sank into water
and mud up to our thighs, and leaning against the side of the
ditch, we cursed our vilest. There were five of them in formation,
big silvery trimotors, and they flew by, serene and unafraid.

But suddenly, from the hills outside of town, we heard a
familiar sound. There, a few kilometers in the hills, we could see
the flash of the guns and then, looking up, the white puffs in the
sky around the planes. The anti-aircraft was in action, and the
planes wheeled and left, without dropping any bombs.

"It's our outfit," I said. "Sure enough," added Eliot. "Let's get
to them."

We picked ourselves out of the ditch and headed in the direction of the guns. The hills were steeper than we thought, and it
was tough climbing, but we reached them just as it was growing
dark. The guns were placed on a small plateau surrounded by
rocks that cast huge shadows. The gun crews were starting small
fires, as it was now too dark for flying aircraft.

It felt good to be back again with these tattered and hungry
men. The young Czech commander greeted us very warmly and
in broken English said:

"Comrades, I thought you were dead—kaput. Salud." John,
our section leader, was beaming and happy. The Americans
hugged us and slapped our backs, and wanted to know what had
happened to us. Louie had reached the outfit that morning.
Crosby, he told us, had been too drunk to continue on with him.
He had left him asleep by the side of the road.

While we hungrily devoured some cold chick-peas, they told
us of all that happened since we last saw them. This was the first
position they had been able to set up since the fascists had
broken through at Belchite. We were not the only ones who had
been left behind. Seven Czechs and two Hungarians were still
missing.

It was very dark over Aragon, and sitting around in groups,
talking, we loved our comrades. The long, menacing guns set up
in a square seemed warm, familiar, and protecting. For a brief
moment we forgot the coming dawn and the many more dawns

until the fascists chased us to the sea. We were back with our
battery, where, it seemed, we had lived forever.

BEN ICELAND was born in New York City and graduated from
New York University, with a major in classics. He worked for
the Department of Welfare until he left for Spain in 1937. He
fought with the Czech anti-aircraft battery from the battle of
Teruel through the April retreats. He then joined an anti-tank
and heavy artillery battery. During World War II he was
classified as a "premature anti-fascist" and served with an anti-
aircraft outfit that was confined to California—one of the many
instances of discrimination against Spanish vets in the armed
forces. After the war he worked as a mechanic and social
worker, and then farmed in upstate New York. He earned a
M.A. in Latin and taught until he retired in 1976. In 1982 he
became the editor of *The Volunteer*. This piece was written in
1939.

· Theodore R. Cogswell ·

International Brigade Song

This is a story
That happened long ago.
You've got to sing it sad
And you've got to sing it slow.

For eighty-seven riflemen
Who tried to hold a hill
And for the one beat-up old Maxim gun
And a gunner name of Bill.

Tanks kept coming
And we started in to cave,
88s got ranged in
And the left flank gave.

Whole damn division
Trying to take that hill,
And no one left to hold it
But us and Bill.

Troops on our right,
They was brave but they was green,
Wasn't used to tanks
And they got run off the scene.

Nobody left
To hold that hill
But a beat-up battalion
And a gunner name of Bill.

We was awful low on ammo
And we couldn't hang on.
Weren't no point in trying
When our flanks were gone.

Captain blew his whistle
And we started down that hill,
A-twisting and a-dodging
All except for Bill.

Bill just laughed
When we started in to run
And checked the feed
On his Maxim gun.

They was dug in good
On the top of that hill,
And they started in a-talking
The Maxim and Bill.

Well, we went and lost the battle,
And we went and lost the war,
And the living are all scattered
And the dead don't care no more.

But I can't help thinking
Of that torn-up hill
With no one left to hold it
But the Maxim and Bill.

I couldn't help the running.
But I can't forget the stand,
So I've made me up some music
And I've set some words by hand,

> For eighty-seven riflemen
> Who got shoved off a hill,
> All except for one old Maxim gun.
> And a gunner name of Bill.

THEODORE R. COGSWELL was born in 1918 in Coatesville, Pennsylvania. He spent thirteen months in Spain, serving as an ambulance driver. On his return he enlisted in the U.S. army air corps and served in the China-Burma-India theater. He then returned to university and earned a B.A. and M.A. in English. He has published two collections of short stories, a science fiction novel, and was national secretary of the Science Fiction Writers of America.

· John R. Gerlach ·

Behind Fascist Lines

It is early morning. Quiet prevails as though the war is not on; neither heavy guns, staccato machine guns, nor intermittent rifle fire can be heard.

We're on the run—have been for days.

The fascists are pushing. Otherwise you would almost imagine this is a hike, an excursion in the countryside. Fortunately for us, the enemy does not know where we are.

There are no more than fifty of us—a remnant of the Fifteenth International Brigade of the Spanish Republican Army. Some of the units of the Fifteenth managed to cross Mora de Ebro bridge. Others encountered fascist Italian units and tank formations south of the Ebro and scattered. We somehow got caught off the main road leading to Gandesa because we suspected the road and town to be fascist controlled and occupied. The nearby countryside is swarming with fascist units, pushing toward the Ebro and the Mediterranean.

Momentarily, we halt on the wooded rise to take stock of our situation. We suspect we are behind the fascist lines. The only staff officers present are Dave Doran, Bob Merriman, and myself. To the not-too-distant right we can see Gandesa. Off to the left lies Corbera.

After a hasty huddle, we move down into a gully and climb to a plateau overlooking Gandesa with a stretch of barren, freshly plowed fields extending to the city's outskirts. Before we can decide what to do next, we look across the gully and see an enemy calvary unit, obviously an advance scouting party, about to bridge the gully we just crossed. There is a burst of machine gun fire from our side. They stop and turn back. It seems easy.

We bunch together and decide to explore the Gandesa direction, on the premise that the main road would be faster, providing it is open and safe, whereas the open field to Corbera would slow us down. Such was our rationale. Merriman and I dispatch ourselves toward Gandesa to explore and see. It is evident that formalities as to who must do what don't mean anything anymore. Neither courage nor bravery prompts me to join Bob to attempt to save ourselves. Simple self-preservation moves me. If I die, I die. It will not be the result of failing to act. In the face of death, there are no good intentions of fare-the-wells. If there is a chance to survive, I'll help it happen. Such was my motivation. Such were my random thoughts.

If one acts, he governs his fate. Of course, there is luck.

We slide down the high bluff, skirting the open, plowed field with caution. The spot is barren except for scattered, ancient, gnarled olive trees. Bob and I stop, trying to size up the terrain. This pause saves us. Just as we are about to move forward, a soldier dashes across the field. From high on the ridge, where we just came from and where our contingent awaits, sounds the familiar machine-gun fire. Puffs of dust follow in fast succession, and the hapless soldier crumbles, like a sack of potatoes.

The situation is obvious. We hastily climb back to our contingent on the bluff and on the run made a decision to move fast, hopefully, unseen and undetected, out of the way of the fascists' gun placement. We head in the direction of Corbera. Just exactly what, earlier, we were reluctant to do and must do now. . . .

It is now late afternoon. Luckily we made it this far without any mishap or loss—without suspecting the night tragedy to come. At this point, Bob gets two scouts to go ahead and reconnoiter. We are in enemy territory. As it turns out, this precaution only slows us down. The two scouts return with no useful information or observation.

Silence prevails. What's to say? What to do? It becomes painfully evident that there is only one goal to pursue—forward to the Ebro, our side, or perish. I volunteer to go ahead and scout.

Silent acquiescence confirms my burden. The others follows, about twenty feet behind. After a while, we reach a road between Gandesa and Corbera, perpendicular to the main road and leading to the Ebro.

We all crouch or sit on the high enbankment overlooking the road, out of the possible view of anyone there. A slow-moving armored vehicle goes by on patrol. After a pause, to make sure no one else is on the road and convinced it is safe, we all move across and scamper up the opposite enbankment. The sun is slowly receding behind us. Shortly, the night will be upon us, making our movements safer and easier. We wait while Bob goes up and down the line to make sure we are all accounted for.

Now the night is with us. We can hardly see each other, but we are getting used to the darkness. A hasty exchange with Bob adds to my confidence that I know where we are since, only a short time ago, the whole brigade bivouacked near here and I visited our units daily. We move ahead. Nearby, I spot Lenny Lamb. "Come on, let's go," I whisper to him, seeking confidence and courage in his presence and company. We move.

Less than a few hundred feet, with Lenny beside me, to our left a guard suddenly hurls the challenge at us. We freeze. We do not respond. The rest of the contingent piles up on us. "Follow me," I shout to Dave and Bob. They follow. In the dark to our left, presumably from the same guard, we hear: "Rojos! Rojos!"

We swerve slightly to the right down a path leading somewhere. After a few seconds, I determine in my mind that the path leads to Corbera—and if there are fascists about they must be in Corbera too. I swerve to my left, with footsteps behind me, coming suddenly to the edge of a high terrace. In the darkness, I can see olive trees with overhanging sturdy branches.

"Jump! Jump!" I shout. At the same time, I grab a branch and swing over the edge. The others are still with me. I know they see the terrace, which at night might have looked bottomless. They stop momentarily as I ease myself down without any harm. I stop and listen. There are others about me. Some follow. Some remain on top of the terrace. We remain silent. High above we hear footsteps on the terrace and a few seconds later we hear a command: "Manos arriba! Manos arriba!"

After a moment, I whisper, "Let's go" to those nearby. I realize that those who did not jump are lost. Soon we are near the main road where we rest momentarily and make certain there is no one about. We listen. Behind us only darkness. No more footsteps. No shouts or shots. Only silence!

There is no record of what happened to Dave and Bob—they delivered themselves into the night in the greatness of their faith. I failed to lead them to safety. They perished without reward. Two days later, we sit on the bank of the river Ebro with sun high above and the hum of quiet. Tears of despair streak down my face. Shortly after that we crossed the Ebro.

I often wonder why they didn't follow when I called.

Yes, I wonder and remember those savage times. Today, I hear their echoes—ravaged youth in their faith and glory who repose under some unmarked and unknown olive tree so that Spain, tragic Spain, could sleep at ease and her children be free. O Spain, you were my mad passion. I escaped your deadly embrace.

JOHN R. GERLACH grew up in Detroit. He went to Spain in 1937 and served for nine months as an intelligence officer on the staff of the International Brigades. After the battle of Belchite, he became chief of information on the staff of the Fifteenth Brigade. When he returned from Spain, he worked as a mechanical engineer and served as a CIO representative. He is now retired and writes poetry, short fiction, and satirical vignettes.

· John C. Blair ·

Prisoners in Franco's Prisons

My first five months as a prisoner of Franco were spent in various hospitals and in the concentration camps of San Pedro de Cardena; and it was in those places that I learned what was really happening to the Spanish Republicans unlucky enough to have been captured by the Franco forces.

I was in the Deusto University in Bilbao, which was being used as a hospital. There were about fifteen Internationals in my room, which was probably a class in normal times. I had only arrived an hour before with four or five other prisoners from Zaragoza.

A man in a bed to the right of me and somewhat to the rear was screaming in pain. He appeared to have an injured leg. Shortly, a large husky man came in and sat next to the bed. I thought he might be a doctor as he was dressed well in civilian clothes. But suddenly I saw him bring his arm way back and then strike the patient with all his might in the face with a large beefy hand. The patient stopped screaming and I heard the huge bully speaking in a threatening tone to him.

The fascist bully left but the patient continued to groan. Shortly after, they moved him to another part of the building, where he died within a couple of days. I was told that he was a Brazilian who had part of the calf of his leg shot away and had developed gangrene because of lack of proper care.

It seemed to be the policy of the fascists to only treat the surface of the wounds. Several prisoners in this room had bullet wounds through their bodies. One U.S. prisoner had one through the intestines and passed blood for some time but his body healed itself; otherwise, he would have died.

There was a large Englishman in a bed next to me whose only injury was a broken arm caused by being struck with a guard's gun-butt after he was captured. The broken arm was never set and caused a series of problems with the result that the fascist bully appeared one day, stuck a 45-caliber pistol muzzle against the head of the Englishman, and told him any further problems would get him shot.

Most of the common labor was done by Basques, whom we could trust in most matters. They told us that a sister of Pasionaria was working in a place and made arrangements for her to appear one day. They got her to come into the room for about half a minute so that we would all get a good look at her and then left. She certainly had a strong resemblance to her famous sister and appeared to be as old, or older.

In the room we occupied there was a Finn who had been wounded in the leg. Lack of proper care caused the leg wound to heal in such a way that the tendons could not function and he had to hop around on one leg with the other several inches above the ground. I suppose if the Englishman with the broken arm survived, it would require a considerable operation to restore use of that arm, if possible at all. A young Welshman named Morgan lay on the battlefield for two days and a night with a shattered arm and bullets through the legs before being picked up and brought to town by peasants. His arm was amputated without anesthetics after he was given a shot of cognac.

After three weeks or so at Deusto University we were finally sent on to San Pedro de Cardena. The Englishman with the broken arm remained behind as did a couple of others who were thought to be in too poor health to be moved. I heard from other Englishmen later that their countryman died or was killed. At San Pedro we met a few prisoners who had been in prison with Spaniards on their way to San Pedro, and we heard of the executions taking place.

After a couple of months at San Pedro I was sent to Zaragoza, with two other Internationals following at short intervals. Here, for the first time, we were among Spanish Republican prisoners, 1,000 to 1,500 of them, and saw how they were dealt with.

They got no trial in any real sense of the word. Those brought before the court heard themselves charged by the prosecutor, heard an immediate verdict and sentence, and then were allowed to make a statement if they wished. There were a great number of death sentences, a large percentage of thirty-year sentences, then twenty-year sentences, and a very few given ten years. A volunteer in the Republican Army was almost certain to draw the death penalty. Then the days would pass until the last two days of the month, when it was usual for executions to take place.

This was a new prison that was completed just before the civil war began. It was a two-story affair with four wings that jutted out from the central portion. Between these wings, on the ground level, were the patios where most of the prisoners spent the daylight hours and then returned to their sleeping quarters in the second floor of the wings, where meals were also served. I was told that the contractor who built the prison was an earlier prisoner here. After being in prison for some time he was taken out and shot like so many other Republicans.

It was some time in August 1938 that I came to prison and was soon instructed in all the details of prison life by other U.S. prisoners who were here before me. All told there were eight from the United States out of a total of about twenty Internationals. Most of the prisoners slept in large rooms on the second floor. When coming down to the patio, we came down iron stairs to the large open space on the ground floor, called El Centro, and walked to the right along the wall until we came to the door of the patio assigned to us. In the center of the open space was a small guard room with a guard always on duty to watch the prisoners as they moved along.

One morning, one of my friends who had been here for some months, said, "You will notice that it will be very quiet in the patio this morning." He said this as we were circling El Centro and approaching the patio door.

As soon as we stepped out of the doorway onto the landing, of several steps leading down to the patio, I understood what my friend had meant. On a usual day when we entered the patio there was considerable noise from the moving crowd. Prisoners were talking with one another, often walking up and down in twos and threes. Sometimes simple games were being played. There was some shouting to one another from a distance. Today was different. Many small groups were clustered around one or two of those who slept on the floor of El Centro or others who had seen those taken out for execution this morning.

It was almost totally quiet as I entered the patio. There was a very soft murmur like the sound of a slight breeze springing up in the morning and rustling the small leaves on an early spring day. This sound came from the small groups talking quietly with the witnesses who had seen those taken out for execution on this morning. It would be an hour or so before the sound returned to the volume of the average day.

In the large sleeping rooms on the second floor of the prison, the crowding was the greatest of any place I stayed in the prisons of Spain. The prisoners slept on single mattresses, which sounds not so bad until you find out that they slept crosswise. We filled in for pillows with a bundle of our jackets, etc., because our heads were stuck out beyond the mattress. At the other end we used our shoes and any other stuff we could to get our feet level. The prisoners slept on their sides with no room to spare. When one went to the toilet at night he had to fight his way back in, because the space he had left would close up.

The glut of prisoners was so great in this federal prison that they could not be crowded into the large rooms upstairs where most of them slept. As a result, many slept on the floor of El Centro, in passageways like those in front of the cells where those with death penalties were held, etc. I was surprised to find a sleeper in front of the urinal, at the entrance of the toilet for our sleeping room, when I went into it one night. The passage in front of the urinal was about three feet wide. The prisoner was crowded over against the wall so that about ten inches was left for those passing or using the urinal.

The prisoners taken out for execution were lined up before the tall wrought-iron gates that led to the outside from El Centro. Those prisoners sleeping on the floor counted the number taken out and usually identified most of them. There were usually fifteen to twenty taken out each day while I was there. Some of those being taken out occasionally showed their defiance of the fascists by shouting slogans for the Republic. The sleepers sometimes responded, but if identified by the guards were beaten and perhaps put in isolation cells for it.

One chilly morning one of the prisoners was brought out without any trousers, just in his drawers. This did not occasion much comment from those who saw this. The Republican prisoners were often poorly clothed. The complete story of this prisoner without the trousers did not come out until some time later. It seems he did have trousers, a good warm pair of them. He felt it would be wrong to take them to the grave, when so many of his comrades needed them so badly. He had discussed this with those in the same cell. The cells, which were built for one or two prisoners, were now crowded to a new capacity. So when the guard called his name at the door that morning, he came without his trousers, simply leaving them behind. Those left behind knew what to do. They saw to it that his trousers found their way to the patio one day, somewhat later. There they were given to another Republican soldier whose pants were thin and in rags. It was all done so carefully that the person receiving them did not know where they came from. He was told that they were from a friend who had gone on to another place—just in case he might have some compunction about wearing a dead man's clothes and so that the fascists wouldn't step in to counter this expression of solidarity.

I saw a young man squatting in the patio with a nice-looking pair of trousers folded on his lap and talking to a poorly dressed young prisoner. I did not know what was happening until someone explained to me about a month later. I was to find that somewhat similar instances were quite numerous before I finished my stay in Spanish prisons. Surely, it seemed to me, a movement that can furnish such exponents of humanism, compassion, and solidarity must find its way to triumph in the end.

JOHN C. BLAIR grew up in Wisconsin in a family of French-Canadian extraction. He became a tool-and-dye maker and a member of the International Association of Machinists, and then an organizer for the United Electrical Workers. In Spain he was captured and imprisoned. After the war he lived in California, where he died in 1982.

· Carl Geiser ·

Christmas in a Franco Prison

The outstanding event in our life in the concentration camp at San Pedro de Cardena was our Christmas Eve performance. Bob Steck, a member of the Workers Laboratory Theater in New York and of the staff of *New Theatre Magazine*, arranged the program; Rudy Kampf, a graduate of the Heidelberg Conservatory of Music, provided the music and organized a large chorus.

Singing had been banned, but the major agreed to lift the ban if no "revolutionary" songs were sung. We invited him to attend the concert with his officers and soldiers, for we hoped the performance would improve our image in their eyes. We had not been certain he would attend, or how many he might bring with him. I was relieved to see him come cross the courtyard with about thirty men and officers, including Sticky and Tanky—without sticks or arms.

I welcomed them at the doorway. The major, motioning to his officers and soldiers, followed me up the dark stairway, through the poorly lit narrow corridor to the last archway, and then into the larger room, since we had filled all except that end with seats made of doubled-up sleeping sacks.

I showed our guests to the two front rows. "We are sorry we cannot offer you chairs. We hope you will find our straw sack seats comfortable." Then I squeezed in behind the major, where I could watch his reactions.

Three weak, unshaded light bulbs hanging from the ceiling, one near each end of the room and one in the center, dimly revealed the many rows of wall-to-wall prisoners seated on similar straw sacks. However, I could see that our guests' main interest was not in the prisoners behind them but in the curtain immediately in front of them. I knew that all except one wondered where we had obtained the wire over which we had hung four of the blankets we had received recently from the Friends of the Abraham Lincoln Brigade.

When all were seated, Bob, as master of ceremonies, rose and with a friendly smile said in Spanish, "Major, officers, and soldiers, we are happy that you have joined us to celebrate this Christmas Eve, which unfortunately both you and we must spend here. To make this evening a pleasant one for all, we have prepared a program appropriate for the season. We will begin with Christmas and folk songs from Germany, Poland, Italy, the Slavic countries, Cuba, England, and the United States. After that we shall present a short adaptation of *The Barber of Seville*, followed by short skits. Our concert will conclude with a Bell Song especially adapted for this occasion."

The curtain parted in the middle and was drawn magically to each side. Eight German prisoners faced us, about to sing. But what drew the attention of the major and Sticky was the charcoal mural on the wall just behind the prisoners. We remembered that the major had angrily ordered all walls whitewashed to blot out our class outlines, and had warned us there had better be no further desecration of the walls. Now one whole wall had been used to depict a winter scene in a small village in the Austrian Alps. One looked down past a church belfry on a street lined with two- and three-story houses nestled in a valley between the mountains on either side. One could almost hear the bell's joyous peal this Christmas Eve.

I caught a "Bonita" from the major to Sticky, as a soft tenor "aaaaa" preceded the opening bar of "Heilige Nacht." The perfect harmony of the eight separate voices, ranging from a deep bass to a high tenor, startled the seated soldiers and prisoners into absolute silence. Stone walls three feet thick, with deeply indented alcoves every ten feet, carried even the softest tones to the last row and produced no echo from even the loudest passages. Forgotten were the straw sacks and the concentration camp; there was no reality except the song and the chorus.

Tears came to my eyes as I listened, exulting in the artistry of our German comrades, for whom our jailers had always reserved the most brutal treatment. I could also sense the elation of the prisoners behind me and see the astonishment in the faces of our guests saying, "These are our prisoners? They can sing like this?"

"Tannenbaum" was next. The strong plaintive voices aroused a deep feeling of nostalgia as we thought of our families and our faraway homelands, and the happier surroundings in which we had sung this favorite. This was reflected in all our voices as, six hundred strong, we joined in on the choruses, flooding the room with emotion-packed harmony.

The Poles and the Slavs, inspired and challenged, made their unique contributions to a varied program. The superb quality of all these voices was due, I was told, to the large role group singing plays in the culture of their native lands.

The British chorus favored us with several old ballads, including "The Twelve Days of Christmas" and "What Will I Do if I Be an Old Maid in a Garret." The blending of Scotch, Irish, Welsh, and English accents, each expressed clearly in short solos, provided a pleasing effect and was warmly received. Even Tanky applauded.

The Ukrainian Canadians with their powerful voices sang the "Volga Boatman" while slowly pulling on a rope cleverly made from tightly rolled blankets. The Cubans were especially well received by our guests, since they sang Spanish songs.

While as a whole Americans could not sing as well as the Europeans, Max Parker did get up a respectable quartet in which he was joined by John Hollis Jenkins, Henry Megguier, and Eugene Poling. They presented a very creditable rendition of two labor ballads, "Joe Hill" and "Casey Jones."

"We should have an intermission at this point," announced Bob, "but since our refreshment and promenade areas are still to be constructed, we shall continue our program as soon as we can arrange the scenery for the *Barber of Seville*. Rossini's opera was first performed in Rome in 1816. One of our operatic experts has undertaken to modernize it for our times, and to adapt it to our stage. So with apologies to Rossini, and for your enjoyment and entertainment, we present a modern-day *Barber of Seville*."

This brief introduction had provided enough time to prepare the scenery—four stools in a row facing us. Against the wall on each side stood a man, waiting. For a long moment nothing moved. Then a man came through the archway and was motioned to a stool. Another wait, and a second man entered, to be motioned to a stool. Absolute silence.

A third man entered and was motioned to a stool. Only when the fourth man had entered and sat on the remaining stool did the two men leave the wall and spring into action. Each took one end of a two-foot-wide sheet, goose-stepped backward, then sidestepped two steps to align themselves with the four men. With one quick flourish, the sheet was raised and lowered, and four heads were sticking above four holes in the sheet.

The head barber now stepped forward, while his assistant grabbed a pail of suds and a wide brush. At the head barber's command, "Ojos a la derecha!" the four heads looked to the right and the assistant with one sweep of his brush lathered one side of all four faces. "Ojos a la izquierda!" and another pass of the brush lathered the other side. "Ojos a la derecha!" and one pass with a large wooden razor shaved one side. "Ojos a la izquierda!" and the job was done. All that remained was to wipe the faces, and that was quickly accomplished, each barber grabbing one end of the sheet and lifting it with a see-saw motion. The four men stood up as one, bowed stiffly to the barbers and marched out as the curtain was drawn.

The prisoners applauded this satire uproariously, but I noted that the major and his officers applauded politely and briefly.

Next the Cubans put on a parody on a night club. Several were dressed as women; we all wondered how they had obtained the clothes. The dancing and singing were hilarious, and drew much laughter and applause from our guests and ourselves.

The French skit overcame all language barriers. It depicted in pantomine the life of a tramp, keeping the audience laughing without a word being said. Then there was a juggler, and finally two Polish Ukrainians performed an acrobatic Russian dance that amazed us all.

A large number of Internationals had unobtrusively moved

out of the audience into the corridor. Bob now announced, "May I take advantage of the few moments required to prepare for the next number to tell you something about it? Rudy Kampf has prepared a special adaptation for a chorus of eighty male voices of the Russian song 'Evening Bells.' It is with great pride and pleasure we present to you Rudi Kampf and the 'Bell Singers.' "

The curtain was drawn back slowly and steadily, revealing Rudi in front of eighty men standing shoulder to shoulder in four rows. After a small bow to the audience, Rudi turned and faced the men. As he raised his hands, audience and performers observed absolute silence. A momentary wait, a slight motion of the hand, and somewhere from the depths of the group came a slow steady "Ding, Dong, Ding, Dong" followed by the opening theme sung by the entire chorus. The purity of the voices and the perfect coordination between the various groups of voices were thrilling even to the least musically educated listener. The smallness of the room in relation to the size of the chorus brought a tremendous range of intensities to the listeners' ears. The softer passages, where one again became aware of the "Ding, Dong" background, alternated with full-throated passages, providing a second level of counterpoint in addition to that developed between the groups of voices.

I stole a glance at our guests. All were frozen motionless. Tanky's face was a study in astonishment; a pleasant smile of appreciation played on the major's face. And I knew the men behind me, who had listened to the low-voiced rehearsals of groups in dark corners, were as astonished as I was by the stunning effect of the complete chorus in full voice. And the men on the stage? It was as if, rebelling against the dehumanization of life in the concentration camp, each was pouring out his soul in a conscious act, creating beauty with his fellow men, for his fellow men.

Gradually the voices became more subdued, and more and more joined in the "Ding, Dong" background. Finally only the background could be heard. Its quiet regularity bred an air of expectancy. Suddenly a high sweet tenor rang out from the midst of the chorus, carrying a haunting melody. My spine tingled and tears again came to my eyes. The unwavering clarity of the high notes called out an emotional response that electrified the room. Every man, both in the audience and in the chorus, was thrilled by the sureness and purity of the tenor voice. It brought to my mind a line from Shelley's ode "To a Skylark": *And Heaven is overflowed.*

All followed the melodious rise and fall of the song, now quickening, now hauntingly slow, always perfectly joined to the muted "Ding, Dong" in the background.

Slowly voices began leaving the background and resuming their usual role, and gradually the tenor melded in with the full chorus. The performance of the chorus, as if inspired by the tenor voice, was yet more precise, more harmonious, and rang out more firmly. How long the song lasted I cannot judge, for the beauty of it made keeping track of time impossible. At the closing "Ding, Dong," there was complete silence for a brief moment. Then the entire audience rose to its feet, clapping hands vigorously and shouting, "Olé! Olé!" the distinction between prisoner and jailer lost in the wild applause. It was a performance we all knew we would never hear equalled, an evening no one would forget.

The exhilarating effect of the performance lasted for many days. It was the main topic of conversation. Those suffering from ailments were much improved. The bond of international solidarity was greatly strengthened as we congratulated each other on the contributions made to the evening. There was no doubt our jailers now looked at us with new eyes, and they used their sticks less when giving orders or reprimanding "offenders." Even Tanky, for a few weeks, stood at the doorway without swinging his stick. Bob Steck and Rudi Kampf, modest in manner, must have obtained much satisfaction out of the evening, as did all the others who had played a part in that memorable performance.

Two days later we received a request to repeat the program on New Year's Eve. The major wished to bring several of his fellow officers from Burgos to our performance. We gladly complied, for we ourselves wanted to see and hear it again. The second performance was more polished and delivered in a more professional manner than the first; it may not have had the excitement of surprise that the first performance had, but it was still the most memorable New Year's show I have seen.

It should be noted that at each performance, some of the fleas in our straw sacks left us and established new residences with our guests.

CARL GEISER was born in Orrville, Ohio, in 1910. He studied electrical engineering in Cleveland and then earned a B.S. in psychology from Columbia University. He was in the first student group to visit the Soviet Union and was member of a number of radical student organizations. He went to Spain in 1937 and rose from ammunition carrier to battalion commander. After being wounded at Fuentes de Ebro, he returned to the front as commissar for the Mac-Paps and was captured. He was among seventy-one Americans exchanged for Italian prisoners in April 1939. Back in the United States he worked in aircraft instrumentation plants until he retired. This selection is excerpted from *Prisoners of the Good Fight* (1986), his history of the Americans captured in Spain.

The

EBRO
OFFENSIVE

and the

WITHDRAWAL

The demoralization that accompanied the retreats was virtually eradicated by the intensive preparations for the last great Republican offensive, which began on July 25. It was here that the International Brigades were to demonstrate the full extent of their courage and heroism, as did the Spanish soldiers. General Vicente Rojo, the officer who planned the

strategy, later described the offensive in his book España Heróica *(cited by Arthur Landis in* The Abraham Lincoln Brigade*):*

> *Our troops effected the most audacious operation of the entire war. The Ebro was crossed to a depth of twenty kilometers and a wide breach was literally torn in the Rebel eastern front. The enemy rear guard was seriously menaced and his command was immediately obligated to terminate its offensive against Valencia, and withdraw troops from that front to be sent to the Ebro: all his plans had been totally interrupted.*

But such enthusiasm was soon dissipated, as the enemy responded by massing a force of planes, tanks, artillery, and men far beyond any previously mobilized in the war. Art Landis wrote:

> *Just as the crossing of the Ebro would be the Republic's greatest attempt for victory and stability, so would the now monstrous juggernaut of the Rebel armies' response be unparalleled in its total commitment of men and matériel. For three months the great mass of the two armies would be locked in a maelstrom of destruction.*

On September 21, while the battles were still raging, Dr. Juan Negrín announced before the League of Nations that the International Brigades were to be dissolved. It has been speculated that he hoped that such a gesture would lead the Western democracies to demand that Hitler and Mussolini withdraw their "volunteers." However, at that very moment Neville Chamberlain was in Munich agreeing to Hitler's most recent demands, the appeasement posture that was the backdrop for World War II—six years of unprecedented barbarity and bloodshed. After the betrayal of Germany at Munich there was no ground for hope that the leaders of England, France, and the United States would aid the Spanish people in any way.

The Lincolns' last day in action was September 23, 1938. Ed Rolfe wrote of the battles on this day that "Each death was more bitter, since the men knew that relief was on the way, that this was the last action." There was an understandable sadness. At midnight the men filed past the battalion command post on their way to the rear. Alvah Bessie described this moment in his book Men in Battle: *"We heard the marching feet, the shuffling feet, dragging on the road, moving toward the river. It was a slow shuffle; there were no voices; there was no singing."*

The war was over for the Americans. Some were chagrined; they would have liked to have stayed until the bitter end. But once the impact of the withdrawal hit home, many—perhaps most—were relieved that they were alive and on their way home. Filled with pride at having served so honorably, Americans, English, Canadians, Swiss, and Latin Americans began to return home. They did so with little difficulty, although they were subjected to considerable harassment afterward. But it was infinitely more difficult, and often impractical, for other internationals, including those who came from Eastern Europe, Germany, and Italy, to "go home." Many of them were interned in concentration camps in southern France; some escaped and went on to serve in the resistance movement.

Some brigade members, particularly those from countries with repressive regimes, stayed on in Spain, many until as late as February 1939. Then, when it became obvious that the war was coming to its tragic end, they crossed the border—only to be interned in French concentration camps. By the time the war ended, on March 31, almost the only brigade members remaining on Spanish soil were those suffering in Franco's prisons.

—A.P.

· James M. Jones ·

Hold That Position!

This is a brief overview of what happened in what some called the Battle of the Ebro, up to this point in my story:

In July 1938 our army crossed the Ebro river from the Catalonian side and swept the fascist forces southward. We recaptured a good piece of Aragon. Mussolini and Hitler continued sending almost unlimited planes, artillery, tanks, and mortars to Franco's fascists. These they unleashed against us. For some time, they succeeded in moving our army only a short distance. In the Sierra Pandols and the Sierra Caballs, and other points on this northern front, our Spanish Republican Army held onto the mountains with rifles and grenades and a few machine guns and mortars. [. . .]

By the middle of September 1938, my closest comrades were out of action. Wounds, exhaustion, dysentery, and death had left the MacKenzie-Papineau Battalion a skeleton force. Ragged, hungry, and almost weaponless, we lay in an Aragón mountain valley. We awaited reinforcements.

When they arrived, these reinforcements proved to be dregs turned out of prison: criminals, evaders, suspected spies. Many were sick. Since I had just been appointed *practicante*, front-line nurse, I went to work to treat the new arrivals' sores. I bound a suppurating foot or scabby neck and got a very close look at these miserables. The thought of going into action with them gave me the shivers. Some could barely walk on festered feet; most had a look of surly hostility.

There at our mountain bivouac the constant heavy pounding of fascist artillery sounded close by. Some large shells swished over us. Then, as we picked up to go into action, we were told, "You won't have to attack—just hold the position."

This was a new way to prepare us for battle and it sounded ominous.

At first light we climbed out of the deep valley and took a winding mountainous path through dry grass into the Sierra Lavall. We trudged up and down, over some three ridges, until we came to a slope that ran up to entrenchments. The entrenchments lay on the crest of a mountain spur that ran northward a hundred yards before it dropped away steeply into a narrow valley.

It was full light as we struggled to the entrenchments. They were cut into rock. Then began a scramble for the most favorable protected positions in the trench. Such a scramble I had never before seen: friendliness, comradeship evaporated.

I started to enter the trench behind a machine-gun emplacement, well fortified in solid rock and wide enough to hold me too. Came the rebuff: "No place for you here, Jones—find another place!" At the next spot in the trench I tried to enter, I got the same sharp rejection.

Rifle and machine-gun bullets started zipping by, some hitting close. This fire steadily increased. I looked for cover, any cover, just behind the trench; found only bare rock. I crouched. Bullets hit the ground around me while I crouched, frantic for cover—crouched there until the bullets peppered too close. With three flying leaps downhill, I landed behind a hump on the slope. I was at the opening of a tiny shallow cave facing away from the incoming fire.

I threw my gear inside. "Gear" was a gas mask case loaded with gauze and strips of cloth—all I could get from the medical lieutenant back in the valley, a blanket, and the book *The Good Soldier Schweik*. A book! I must have believed that we were going to "sit this one out."

Then I took stock of the battalion's position. I wondered how I could reach the wounded while I crouched at the mouth of the small dugout: over a hundred yards of trench, some of it out of sight! I crouched there until so many mortar bombs sailed by that I could glimpse them in the air.

At that point I started popping my head out of the hole like a gopher. As a bomb *shushed* in close, I jerked myself back in—then leaned out to listen for a call for help. Mortar bombs seemed to saturate the air now.

"Practicante—practicante!" At the call for help, I darted out to do what I could to tie up the wounded to keep them alive at least until they got over the first ridge to the rear. A man wounded in the leg leaned on a man wounded in the arm or the head, and stumbled down the backside of the mountain. There were no stretcher bearers.

High concussion shells began landing just below the mouth of my dugout—shattering blast and acrid green smoke.

These blasts made me forget about mortar bombs. My attention concentrated on timing the blast of the artillery shells in order to know when to pop out my head for calls of "Help!" and when to dash to a wounded man.

Few of the wounded made it to my dugout. Some got stopped by the fascist fire while they were in the open and I scooted over to them; others went off without waiting for my first aid.

The fascist artillery was tearing the top off the mountain. Maybe my first aid was only a quickly improvised sling, a pat, and, "That's all I can do—get moving!" I was too busy to stay alarmed. "I'll tie your arm so that it doesn't dangle and bump"; then, "Pick up Henry at the cave there—get him to the rear with you. His foot is smashed."

Was it three hours, or was it more, that the fascist shells and mortar bombs smashed at us? I remember that it occurred to me, "You did not jump back that time; you were blown back!" Stunned by concussion, I moved without thinking. Sometimes *blown* by the blast. Came a call for help: "Ayuda!" Then a dash to the wounded. Then back to the hole, straining to hear calls in the uproar. Dodging in and out.

My gauze was almost gone.

The fascist artillery shells blasted us without letup. Fortifications disintegrated. Our men were at the mercy of mortar and machine-gun fire, most of their shield of rock gone.

The flow of the wounded became a steady stream, until I heard yelling, indistinct, up and down what was left of our trench. I couldn't catch the words. The stream of wounded turned into a stampede, the wounded joined by men carrying rifles.

"What's going on?" I demanded of those rushing close by me.

"Retreta"—"Get out!!"

The fact that our men were in full flight did not hit me until I turned into my dugout to pick up my bag. Then I moved so fast that I left behind my blanket and the copy of *The Good Soldier Schweik*. Down the mountain I raced, bag bouncing on my back. By the time I reached the bare face of the next steep slope upward and started to climb it, the fascists had a machine gun trained on me.

Back home in the Sierra Nevada in the snow and miles away from humans, I have slept alone while big cats whimpered around me; and in notorious rattlesnake country like isolated Pate valley, I hiked when it would be more than a week before you saw another person. But never before had I felt so helpless, so exposed as now on the slope of this bare mountain.

The machine-gun bullets followed me up the slope. It was as though the fascists were trying to spray me, the last straggler, off the mountainside. Though I was close to all-out panic, I managed to fight off despair. My breath was coming in gasps and it was a living nightmare to make my legs move.

Throw off their aim! Zig-zag, I told myself. Strength was gone, but I made myself stagger a few steps from side to side. Then it was hard to regain momentum upward. The top of the slope was not yet in sight, so I felt like a very tired swimmer who cannot see shore. [. . .]

With each step I deliberately lifted my leg and placed the foot away from the biting bullets. After this painful feint, legs leaden, I weaved upward again. Almost crawling, I lost the pursuing machine gun; I paused over the crest of the ridge.

Years before, caught in a bad place while scaling a mountain or a canyon wall, I exhorted heaven to help me. Here in the Sierra Lavall, I depended on myself alone.

Still trying to move fast, I found myself on a mountain trail sheltered from fascist fire. A few hundred yards along the trail I caught up with slowly moving young Spanish comrades—some in the group wounded, the others helping them along.

I might have passed them because the fright from the machine-gun bullets licking at me, on the side of the mountain, was still with me. My legs wanted to move to the rear. Then one of the Spaniards at my side said, "Please repair my hand—it is shot through." He almost begged.

Gauze gone, I had only a strip of cloth. While we shuffled along the dirt path, I swathed his gory hand.

A little farther along the path a group of three or four knelt around two comrades laid in low bushes. The Spanish boys urged me, "Morfina, por favor, camarada practicante!"

I had no morphine for the two wounded whose faces twisted in pain. The boys' eyes said to me, "What good is a scared *practicante* without morphine, without even bandages?" I helped shift the two badly wounded into the bushes so that they were better shielded from the glowing sun.

Next, I found a group of wounded gathered under some trees. One was shot through the face, another through the stomach, and the others were smashed and bloody in several places.

"Forget your fright, your exhaustion. Find them morphine and bandages!" I spoke to myself. Where could I find supplies? There were no markers in the mountains other than an occasional winding goat trail. Finally, in a deep gulch, I encountered soldiers of another battalion sprawled at rest, indifferent to the heavy fire whistling and whooshing above them.

I went from person to person, pleading, "Where is a field station with medical supplies?" These battle-worn men were vague: with medical supplies?

Finally, in a gully I found a field hospital of sorts. A dignified Englishman in charge of the field hospital brushed aside my urgent begging. Supplies for his own battalion were scarce. I had to insist until this *médico* gave up two shots of morphine.

With these and a few bandages I started back over the serrated mountains. I decided to take a shortcut to the group of wounded lying under the trees because my sense of direction is usually good. In haste, climbing and sliding, I missed them.

Still headed in the direction of what I thought was our broken battlefront, I searched for the wounded. I came out on a high point blasted clear of bushes, to look for a landmark to tell me where I was.

A soldier suddenly popped up in front of me, fifteen feet away. A dark-olive uniform strange to me and a revolver ready at his hip: he was obviously an officer. This dark, forbidding figure sprang from the bare rock with no troops or fortifications showing.

I stopped in my tracks.

"Qué quieres?" Menacing, rock-hard lean, he demanded to know what I was doing there.

Quickly, I answered, "Dónde están Los Internacionales?"

Voice guttural with disgust and with a sweep of his arm to the rear, he answered my question, "Al otro lado del Ebro!" The Internationals were gone beyond the river.

This stone-hard man made it plain that he wanted to get rid of me, the intruder. I deliberately turned and walked off.

He did not shoot.

While I made my way back from the new battlefront I realized that I had lost my fright.

After some twenty minutes travel over a mountain trail, I found the remnants of our forces. Two commissars were rushing around trying to round up the scattering of men who were not injured badly in order to drive them back into battle. They had a panicky urgency.

I refused to take a gun and be herded: I was a *practicante*, I insisted. Then I joined another *practicante* who was caring for wounded collected in a small hut made of reeds and branches. The hut lay in the open on the bare rock. My partner *practicante*, slim, grey-eyed, clean, and neat, steaded me with his calm in-charge manner in that *chabola* full of badly wounded. Leslie: he told me his name.

Leslie took my two shots of morphine, and while he used them I set to work to staunch the bleeding and to comfort the dying. A soldier shot through the stomach was propped up in a sitting position to make him more comfortable and to keep him from vomiting blood. Between low groans, he whispered for a drink of water. His eyes pleaded. We had no water.

Next, I tried to figure what to do for a man shot through the face. His jaw was shattered and his tongue partly severed. Fashion a stirrup bandage in order to keep the pieces of his jaw from grating; but how to wrap him without strangling him? Leslie made suggestions over his shoulder. The face-smashed man sat patiently, burbling glug-glug as he swallowed his blood to keep from choking on it. I had to almost cover his head with bandage in order to hold his face together.

Then the *Stukas*, the dive-bombers, came. In a rushing roar they circled over us. Next circling, they swooped low to let go screaming bombs. The bombs exploded and flew out broadcast on the solid rock: one close hit would demolish the flimsy reed hut and us in it.

The man shot through the stomach was gray-faced from loss of blood, from shock. There was more hurt in his eyes, now blinded in pain—he must have wished that the bombs would end his misery. The other wounded also showed resigned weariness. Leslie continued calmly bandaging.

Fright was hitting me again. I could not ignore the bombs. Leslie was whispering to me, noticing my anxiety, "Why don't you grab that canteen—look for water in that reed thicket over there?" He pointed to a spot two hundred yards away.

Glad to get moving, I made it fast over the rocky interval without getting hit. A path through the reeds led to an ancient waterhole flooding six or seven feet across. As I knelt to clear a spot in the slimy water, I sniffed like an animal. It was too quiet here. I cleared the greenish goo from a spot in the water—took a long drink. The water was deliciously sweet.

Just as I was about to push the canteen under water to fill it, came the thought: Why is this spot abandoned? I got very uneasy. As I wondered, a kind of clicking sound off behind alerted me. Then, at the same time my ears picked up a hissing sound, I jumped like a cat. I must have sprung six or seven feet. While I was still in the air a *plunk* sounded in the mud. A projectile had disappeared where my knee-marks showed. Canteen full, I hurried out of the thicket.

Back at the first aid hut, Leslie was still working calmly—fixing a bandage or adjusting a helpless man to a more comfortable position. Leslie had thrown a tattered jacket over the chest of the soldier shot through the stomach. He had slumped, face greenish, and as the water touched his dry mouth he worked it like the beak of an exhausted bird. When I made motions of giving the dying man another sip, Leslie nodded his head in approval. Leslie doled out the rest of the water to the others while I checked the man shot through the face, to see that he could breathe. The bandage was firm.

We moved out our wounded at nightfall when we got bearers. They helped us improvise stretchers out of tree limbs, rifles, and coats and blankets.

Aboard the *Ausonia* on the North Atlantic, a few months later, I encountered the man with the smashed face. He took food through a straw. His patched face with the jaw wired up by plastic surgeons was healing.

JAMES M. JONES was born in Chicago in 1904. He was educated at Dartmouth College, the University of California, and Sonoma State University, where he combined his education with trade-union activity. He was a member of the Piledrivers' and Bridgebuilders' Union, the West Coast Longshoremen's and Warehousemen's Union. He has also lived in, and has written about, Latin America. The selection here is taken from his *Pain in Spain.*

· Jim Lardner ·

"A Good Soldier Is Hard to Hit"

In January 1938, James Lardner, son of the famous American humorist Ring Lardner, was working on the Paris edition of the New York Herald Tribune *and thinking about the "civil war" in Spain that was ravishing that small nation. He then traveled to Spain and joined the Lincolns. He was wounded, returned to action, and was reported missing. Here are excerpts from letters he wrote to his mother and his brother, Ring Lardner, Jr., that winter and spring, as well as a few pieces from fellow journalists and veterans.*

March 23, 1938

Mother, darling,

I suppose this is bad news, but I am rather excited about it. I am going down to Spain for my vacation. I shall be very careful and not get mixed up in any fighting, as most of what I want to do is behind-the-lines research. Mr. Hills wrote me a letter enabling me to fix up my passport as a *Herald Tribune* representative and said he would take any stories I might mail out or write afterward, but I am also negotiating in various quarters for other pieces. If things work out well, I may write a book.

March 31, 1938

Mother, darling,

This is a letter I started to write on March 10. At that time I thought I was going to have to break the news to you gently, but you seem to have heard it before I had the chance. I have kept putting off writing you because each day it seemed as if on the next I would know what I was going to do and where I would be stationed. I still don't know exactly what the situation is, but I am leaving in half an hour for Badalona, about seven miles up the coast, where I will learn the rudiments of artillery in company with a new mixed international unit. It looks as if French will be the medium of instruction. I shall let you know more as soon as I can.

This is a most elusive army. It has taken me twelve days of going from person to person and office to get where I am. I have listened to advice of all varieties, a large part of it against my enlisting at all. The decision has been very much my own, and I took it after a great deal of consideration. My closest friend and principal adviser here has been Vincent (Jimmy) Sheean, who told me not to join, which shows you how stubborn I am, if you didn't know. Ernest Hemingway's advice was that it was a very fine thing if I wanted to fight against fascism, but that it was a personal matter that could only be decided by me.[. . .]

If you still consider me one of your sons, you can send me an occasional letter and possibly a package now and then. My address here, I think, will be in care of the *Brigadas Internacionales*, but for awhile I think it will be simpler to communicate through the Sheeans. Anything edible would be appreciated, milk chocolate or raisins, or anything in cans that does not require preparation.

Barcelona
May 8, 1938

Dear Mother,

I know I shouldn't be writing from Barcelona, but that is where I happen to be today. Four days in Badalona were enough for me to see that there is not much chance of my getting into the artillery just now. There are too many trained men and not enough guns. The International Brigade administration is very disorganized at present, having just moved precipitously up from Albacete in the south, and anyway there exist no regular channels for a foreigner volunteering in Spain. If I stayed around here or at Badalona and waited to be placed, it would take weeks and weeks.[. . .]

May 27, 1938

Dear Mother,

We seem to be about to go into action, but I am not at all nervous. Just excited in a peaceful way. By the time you get this letter I may be out of the lines again. Anyway, as soon as I am I shall try to let you know rapidly that I am well.

For three days now I have been a corporal, commanding four men, three Spanish and one American. The Spaniards are eighteen and nineteen years old and have never been to the front, and the American is not too bright; but we have a sergeant and a lieutenant above us with plenty of experience.

June 6

[Dear Mother]

You asked me how long I enlisted for. There is only one way of enlisting: for the duration of the war. Sometimes Americans are sent home, but it is only if they are incapacitated, or for propaganda purposes, if they have been in the lines for many months. Don't pay any attention to the plans of the Non-Intervention Committee. There is no chance of Hitler or Mussolini's withdrawing support from Franco before it is all over, and the government has no intention of being tricked into weakening its forces. These are facts. What the committee announces are just words.

I don't mean to be cruel. But it is better that you should resign yourself to my being in Spain indefinitely. A good soldier is hard to hit and I am going to be a good soldier.

June 27 & 28

Mother darling,

I am just back in the battalion after spending ten or eleven days at a school for corporals in a nearby town. The rest of the company, except for a few other corporals and the guard, are away somewhere or other on a maneuver, which gives me my first free afternoon in a long time. As you may have gathered, we are still being held in reserve.

There were about one hundred Fifteenth Brigade corporals at the school and we lived in a large house, going into the fields mornings and afternoons for instruction. The work was a little more mental than physical, but it filled the day even more completely than ever. And what little spare time I had, I had to devote to writing for a wall-newspaper for the school.

The daily program was something like this: 6:15 A.M., got up and washed, march across town for exercises on a playing field, march back; 7:00, breakfast and clean rifle; 8:00–12:00, theoretical and practical instruction; 12:30, lunch; 2:00–3:00, political or language work; 3:00–6:30, same as 8:00–12:00; 6:45, supper; 9:30, roll call.

The instruction was very good. On the last day, yesterday, we had a series of tests on the course. I did pretty well.

July 13, 1938

Dear Ring,

Life here is surprisingly peaceful. Since I joined the Lincoln-Washington Battalion, Fifteenth Brigade, more than two months ago, we have not been near a trench nor put in a single day's fighting. This in spite of the fact that we are supposed to be shock troops. A lot of planes have passed overheard but none has condescended to notice our presence.

Nevertheless I am kept pretty busy learning and practicing infantry technique. There is more to it than you might think, though not so much that I am not getting a little bored and anxious to see some action. Two or three times we were sent off [*one-half a line faded out or erased accidentally*] led for the front, but each time it has been a false alarm for one reason or another.

I suppose you expect me to give you the inside dope on the war, but it is really harder to follow it from here than from California. It looks as if it would drag on here until some big change in the international situation decides the outcome. Fortunately, almost any change would favor us.

Bloms,
St. Margaret's Bay (Kent)
August 20

Dear Mrs. Lardner,

You will have been told, or read in the papers, that Jim was wounded in the offensive across the Ebro a couple of weeks ago. I have just now heard from Leigh White (a colleague down there) about him. His wounds, although rather painful, are not serious. One piece of shrapnel (from a bomb) went into the inside of his thigh and another into his lower back. If you are going to get shrapnel these are good, harmless places. It has the further advantage (from your point of view, not his) that it removes him from the front lines, where the fighting just now is pretty terrific, with constant bombardments from the air. He is in the base hospital at Villafranca, no doubt with American or English doctors and nurses. He will undoubtedly be all right, and I hope you don't worry unduly about him. He may fret a little at being in hospital, but that's the worst that could happen to him.

I am going down to Spain again in about a month's time and will go to see Jim, of course. I'll write and let you know all about that when I return to Paris. In the meantime he is well cared for and has lots of friends down there, so we can always keep track of him. The press correspondents always keep an eye on him— partly because they all know and like him, and partly for professional reasons. I'll be hearing again in a few days, and will let you know what I'm told. It is possible that his wounds are of a sort to justify his discharge from the brigade, in which case he'll be back in France again before long. I'll find out all about that and tell you. And don't be too anxious. He's much safer in hospital than at the front: there's that to be said!

Best,
Vincent Sheean

August 2, 1938

Darling Mother,

I don't know whether you are aware of the sad fact that I was wounded six days ago and am taking it easy at a popular Mediterranean hospital. I didn't have the money or facilities to cable. Anyway, it is nothing serious, just enough to keep me out of action for a couple of weeks.

It seems that after a couple days of forced marching and patroling on the far side of the Ebro River we encountered the enemy and rapidly took two hundred prisoners. I was one of those sent back with them as a guard. We reached the river in the afternoon of the twenty-ninth very tired and hungry, and were ferried across.

I heard a rumor that there was an orchard two hundred yards away and, not having eaten all day, got excused and headed for it. There were some unripe pears and apples and peaches, which were better than nothing, but my attention was soon distracted by one of the frequent duels between anti-aircraft guns and bombing planes. The small round white puffs of smoke where the shells explode keep appearing all around the bombers until either one of them lands and a plane comes down or, much more often, the planes fly away after dropping their loads.

This time the bombers were coming directly overhead. I began to wonder what were the chances of my being hit by one of the anti-aircraft shell fragments. It didn't occur to me that there was any danger of being bombed all by myself until a munition truck three hundred yards away burst into flames with the explosion of a bomb.

I was lying on my stomach when the planes passed over, but the bomb was a little too close. The explosion and concussion were terrific, but I didn't discover I was hit right away. In fact, I walked over to where my rifle, munition belt, and canteen of water were lying, picked them up, and started back. Then I began to notice that my left calf and the left side of my behind were hurting. I felt them and found my trousers were covered with blood. A little further on I found several soldiers waiting in a trench for all the planes to go. I joined them, and one, a Negro friend of mine, went for a stretcher. The stretcher bearer dressed my wounds and took me to an ambulance. Since entering the trench I haven't been able to put my weight on my left leg. It seems the flying shrapnel hit me in the flesh and muscle, picking very soft and fortunate spots. It will be about ten days more, I think, before I shall be considered cured. I hope to get a few days in Barcelona before returning to the front.

This hospital is clean and sunny, but nothing to read. I am going to write a piece on my recent adventures, which I shall retail through Walter.

IT SEEMS TO ME

Heywood Broun

James Lardner, Ring's boy, has been wounded fighting for the Loyalist army on the Ebro front. A bomb burst near his trench, and he was struck in the back by a fragment, but they say his wound is not serious. Nevertheless, I hope that he will be invalided back to his own country, for I think he may have much to say which will be useful to democratic Spain and democratic America.

Many American writers much better known than young Lardner have come out for the cause of the Spanish government, and quite a few have seen some portion of the war. And yet I think that Lardner's testimony may have a special significance.

In small part this is personal. I have not seen James Lardner since he was one of four chubby children who all looked exactly alike. They lived in a big house in Great Neck across the lawn from the Swopes. I saw a lot of Ring in those days, and I try to grab back things he said or did, because I imagine he was the only man of genius I ever met.

It would interest me enormously to know just how Ring would have reacted to Jim's enlistment with the Loyalists. For the life of me I can't remember Ring's ever saying a word about politics or economics or world affairs. It was a long way in those days from a Great Neck lawn to the Ebro. I suppose everybody would have been surprised if some soothsayer had pointed to the chunky kid playing Indian and said, "When he is twenty-four he will be wounded fighting fascism in Spain."

Of course, the word "fascism" would have been meaningless to us. But I think that in a way which is curiously remote Jim has carried on the tradition of his father. Under an insulation of isolation and indifference, Ring boiled with a passion against smugness and hypocrisy and the hard heart of the world. He used to sit up until 6 o'clock in the morning telling cockeyed fairy stories, and so I got the impression that he didn't like Great Neck.

I used to sit up with him when everybody else had gone to bed, because I knew that Ring was a great man. But the stories were very long, very involved and, on the surface, a little pointless. At that time I had never heard of Freud, nor was I familiar with the modern connotation of "escape." So I retained only an occasional phrase.

There was a story which began, "I turned the tap on in the bathroom and four Czechoslovakians jumped out." In those days "Czechoslovakian" was a comic word. But time, which makes jokes as well as dreams come true, did not turn on the tap. And when streams were loosed in Middle Europe there were drops of blood upon a lawn in Great Neck.

I hope Jim Lardner comes home and speaks his piece. In arguments about Spain one debater always attempts to disqualify the other by identifying him with some political, economic, or religious group. But here is a brief biography of James Phillip Lardner, son of our great native American humorist:

He was educated at Andover and Harvard and joined the staff of the *New York Herald Tribune*, where he conducted a column on contract bridge. Later he became a war correspondent for the European edition of the *New York Herald Tribune*, and after three weeks as an observer he said, "I think something has to be done by somebody. I've seen the front, and I know what I'm going into. This is a fight that will have to be won sooner or later, and I'm in favor of doing it here and now."

You may agree or disagree with the decision at which Ring's son arrived. But nobody can justly say that he was put up to it by "subversive influences." He saw with his own eyes, and he made his own choice. Ring and the rest of the Lardners always did run without blinkers.

The World (New York), August 1930

Barcelona,
September 2, 1938

Dear Mother,

This paragraph is confidential and possibly inaccurate. From a number of events and rumors and opinions I gather that a gradual and lengthy process of removing the I.B. [International Brigade] from Spain has begun. Herbert Matthews, *New York Times* correspondent, with whom I had my first whisky and soda in many months yesterday, says he thinks it will take six months or so. I, of course, would be one of the last to be withdrawn. All this is unofficial and by no means certain, especially if we receive any serious setbacks at the front. At present, the situation is promising militarily but not so good among the civilians. Catalonia is way overpopulated now and there is a shortage of food. If we get through the winter all right I foresee victory next year.

I arrived three days at Las Planas, the I.B. base through which all convalescents pass on their way back to the front. Probably in a day or two I shall be sent to Mont Blanc, a training camp, for a few more days and then to the Brigade, which is now at rest after two very hard-fought actions near Gandesa. Las Planas is an old sanitarium situated on a very high hill among tall pines and overlooking Barcelona, which is a much more attractive city when viewed from above than I had ever realized.

Day before yesterday I got permission to come down here to

the city, and I am to return tonight. The first thing I did was to go see Johnny Murra at the hospital. He was wounded the day after I was. The bullet entered his shoulder, traversed his left lung lengthwise, missed his heart and other organs, and came out right next to the base of his spine. His lung was filled with blood and other extraneous matter and his legs were temporarily paralyzed. He had to lie in no-man's-land within easy range of the enemy from 7:00 A.M. to 11:00 P.M., most of the time in the blazing sun, before he could be brought back. This is just to show you how hard it is to get killed. He is going to be sent home when he is a little better and will recover completely. My other closest friend in the company, Elman Service, also was wounded, but I haven't seen him since.

The next step was to come to the Majestic, where [Joseph] North had left four letters, a cablegram, and a carton of Camels for me. The cigarettes being from Walter at my request. Then I had a long talk with Matthews about the European situation in general. I had supper with five other I.B. members at a semi-private Jewish place. There was a gefilte fish, an excellent vegetable soup, fried potatoes, a fried egg, and some wonderful peach strudel. The price was thirty pesetas, which is way over the head of wage-earners, and I think only semi-legal. Then I went with two other comrades and rented a room with three beds for the night. This arranged for, I called on Leigh White, whom I must have mentioned to you sometime. He is about a year younger than I, came to Spain to drive an ambulance and later became a foreign correspondent. He speaks beautiful Spanish and knows the country better than any of the other correspondents I have talked to. Recently, he was substituting for the correspondents of the London *Telegraph* and *Post*, simultaneously, while they were taking vacations outside the country. He is about to marry an attractive, vivacious Asturian girl, whom I met early in May. We talked so late into the night that I spent the night in their spare room instead of returning to the other lodging.

After breakfast in their apartment I got in touch with Douglas Flood, American Consul, and as a result today was returned 450 francs I had left with the Consulate in May. I sold the francs to

Leigh for transportation to Paris when he leaves the country with his bride in about two weeks. He is going to try to get a job in Paris, with the *Herald* or elsewhere, and if unsuccessful go to Mexico for a while. He doesn't like the United States. I forgot to mention that before I left he gave me his old ambulance driver's uniform, which is the best I have had in a long time, three books that I have wanted to read, and some detailed maps of Spain that I gave him when I entered the I.B. Also my wrist watch, newly cleaned and repaired.

Yesterday I had lunch at the Majestic and dinner at the White apartment, again staying the night. Now, since I have eaten Leigh and bride out of all their food, I am taking them to dinner at the Jewish place. I have done a lot of errands for myself and others and am at present trying to think of a good wedding present, being very rich. And I just had a hot bath and put on all new or clean clothes. Those are all the luxuries of city life I can think of offhand, except that Johnny Murra gave me six caramels and part of a bar of chocolate.

There are still some phases of war that I haven't seen, so that I am not sorry to be returning to the Brigade, but for your comfort it is very unlikely that we shall see action for some time. There is a lot of reorganization and remoralization to be done. One thing that makes me more satisfied with life than ever is that I have a very good idea of what I am going to do with my life. Some of the details may not work out, but I shall work hard toward a definite end, and I guess there is nothing better than that.

A PERSONAL NOTE
Alvah Bessie

I had been removed from the battalion a few weeks before this and appointed a front-line correspondent for our newspaper, *The Volunteer for Liberty*. Exhausted by running from one battalion to another for news, I asked the command for Jim

Lardner, to act as my legman and relieve me of about half the work.

The command said he would be a much better writer after he had seen more action and I said, "Yes, if he survives it." "Of course," said the command.

On September 21 Prime Minister Juan Negrín, speaking before the League of Nations, announced the intention of the Republic to withdraw all its volunteers from action immediately. On the twenty-second the Lincolns, knowing a Spanish brigade was coming to relieve them, moved up to help hold the weakening lines against a deadly artillery barrage. That night was their last action.

Jim Lardner was sent out that night in command of a three-man patrol to try to locate a missing platoon. They heard the sound of men digging: Jim stopped and challenged. He heard no reply so he moved out alone and the two men he ordered to lay low heard rifle and machine-gun fire burst out and hand grenades exploded around them. One of his comrades, a Spaniard, was killed; the other, Anthony Nowakowski, an American, returned alone.

Jim's body was never found.

Socorro Rojo 101-S
November 12

Dear Mrs. Lardner—

My name is John Murra and I understand that Jim wrote to you about me. We used to be in the same company for several months and together with Elman Service we formed a trio that got along rather well.

For quite awhile I was thinking of writing to you. And there is nothing much I could write to you—unless I wrote about Jim, my friend.

He came to our company preceded by considerable publicity. Now, you know how men in a fighting unit are—they don't like ballyhoo and we were on our guard. This reserve lasted for a while and then we gradually took him in. He was so obviously honest and sincere, he was not highhatting us. One of the marching songs popular with us had a soldierly obscene quality. It seemed to shock Jim, not through its quality but, as he explained it to us, because he found it among us—a rather unusual type of army. But the day came when Jim was marching at the head of his squad—he had been made a corporal—and was singing along. From that moment on he really belonged.

In the months preceding our Ebro campaign, we got to be friends. We talked and we read each others' letters and Jim kind of worried along about our problems. Journalism interested Service and even me. He used to talk about his newspaper work, about Paris—he was older than both of us and had seen more. Just before we went into action we planned in a jocular sort of way the publishing of some magazine when we got back.

Before going into action one always seems to be making plans; one really tries to conjure fortune. Then we both got wounded, only my wound was more serious—a lung shot and I am still in the hospital. On September 1, upon recovery, he came to see me and we spent a day and half together. We talked some more; he told me he was going back to Brigade. I gave him some tobacco to take along to the boys and he was supposed to come and see me again next day. But then they evacuated me to another hospital. Eddie Rolfe brought me later the news of his death.

Jim would have liked me to write to you, I am sure. There is nothing else to say about your son and my friend and I beg you to believe that we, his comrades, will continue to fight for the cause for which Jim lost his precious life.

John Murra

JIM LARDNER, son of the famous American humorist Ring Lardner, was working on the Paris edition of the *New York Herald Tribune* when he decided to go to Spain. He arrived in early 1938, intending to work as a journalist, but he quickly resigned from the newspaper and joined the Abraham Lincoln

Battalion. He was killed on September 22, the last night that the battalion spent in the lines, while trying to locate a missing patrol. His body was never found.

JOHN MURRA is now a professor of anthropology at Cornell University.

· D.A.N. (Alvah Bessie) ·

120 a Minute

Men of the Lincolns are not likely soon·to forget that hill in the Sierra de Pándols, which for purposes of military information was known as 666. No matter how long they live or how much modern warfare they may see, that hellhole will remain in their memory, a nightmare come to life. They lost some of their best comrades there and they proved, to the satisfaction of Brigade, Division, and possibly to themselves exactly what sort of stuff they were made of.

Our introduction to the scene should have been a warning. God never made a more desolate stretch of terrain, and man never contributed more to its further desolation. From the main road, at night, we climbed for hours over broken rock; the men sweated and groaned under the weight of their equipment, their guns. As we climbed there was not a man who did not think: "It's going to be tough getting food, water, and munitions up here; it's going to be tough for the wounded." Rock walls bordered the goat trails that led to the wind-torn summits. Near the crest we came upon terrain that had been fought over, lost, and recaptured by the famous Eleventh Division. Here they had withstood constant shelling; here the fascist planes had rained incendiary bombs and, temporarily, driven our men off. It looked like a landscape on the moon—tumbled, crumbling rock, black and slippery; burnt-off shrubbery that caught our trouser legs and tripped us up. We slipped and fell, stumbled and cursed; there was a bitter wind and the smell of wood smoke.

Even before dawn it was possible to see that there was no cover here; there were no trees; there were no bushes; there were no natural cavities in the rock; the earth itself was stone—you could not dig in it. And there were no fortifications facing the enemy. The men of the Eleventh Division had done the best they could; they had scraped shallow trenches into the crest of the hill and they had erected stone parapets topped with a few sandbags. These were the lines we had to hold; and they were held. The men suffered from the sun's heat; from thirst; from nervous exhaustion. Many must have thought that the old saying that there is a limit to what flesh and blood can stand was scarcely true. For there seemed, for those five days, to be no limit.

The first three days were relatively quiet; a little mortar fire, a little machine gun, and the attack we made, which did not attain its objective. It seems absurd to speak of an attack as being relatively quiet, but the men who went through it will agree that it was vastly preferable to what followed with noon of the fourth day. At that time the fascists, having set their guns and mortars, opened up. They opened their guns and the guns remained open for seven and a half hours, from noon to seven-thirty that night, they gave us everything they had, and it was plenty. Artillery and mortars, big ones. There are those who say they prefer artillery to mortars, because you can't hear the mortars coming; well, you may have your choice; it matters relatively little. Our parapets were pounded; they had the range and they kept the range. As each moment followed the moment before it, they hammered our parapets from left to right and back again; they covered the back side of the hill; they covered the left and right flanks. Munitions and water had to run that gauntlet; stretcher bearers carried wounded men through that rain of fire that seemed to fall wherever it pleased. The fascist gunners knew just where we were.

Hour after hour the shells and the mortars fell; the antitank guns hammered at our parapets. The sandbags fell in; the rocks tumbled; the men withdrew from one section of the trenches to another. And the man who says he did not want to run is a liar; but the men did not run. In the face of this barrage, which fell wherever it pleased and which was unopposed, the men stayed put. They cared for their wounded; they stuck with their guns; they lay in their pitifully shallow fortifications and talked and smoked, waiting. Waiting for what? For the next shell, the next mortar, the next piece of whining shrapnel. They knew that these positions must be held; they knew the strategic value of these hills; that they dominated our objective; that if they should pass again into enemy hands, the enemy would possess positions from which he could shell our bridgeheads across the Ebro and make communication with our rear impossible. And so the positions were held. And what is more, they were held the next day as well, when the enemy opened up again with a slightly less intense but considerably more concentrated and accurate fire. The shells and mortars were not landing at the rate of a hundred and twenty a minute, as they had the day before; they were falling more slowly, but with greater deliberation and more demoralizing effect. The fascists were calling their shots; they seemed to take a devilish delight in hammering away at the same point on our line, and it hurt. It hurt in much the same way that a sore knee hurts when you clumsily bang it time and time again. But again, as the day before, they got nowhere. The night before, after the barrage lifted, they tried an attack, an attack that was pitiful, that was laughable. A few of them came forward; our men hurled grenades; the machine guns spoke and the enemy withdrew. And thus they demonstrated again—as though it needed further demonstration—that against our infantry, their infantry is worthless. They demonstrated again how they have made their past gains in this war—that without their superiority of mechanized equipment they are licked.

For we licked them on Hill 666 as surely as though we had taken additional terrain. They hoped to blow us off that hill by sheer weight of flying steel. They had seen it work in the past—there wasn't an inch of that hill and its surrounding heights that was not pocked with shell holes, that was not littered with broken shrapnel. They figured that if they hammered us hard enough we would withdraw; that through our broken lines their soft and unprotected infantry could then advance. Well, they hammered us; but it was not hard enough. And we did withdraw.

But when we withdrew we left, for our relief, a line of fortifications that was stronger than the one that we had found; the parapets were rebuilt and strengthened; the sandbags were replaced and added to; the hill called 666 (for purposes of military information) was still within our lines. And it is likely to remain so. For there seems to be no limit to what flesh and blood can stand: men can lie athirst in the broiling sun for days; men can carry food and water and munitions up precipitous grades for days; they can carry their wounded comrades down to safety; they can lie under a shower of howling steel and wait; wait and hold on. Because they know what they are doing, and why they are doing it.

That's more than our enemy can say.

ALVAH BESSIE (D.A.N.) was born in 1904 and died in July 1985 while working on this anthology. In Spain, after months as a soldier, he was frontline correspondant for *The Volunteer for Liberty*, the organ of the Fifteenth Brigade, from which this piece is taken. He was the author of several novels, a contributor to many books, wrote screen and radio plays, and was published in magazines and newspapers around the world. He was the editor of *The Heart of Spain*, published in 1952 by the VALB, and wrote his personal account of the war in *Men of Battle*. He was one of the "Hollywood Ten," and spent a year in prison for refusing to answer questions about his membership in the Communist Party.

· Jacques Grunblatt ·

Forever in Spain, III

Mataró, March 1938 to February 1939.   Mataró was my last post in Spain. Oliva was assigned to the same hospital, which had been an old monastery. The wards for the patients were in the main building. The personnel were housed in several small buildings on the grounds of the monastery.

Oliva and I had a two-room apartment. We adopted a dog, a terrier, which we named Roli. She was a fine watchdog. Her only bad habit was to attack cars from the front. We were always afraid she would be killed.

Oliva had her work in the hospital; the laundry room was under her jurisdiction. I worked on the wards, which were filled to overflowing. Here I saw only the victims: the wounded, the dying.

Doctor Hart, an Englishman, was chief of surgery. As long as my Spanish was better than his, I often had to be the messenger. It was not always a pleasant task.

We had a Spanish soldier on the ward with a badly shattered leg. I had hoped we could save the leg, but Doctor Hart was certain it could not be saved. We temporized for two days. Then I had the heartbreaking mission to tell him that his leg would be amputated the next day. With tears in my eyes, I hugged the man.

I assisted at an autopsy that was being performed by Doctor Leo Eloesser in a primitive setting. I met him only once in

Spain. What an impression he made on me! A mental and
human giant!

One double amputee, a Yugoslav who, after the operation,
needed a blood transfusion. My blood matched his and was the
only one available. I did not mind when he screamed, "Take his
blood! He's strong! I need it! I'm weak!" I gave him all I could.

The patients in the hospital were recovering from wounds;
many were in casts. At that time we believed that maggots in a
wound cleaned it better than any antiseptic. As a result of this
treatment, many patients had maggots crawling over casts and
wounds. The wounds looked clean, but we had a hard time
getting used to the sight of so many maggots.

A very important soldier developed gas gangrene. I do not
know why a visiting doctor advised a blood transfusion to
strengthen his defenses. Blood transfusions at that time were
done directly from donor to recipient. A beautiful girl of about
eighteen and a member of the Communist youth offered to give
her blood. The results were tragic. Both died; the donor, because
of contamination from the gangrenous blood. The entire village
of Mataró attended their elaborate funeral.

At that time the food supplies for the Republic were dwin-
dling. Our staple diet was garbanzos or chick-peas. We lived on
them for several months.

I do not know if it was the hard work or insufficient food, but
Oliva developed a cough and hemoptysis. I took her to a hospital
in Benicasim, where she was suspected of having tuberculosis
and was kept there for four weeks. After her release, she returned to work in the hospital in Mataró.

I did not stay in Benicasim but returned to work in the hospital. During my absence, neighbors took care of Roli. She was so
upset that she never left the room and ate nothing.

Traveling with a dog was an ordeal. Once I had to pass
through crowded Albacete. We checked into a rooming house. I
had errands in town and Roli came with me. By the time I
wanted to return to my room, I could not find Roli anywhere. I
finally gave up searching and headed back. When I arrived
there, Roli was waiting at the door. How clever she was! I had
been to that room only once that day.

On another occasion, Oliva and I stayed in line for a movie in

Madrid. The line was long, and so it took a long time to buy the tickets. Roli had accompanied us. By the time we had them, Roli had disappeared. I organized some children into a search party and gave them some money to look for her. She could not be found. Downcast, we went back to our place. Oliva suggested we follow the same route we had taken to come. There on a corner little Roli stood, watching every passerby.

Another trip took us to Morelia, a beautiful city on a mountain with a medieval castle dominating the whole town. We walked the streets of the city. At a certain house, Roli stopped and would not follow us. She sniffed the house, wanted to explore and go into it. She climbed some steps. A woman passing by exclaimed, "Look! The lawyer's dog is back!" It was her former home. After a while, when she could find no one, she followed us.

· Maury Colow ·

The Last Day in Spain

We were in the small town of Ripoll near the Spanish-French border. I awoke at dawn and and walked outside the barracks. A soft wind was blowing the mist away from the mountains. Memories stirred as I walked down the road. My God, there were no sounds of artillery or rifle fire. I heard the clip-clop of a peasant and his burro. "Salud." "Salud," I answered. Then again that uneasy quiet. The war seemed remote. My thoughts were of the comrades who wouldn't return; how lucky I was to be alive and how sad it felt to leave Spain.

When I returned to the compound there was little of the usual banter. Everyone seemed to be off on his own memory kick. However, we all felt the tension. When we sat down to breakfast, it was the quietest breakfast I had had in Spain and with little eating going on.

We grouped into a motley formation and were marched off to the railroad station. The train was waiting for us and we were quickly mustered aboard. The mayor, the town council, and various citizens were at the station to say goodbye. Our train jerked as it steadily climbed toward the French border. The mountain silence was broken by our clattering locomotive. After an interminable time we arrived at the Spanish border station, Puicgerda, a small village; a few homes, a border barracks. Again, as in so many areas of Spain, the populace turned out to bid farewell with raised fists. We halted for a few formalities and moved across a bridge just ahead. On the other side was the town of Bourg-Madame, in France. We moved quietly across the tracks. I noticed how bright the sun was and the endless sea of blue sky.

We arrived on the French side to a beautiful greeting. Townspeople, officials, even French soldiers and police embraced us. There was what seemed like a full block of tables laden with food—bread, butter, cheeses, wine, sausages, and home-baked cakes. And we were starved. For some of us, this kind of food hadn't been seen for years. And how great it was to be basking in the warmth of French friends.

Suddenly we heard anti-aircraft fire from the hills on the Spanish border. Then we saw fascist planes dropping bombs on the small railroad town of Puicgerda. As some of the fascist planes flew over French territory, French anti-aircraft batteries opened up, but there was nothing we could do. I looked over at Spain, the Spain I had grown to love. So many bitter and beautiful memories, and it was in smoke and on fire. An uncontrollable emotion welled up within me. I walked behind the freight cars and cried.

MAURY COLOW was born in 1917 in New York City. Before he left for Spain in 1937 he was a factory worker and part-time student. In Spain he served with the Eighty-sixth Brigade on the Cordoba front, and with the Second Company of the Mac-Paps during the crossing of the Ebro. He was wounded during an air raid at Valsequillo on the southern front. On his return, he worked as a trade union organizer for the Leather Workers' Union, and then served in the U.S. navy in the Pacific. He is now a sculptor and painter, and has been involved in anti-nuclear activities. He recently led the VALB delegation that delivered nine ambulances to the government of Nicaragua.

· Sid Kaufman ·

The Flight

[. . .] Half of Spain must be on the move north—so many women, kids, people have passed through today. Noted here in my diary that there are disgraceful scenes of the *carabineros*—being used as police, brutal and unfeeling—The *intendencias* were certainly corrupt to have bulging luxury supplies. Hear rumors of what will happen to us. The border is wide open—women, children, and soldiers will probably be interned—some sent to the Levante by ship, others *no lo sé*—good thing we carried plenty of canned goods with us—liable to be tough until things get organized—trucks, equipment, arms going over with us or destroyed—no help to the fascists. Love to get one of those new Czech automatics through (sub-Thompson type) but impossible.

Finally cross the border at 5:00 A.M. February 7 [1939]. Mountains of arms piled on the French side—weapons of all descriptions confiscated. We cross at La Junquera (Spain) to the French Le Perthus. A long roundabout way from original start at Casa de la Selva. We send the truck on ahead. Now start long walk to the coast and internment camp at Argeles Le Plage about 18 km. It's John Murra, John Palu, Nancarrow, Fontana with me—suitcase on my back—pleasant talks along the way—we're "free"—see in French paper. Hell to pay in Spain—might have expected as much from Azana Caballero, and Luis Companys. Spent another freezing night outdoors—but on French soil—filled up on milk and chocolate, etc.—going for salmon, tomatoes, coffee without milk.

February 8.—Argeles—What a sight! tens of thousands of people—no shelter—make do on the beach in the sand—the whole thing is practically organized in French-Albacete style—but control is excellent considering no one has a "sou" in his pocket. The panic in some of the guys was disgraceful, not having the patience to stick together in a group to go over the border in a unit—when only 5 km. from the frontier.

André Marty truly discredited with his attempt to have the I.B.'s return to the front after Negrin assured the outside world that all the International Brigades had been withdrawn. Many German and Italian I.B.ers killed as a result—*L'Humanité* carried his statement that eight hundred I.B.ers were "lost" in the mountains.

Hope the American papers are carrying some of the pictures of the refugee camps. The French papers are full of the story. The "deserters" show up to scrounge on our food. Among our American group in the camp were Murra, Palu, Nancarrow, Stockstiel, Schutt, John Stuvenberg, and Stanley Postek (whom we encountered wandering on the road, released from a hospital, with an airplane splint—festering wound etc.), Fontana and others I can't recall—we held on to one *camión* and some sacks of rice—canned goods, etc., so were better off than most other groups—but don't know of our future. Reactionary press here inciting people in this province against us—"Colonization of France"—the French soldiers are very brutal—Senegalese—papers say there will be over 200,000 at this camp alone—camp incidents include stabbings of those who advocate returning to Franco's side.

February 9.—Miserable night, last night—the shits—dysentery and sick in general. "Incidents" still continue in the camp. There are "bulos" galore—understand the French are using many means of provocation—confiscating some of our food as "war materials," etc. Representatives of the League of Nations Commission showed up and apologize for the mess and general disorganization in the camp. The Canadians not repatriated are in bad shape—no blankets, no food, etc.—anarchy crops up all over continually with lots of fights. Before I go into the notes for

February 10 on, I want to back up to an aspect of our long trek starting January 30.

In all the time that the roads were checked with retreating troops, withdrawn I.B.ers, civilians, vehicles of all kinds, the news kept filtering through. *Frente Rojo* and *Treball* (in the Catalan language) were being published right through the chaos—with hand presses—mobile presses—I do not know. However, almost every day couriers on motorcycles would ride way ahead and paste the newspapers to the telephone poles or utility poles, and we'd all take a few minutes to read the dope. This is how we were aware that the fascist armies had taken Gerona and the line was broken behind us. I took some samples off the poles, whitewash and all (and they are now at Brandeis University in the archives).

On February 10, the American consul appears in the camp seeking us out. He brought cigarettes and chocolates. He promised to return the next day, with an American flag, medicine, and supplies. There are now eight of us who can be repatriated plus others whose legal entry into the States was cloudy. He promises to get eight of us out of the camp on the eleventh—uplifting to say the least. Former brass from Albacete try to carry over I.B. Organization into France.

February 11.—Feeling low—gas pains, the shits, etc. At 2:00 P.M. consul had not arrived—attempt to censor our mail of all things—consul still doesn't show but Smith (assistant to Fred Thompson in Paris), Noel Field (Quaker—American representative on League of Nations Commission), and Steve (Canadian representative) do show. They attempt to get us out of the camp but Field doesn't want to take the chance, without proper authorization. Promise to try tomorrow. How often have we heard *mañana?* Smith is great, brings cigarettes and chocolate and news.

Provocations by the French continue—now convinced the Popular Front is failing—serious discussion, the evaluating of a new formation of the policy in view of France, Spain, etc. Smith says the American consul is very busy and maybe on Lincoln's Birthday the slaves may be freed.

On February 12 a fascist sound truck shows up with an officer, in the name of the French government, to send Spaniards immediately to Barcelona or Hendaye! Truck has to fuck off because of booing and cat-calling. French cavalry comes in to establish "order" (Spahis from Morocco, colorful scarlet tunics—crack troops for dress parades). They use their sabers recklessly—many hurt—later in the morning large groups of visitors—all of the consuls show up—many newspapermen and foreign correspondents—stories of the barbaric conditions in the camps are finally getting out, but the home newspapers in London and New York don't like it. Herb Matthews has been cabled by the *New York Times*, "Why so anti-French?"

Finally escape from "Devil's Island"—Smith does a great job of maneuvering us out (Nancarrow and myself) outsmarting the right people—jumpy all the way to Perpignan—stopped once and searched but got by—stop in a cafe in Perpignan—have my first glass of beer in ages—two glasses and I have a glow.

I am writing this on the night train to Paris. Saw a train in Perpignan railroad station full of "our" people going to the Franco side—the bastards!

Spanish comrades in the camp at Argeles la Plage are so incensed they say the next war has to be against France even if it has to be on the side of Franco! [. . .]

February 13-14-15. Paris—Get re-outfitted—get fixed up. We hear about the deal between Roosevelt and France with the double-cross by Bonnet and Daladier on Spain. Blackmail by France—agree to open the border in return for planes that landed at Toulouse in the south of France. See Larry O'Toole and hear some of the news regarding some of our guys. We hear Matthews has been given an ultimatum by the *New York Times*, on going to Italy. Join Nancarrow and his friends partying in the Place Pigalle—Bob Allen and Bob Oken, newspaper men. Oken was a young reporter in New Jersey on the *Bergen Evening Record* who just happened to be at Lakehurst, N.J., when the "Hindenberg" blew up. He scooped the world on the story and was rewarded by the Associated Press. They gave him a choice and he chose, foreign correspondent. Also in the party was Pepita and little Ziggie, who got everything wholesale, even the champagne in the cabaret. Diarrhea still with me so I can't appreciate the choice grub. Ended the night like typical tourists with onion soup at the market at 4:00 A.M.—wild!

Can't trace my mail or money sent to me by the family. Fred Thompson doing an outstanding job on behalf of the friends of the Abraham Lincoln Brigade. He is Kathleen Norris's brother—she's very reactionary. He the opposite. Told some wild yarns about the arguments around the dinner table at her house. He was able to get Stanley Postek admitted to the American Hospital at Neuilly for treatment. His wound was still festering and draining.

I've been made *responsable* for the eight Americans getting out of the camp by Saturday through his efforts. We're booked for the "President Roosevelt." I promise to look up Babin's wife in New York. We were given VIP treatment on the ship. Ex-shipmates amongst the waiters and room stewards including Al Rothbart from the N.M.U. Pilot Staff.

Arrived back in New York on the twenty-fifth of February. Met by Mom and sisters Ida and Ethel.

The pathetic scene on the docks—the women who carry pictures of their sons who were among the "missing" and ask if we had known them or seen them.

SID KAUFMAN was a merchant seaman who was involved in many maritime strikes. He went to Spain in the summer of 1937 and saw action in the Aragon as part of the anti-tank battery attached to the 129th (Slav) outfit. After the fall of Barcelona he was interned in France and was not repatriated until March 1939. He returned to the sea, but retired in 1979 from International Longshoremen's and Warehousemen's Union, Local 63.

· Jacques Grunblatt ·

Forever in Spain, IV

Withdrawal, February 1939. The Spanish Republic was cut in two; its end was fast approaching although Madrid was still holding out. President Juan Negrín decided to withdraw the International Brigades and send them home.

Several hundred of us started the long march to the French border 125 miles away. The nights were bitter cold. Oliva walked for two days but could not continue. It was then I learned that she was pregnant. She chose to go back to her sister in Madrid.

Even at that time the Spanish population was friendly to us. Many times during our stops there was a spontaneous meeting. Speaker after speaker would come up to the podium and exhort us not to leave but to return and keep on fighting. Those were suicidal ideas and we kept on walking. We reached the French frontier not far from where I, then so full of hope and enthusiasm, crossed in October 1936.

We waited at the border while the French border patrol conducted inspections. Those last few nights waiting for the French to examine us, remove small arms from us, were very hard to take. Depressed, hungry, freezing, and defeated, we were greeted by André Marty, the French Communist deputy, who gave us a pep talk. Then we crossed the border.

I pulled out my French ID card. Much to my dismay, the French officer tore it up and said crisply, "You're a Spaniard! Follow the others!"

297

The French were not friendly to us. We walked until we reached the detention camp at Gurs. We walked; we slept walking; we walked sleeping. I carried an extra pair of shoes on my shoulder and never felt when they slipped off.

Gurs was a large beach fenced in by barbed wire. We had the sand to sleep on and the skies for a roof. The camp did not even have the most elementary hygienic facilities and no medication whatsoever. Many inmates became sick. I became a doctor of a sector. One of my duties was to transport the most severely ill by ambulance to Perpignan.

A loudspeaker was installed in the middle of the camp to give instructions and orders to the inmates. One day I heard my name over the loudspeaker, summoning me to the office. There I met some of my friends from Marseilles, and we formulated a plan. On my next trip to Perpignan with the sick, I left my patients in the hospital, left my ambulance in the parking lot, took off my Spanish officer's uniform, put on civilian garb, and left by train for Marseilles.

I left my Spanish friends behind in the camp. They stayed there two years. When World War II broke out, the Germans took over the camps. They let the old and weak die and took the young and vigorous ones to build railways in Africa. They picked out the Jews for a special reason. Many of the doctors I knew joined the French Underground and paid another toll in life's suffering. [. . .]

· Albert Prago ·

Women in Franco's Prisons

Two civil guards approached one of the cattle cars that had been carrying human cargo from Alicante to Valencia for some three days. No sooner had the policemen opened the door than they were nauseated by a foul stench. Holding his nose, one civil guard asked, "What do you have in there, the pestilence?" One of the women within answered, "Dead children and shit."

It was the spring of 1939, not long after the military defeat of the Spanish Republic. All throughout the war, as the Franco forces won territory, measures of violent reprisal were hurled against the "reds," meaning anyone of any political belief who in any way supported the Republic along with those accused of military rebelliion. The experience gained during the war served the fascists as the basis for the escalation of an intense reign of terror. There exists an extensive literature revealing the fate of the hundreds of thousands of victims of Francoism. But there is not very much about the women victims, whose history warrants separate study.

The persecution of the women exposes most dramatically the depths of Francoist sadism. The fascist authorities provided not merely separate prison facilities but also a number of separate prisons for the tens of thousands of women prisoners. Illnesses, humiliation, indignities, hunger, cold, social isolation, torture, and even death—that's the standard course of treatment for political prisoners everywhere, from ancient times to this twen-

299

tieth century of enlightenment and progress. The new features are vast numbers of victims and to old techniques of torture new ones have been added that simply reflect the development of the physical and behavioral sciences. In addition to the sufferings common to all political prisoners, women were subjected to unique humiliations and tortures. Two examples suffice: the violations of the body by "macho" guards; and, almost immediately after birth, infants born in the dungeons were taken away, forever, from their mothers and placed—it was alleged—in orphanages.

As in Dante's Inferno, the degrees of horror were varied and some levels are almost beyond comprehension. In this brief account I present some examples gathered from conversations with several of the victims and from the written testimony of one woman who survived eighteen years in Franco's jails. Juana Doña, whom the Veterans of the Abraham Lincoln Brigade and our guests are honoring this February 25, 1979, describes the nightmares of those eighteen years in *Desde la Noche y la Niebla* [*Out of the Night and the Fog*]. That title is borrowed, the Spanish playwright Alfonso Sastre noted, from the Nazi slogan "Nacht und Nebel," sinister words of a sinister banner; it signified the Nazi extermination of the Jews during the Third Reich.

Sastre, whose wife, Eva Forest, was jailed and tortured in 1974 (falsely accused of assassinating Prime Minister Carrero Blanco), in his prologue commented on the strong stuff contained in Sra. Doña's unique book about the former women political prisoners. The incident of the cattle cars and its human cargo is but one example of the infinity of barbarisms endured by many tens of thousands of women most particularly during the first twenty years or so of the Franco dictatorship.

In Madrid many antifascists assumed that the pending Casado-Besteiro surrender in the winter of 1939 would be followed by persecution. Therefore, while there was still some faint hope, many thousands fled to the Levante, which was the last strip of territory still in Republican hands. Thousands went to Alicante, where they expected to be rescued by ships to be sent, it was rumored, by the League of Nations. After waiting desperately

and vainly for several days on and near the docks, thousands of
refugees were turned over to the victorious fascist army.

Almost five thousand women and children were taken to a
"camp" located in almond groves where the fascist mercenaries—Italians, Moors, and Germans—were turned loose. In de-
scribing the harrowing scene, one of the women told me that she
still hears the cries of the girls and young women shrieking and
moaning "Mama! Mama!" all through the fearful night.

All were held in the "camps" for about six weeks. After one
month, milk was distributed to women with children. The milk
had first to be boiled—a necessary precaution especially for the
children suffering from dysentery. The Spanish guards refused
to supply a match with which to light a fire: orders of the camp
chief. An Italian officer volunteered a package of matches, but
the Spanish officer in charge permitted only one! Many of the
infants drank unboiled milk; some took ill and a few died.

It was already late spring when a number of women and
children were transferred from Alicante via cattle cars to Valencia. Packed into each car were thirty or more women and as
many children. Each woman was given two tins of sardines and
one canteen of water. In the course of the three days traveling to
Valencia (normally a journey of a few hours) with so little food
and water, with very little air, no light, and insufferable heat,
several children died in their mother's arms. One distraught
woman tried to give water to her dead child. She had mistaken
for perspiration the fetid matter oozing from the infant's body,
decomposing rapidly in the heat of the overcrowded car. The
reply to the civil guard who had asked, "What do you have in
there, the pestilence?" was a horrible truth—dead children and
shit. The civil guard exclaimed incredulously, "Dead children!"
A woman said, "Yes, dead children. What's so strange? We had
no air, no food, no water. Here there is only death."

The guards ordered that the dead children be passed out of the
car and although some of the women were reluctant to dispose
of their dead infants so unceremoniously, they had no choice.

The women were divided according to their town of origin, to
which they were to be transferred. Some of the women, in
recounting their experiences to me, noted that the antifascists

arrested in towns other than where they resided had some "luck" on their side, for when it was possible for specific "identifications" to be made by venemous neighbors, by jealous and ambitious acquaintances, and even by strangers quick to falsify evidence, there were many wild, unsubstantiated accusations quickly followed by summary executions. Being shipped to their home towns might mean release for some, imprisonment for many, and for others, death usually preceded by unspeakable tortures.

How to estimate the number of women killed by the Franco sadists? During the first two years after the war's end, and especially during the first months, there were daily executions in each of the many prisons. The inmates would listen, terrified, to the sounds of rifles and even machine guns mowing down their comrades; then each prisoner would keep a blood-curdling, bone-chilling count of the number of *tiros de gracia.*

Moreover, those formally executed were not the only women to be killed. One must add those who died from torture and from illnesses contracted during the long incarcerations. Fatal illnesses included peritonitis from repeated blows in the abdominal area; diseases of the liver, kidney, bladder, intestines, stomach, and lungs; and skin cancer. Some women died in childbirth. And I would include among the killed those who committed suicide.

To write that many of those arrested were innocent is to assume that any were guilty of some crime. Having supported the Republican government, or having fought in its armed forces, or having been a member of any organization supportive of the government, or accused of any of the above, was considered by the fascists evidence of criminal action. Therefore potentially more than half of the population was liable to arrest. Yet even within that gargantuan net, the wholesale arrests included some absolute innocents, as was Maruja de Diego, who was first arrested in 1939 at age thirteen. She was not charged with anything.

She was arrested merely because she was the daughter of a man sought by the fascists; also arrested were Maruja's mother and three sisters. The father was beaten to death while in jail, her mother and sisters were kept in jail for many months, while she, being so young, was released—after five months. To go out into the street. Without immediate family. Without funds. Viewed by the fascists as a prostitute. That Maruja survived is miraculous. After her family was released, she became an anti-fascist fighter in the underground, and that was an act of consummate bravery. She was subsequently arrested and spent a total of five years in the Franco prisons.

During her first stay Maruja witnessed a mind-shattering event. From the jail in which she was interned, thirteen young women, under age twenty, and forty-nine young men were taken out of their cells one morning and executed within earshot of the inmates. Another witness, poet Angeles O. García-Madrid, with the tears welling, said that the youngsters went to death singing. In her sonnet dedicated to the young women, Angeles described them as thirteen fragrant dreams, thirteen voices, thirteen stars, thirteen ideas, thirteen flowers violently uprooted.

That Maruja spent so short a period (five years) in prison was subject to much friendly kidding by some of the women with whom I and my wife met one night in May 1978 in the Madrid offices of the ex-political prisoners. Cecilia Centeño Cifuentes, whose husband was beaten to death by the police, was condemned to twenty years, actually served sixteen years (one-half day off was the reward for every day of work). Antonia Herrero Muñoz served eighteen years; Felipa Albarrán Casal twenty years, and Carmen Machado Perez eleven years in the Franco hellholes. I believe it was Antonia who was denied the opportunity to visit her husband in the same jail. He had lost a leg in the war, was suffering immeasurably, and was denied medical attention. In desperation one day he seized a pistol from a guard and shot himself.

Amid the multiple horrors of prison life, the will to survive remained incredibly strong. One wonders how that will remained among some, like the elderly who lacked the physical strength to endure. How did the mothers, watching their children die of hunger and cold and illnesses, maintain their spirit to survive? How can we enter the minds and thereby understand the women who were condemned to death and awaited execution for one day—one week—one month—several years? Consider the agony of women who on first arrest were held incommunicado for weeks and even months! Such was the case for Sra. Doña, who was kept in solitary confinement for twenty days, savagely beaten, subjected to electric shocks, and kept another sixty days incommunicado!

With minds and bodies battered it is understandable that some prisoners broke; that so few succumbed is amazing.

What does the Association of Ex-Political Prisoners campaign for? After having been imprisoned for the better part of their lives, what do these men and women demand? What special problems engage the members of this unique organization? Many of these victims of injustice are "now sixty years of age or more, sick, with physical defects contracted in their long years of imprisonment, and are without necessary economic resources . . . social security and pensions would enable them to live on with dignity during their final years," writes Gabriel Salinas, an officer of the association. He states that there has not been "any legislation initiated to date that would aid the large number of widows and orphans of the men and women who were executed or who simply died in prison."

The association has been conducting a campaign to convince "the Spanish administration to recognize and repair the monstrous injustices that have been perpetrated . . .

"We still need the help of all democratic peoples." We still need "the moral and material solidarity of men and women of good faith who, like the North Americans, have in the past encouraged and helped us to bear with dignity the many sacrifices occasioned by our condition as ex-political prisoners."

Do these problems come under the purview of President Carter's concern for human rights?

We, the Veterans of the Abraham Lincoln Brigade, call the attention of our fellow Americans to the plight of our fellow democrats across the sea. By providing meaningful evidence of our solidarity we are but continuing in the honorable tradition that brought us to Spain forty-two years ago.

· María Teresa Toral ·

A Long Night

We called them *guerrillerinas*, these women of the mountains. They had been jailed for having aided wounded and sick guerrillas forced to come down from high in the sierra in search of help.

After being maltreated by the Civil Guard, the women arrived at the prison where, fearful, they rolled themselves up on their mats, with their cloaks barely covering them. They did not talk while they watched the days go by. Perhaps they were thinking only of their poor, abandoned huts and of their children—alone and hungry; perhaps they were given shelter by some charitable neighbors who dared to defy the violator of the people's rights and to risk the possible reprisals of the Falangists.

They made little noise, as if they wished to pass unnoticed. Since they never received letters, nor visits, nor food packages, their names were never called out.

We hardly knew them. Among ourselves, there was constant talk—about our ideas. About our struggles. We approached the *guerrillerinas* with these same concerns; and then, because we encountered their silence, we went on to interpret their apartness from us as an absolute and definitive indifference. It seemed that if they did accept sharing our food packages it was simply because they were hungry, but they did not understand the good fellowship of our gesture. They thanked us with dignity, nothing more—without smiling, without establishing ties of friendly trust; they never expressed confidence in us.

The month of January flew and it was snowing in the streets when the revolt was initiated in the prison. We were five thousand postwar women then in the prisons, and we had decided to go on a hunger strike. But we did not know what the *guerrillerinas* would do, whether they would join us or continue their indifference. We had to speak with them, but it was difficult to find the words necessary to break their isolation from everything that did not deal with their memories and their nostalgia. Sensing our fear, one of them, a young countrywoman from Avila, tall, well shaped, with beautiful but sad, grey eyes set in an austere, weather-beaten Castilian face, approached us.

"Why aren't you taking the food?"

We were pleased to hear her question, since it seemed a good augury that she was interested in what was taking place.

"You'll see. Today a commission was going to come to the jail; they would propagandize how well we are being treated and publicize it in the press. The prison administration has ordered that a better daily ration be given us and thus to prove it to the commission members; instead of the lentils with crawling insects that they give us every day they intended to give us rice and potatoes. At the last moment they learned that the commission would come in the afternoon—then they weren't able to resist the temptation to steal so they did not put out any rice in the prison meal; instead they gave us a small cup of water in which a tiny piece of potato floated. The head of one gallery of cells refused to give his meal to her companions so they have put her in the punishment cell where they will hold her incommunicado for three months. Since she was right, we will not eat until they take her out of the isolation cell. And we'll be able to demand more; for the commission cannot enter the jail because there is a rebellion, and everybody will know that we prefer to die once for hunger than tolerate the treatment they mete out to us, you understand?"

She appeared to smile. We saw her sidle gracefully away, with her peasant step accustomed to skirting stones and brambles. We did not cling to too many hopes, for we could not imagine what her friends would think when she explained to them what had happened.

Accompanied by press photographers, the commission that

had come to visit the jail could not enter a prison in revolt. For the moment we had won, but if the *guerrillerinas* were to eat, the members could return the next day and a number of us inmates might pay with our lives. And the rest of us would be locked up in the cells and our existence would remain in utter silence.

Night came. The jail was dark; cell doors clanged shut with their heavy chains. Nobody slept. In the cells, seated on our mats, we were tense, expectant. In the silence of the central gallery, the noise of footsteps. Bolts crashed and the lights of lanterns dazzled us. The director and all the officials were in the entrance of the cell block.

"Line up! Have you thought of what you are doing? Do you realize that this is a rebellion? Don't you know that you are risking the liberty of those who are to get out and that we can shoot ten, a hundred, a thousand women? Don't be fools! Understand that we cannot retreat even one step, and that we are ready to do anything."

We were silent.

"There is still time to go back. Don't you want to eat the food?"

Our unanimous silence was the response.

"Then suffer the consequences. Those of you who persist in the rebellion are to go out to the central gallery with everything you have—and stay in line!"

Watched over by the guards, we could not talk. Each one grabbed her straw mat and we left our cells and lined up in the cell block gallery. Apparently they wanted us to be concentrated on the highest floor of the jail so as to isolate us from the infirmary, the kitchen, and the service rooms of the officials.

If the *guerrillerinas* did not join the strike, our enemies could point to a triumph.

We did not know what our cell mates would do.

I thought we ought to have spoken more with them to explain things better, to tell them that we needed their help. Now it was too late. In the gallery darkness, broken only at intervals by the zigzagging light of the guards' lanterns, we waited. Suddenly, at my side, a firm voice assailed me: "Compañera!"

Yes, that disused word came out spontaneously from the lips of the *guerrillerina*, who was now openly smiling, illuminating the darkness of her countenance with the sound white teeth of a peasant woman. I looked and I almost did not dare to believe that it was true. Yes. There she was and there were all the *guerrillerinas*, young and old, at our side, as sturdy as trees. Their hands, seamed and deformed from the hard work in the fields, did not tremble while knotting the black handkerchief each had to gather her hair. There they all were, even the very old woman whose arm the Civil Guard had broken and who still wore a sling.

"Compañera," she asked, quite serene, "are they going to take us out to shoot us?" I felt amazement and admiration before the simple heroism. "No," I said. "But, are you ready to die?"

I looked at her with mingled respect and emotion. With difficulty I could discern her eyes, which no longer seemed sad.

And finally I understood. No, it had not been by accident, nor for simple humanity, nor ignorance of the danger, as we had mistakenly believed, that they had given such generous aid to the wounded, to the hungry, to the sick guerrilla, who had descended from the sierra to the village, risking his life in search of fraternal warmth from the people even more than the desperately needed material help. No, it had not been only compassion that explained giving him bread and water, or healing his wounds. It had been the same sentiment that led the women, without a trace of fear, to join our rebellion—because they considered it just.

We remained standing, lined up tired, without having slept nor eaten, frozen by the humidity, cold, wintry air of the Madrid dawn, in the inhospitable prison from which went out to die— on the thick wall or from punishment—so many of our *compañeras*.

It was just about dawn, after a long night.

María Teresa Toral is the widow of composer Lan Adomian, a member of the Brigade who she married years later in Mexico. She was imprisoned in Madrid, where she sang a verse by the poet and martyr Miguel Hernández to music composed by Adomian. After five days of the hunger strike, the women won.

The piece is translated by Albert Prago from the Mexican
literary journal *Cuardernos del Viento,* where it first appeared
in November 1962.

The
WAR
GOES ON

The disbanding of the Brigades by no means signalled an end to the conviction that fascism had to be fought in all its guises. The volunteers never forgot that they had gone to Spain to stop fascism and to conserve democracy. After the defeat of the Spanish Republic, many survivors went on to serve these aims in the armed forces of their respective countries or as members of partisan groups fighting in Europe. They hoped that winning the war would lead to a better world, one ruled by and for the people.

In the postwar years, the veterans remained determined to continue what had come to be called the "good fight." The selections in this last section give some small indication of how the volunteers have fought on, for peace and human dignity. They also show that the experience of the Spanish Civil War is firmly fixed in the minds and hearts of the Brigade members, many of whom have returned to visit Spain, especially since the death of Franco in 1975.

Each year the Veterans of the Abraham Lincoln Brigade come to-gether at their annual dinner to renew old friendships, relive old experiences, and reaffirm their pledge to continue the good fight. One reunion has been particularly important. In October 1986, the International Brigades celebrated their fiftieth anniversary in Spain itself. The volunteers recalled La Pasionaria's farewell speech in Barcelona in 1938: "We shall not forget you, and when the olive tree of peace puts forth its leaves again, entwined with the laurels of the Spanish Republic's victory— come back!" The volunteers returned to a democratic Spain and were thrilled to learn first hand that the Spanish people had not forgotten the International Brigades.

The Veterans of the Abraham Lincoln Brigade's most recent efforts have concentrated on aiding the Nicaraguan people in their fight against the U.S.-supported contras. Remembering the tremendous importance of the ambulances that were sent by American antifascists to Spain in 1937 and 1938, the Lincolns have raised money to send nine fully equipped ambulances to the people of Nicaragua. Fifty years after Spain, the surviving volunteers still carry the torch of liberty, proudly and vigorously.

—A.P.

· Irving Weissman ·

The Return

It is forty years later, and I am walking across the Frenchman's Bridge, which spans the Manzanares. A tinkle of bells floats through the clear air, and I glimpse the flock of sheep, their wool coated with dust, through the bedraggled foliage of the Casa de Campo. They are dawdling as they munch the scant grass, and a skinny black dog, his tongue lolling in the heat, lethargically patrols their flanks. The shepherd ambles into view, a squat man whose broad-brimmed hat shades a weatherbeaten face. A blanket droops over his left shoulder, his bare feet are as coated with dust as the wool of his flock, and his right hand grips a gnarled staff. And now all of them recede through the leaves like an apparition from an ancient and indolent world, until only the ever more distant tinkle asserts their contemporary existence.

Yes, this was that bridge, and this is that park, where, on those cold November days, the blood soaked into the earth, and trickled into the river, and the corpses sprawled among the trees and against the abutments, and the wounded on each side fought to the last breath, knowing that no prisoners would be taken. Yes, this is the bridge to which we came, after our boots had drummed on the cobblestones of Madrid, and our kind of people everywhere in the world knew that there was cause for confidence in the earth to be reborn. Brothers! we were saying, you must not be devoid of hope; we are emerging, all of us, from the inhuman labyrinth of our slavery. Then we went into battle

313

against the Moor and the Legionnaire. The Legionnaire sang, "My Bride Is Death." We performed the wedding ceremony.

A large open-air café comes into sight. Sunlight falling through the leaves of the trees, which have recovered from their old wounds, dapples the tops of the round tables lucky enough to be in the shade. Four waiters, their aprons dangling from the backs of their chairs, are playing a noisy, cheerful game of cards at the one occupied table. I sit down in the shade and wait.

After a few minutes, one waiter slaps his cards down, shoves his chair back, ties the apron around his waist, and comes over to me. He is still grinning over the dispute he has left behind him. He takes my order, returns with the beer, Manchego cheese, and bread, and rejoins the game. I sip the cold beer in the delicious shade.

Pedro warned me to stay away from the afternoon's prohibited demonstration in the Plaza de España. "They will put you on the plane without a moment's hesitation," he said, "and off you go! back to the United States!"

Pedro escaped arrest at the last demonstration. The cops had attacked with tear gas and rubber bullets, and were chasing and clubbing the scattering participants. Pedro ran into a building and up a flight of stairs. Through an open door he saw more than a dozen people bent over ledgers and typewriters. There was an empty desk on which a typewriter stood. Pedro sat down at it, inserted a sheet of paper in the roller, and began to clack away. Two cops, panting, swaddled in tommy guns and pistols, their clubs in their hands, appeared in the doorway. They started into the room. Everyone's head was bent over his work. The cops' breathing quieted down. They turned and left. After five minutes, a woman got up, beckoned to Pedro, and led him out a back way. All this time no one spoke.

"I don't know if you understand what it is to feel terror for ten years, from the time you have committed yourself," Pedro said to me. "In all honesty, I wonder if it is not worse terror than you felt in the moments of battle."

I keep silent. On what scales are the separate terrors of this world to be weighed?

Yesterday we drove to Toledo and were enveloped in medievalism. Over the lintel of the wooden doors of the church of San

Juan de los Reyes a skeleton carved in wood reclines. The ubiquitousness and inevitability of death embedded itself in me. I thought of that same November when the Madrileños, some in uniform, and so many of them in civilian clothes, had stood in the trenches, one rifle for every ten combatants, and picked up the rifles as they dropped from the hands of the dead and wounded. I thought of the July that had preceded that November when, in answer to the treachery of the generals, the untrained men and women in *monos* had gone up against the uniforms, machine guns, and repeating rifles of the Montaña barracks. This people's disdain of death awed and saddened me.

"Why so bemused?" Pedro asked.

I told him my thoughts.

"You're right," he said. "The centuries have embedded it in us, this notion of the transience of life, and therefore of its small worth. So that our contempt of death is all too often a belittling of life. There it is, with deep roots, even in those of us who are atheists and don't look forward to a paradise that will compensate for the hell of this earth. . . . But tell me, my North American friend, do you think this is a good thing?"

"Everything is relative," I answered, with Hegelian complexities in my mind.

"Relative? But I tell you that this scorn of death is really a scorn for life!"

I questioned him mildly. "Is it not Machado who wrote, 'Madrid, tu sonríes con plomo en tus entrañas'?"

"And just how would you translate that? I want to hear it the way your North American ear hears it."

"I would say, 'Madrid, you smile, even while the hot lead burns in your bowels.'"

"Fair enough," said Pedro. "But isn't there more than the endurance of pain in those lines? Isn't there also the certainty of the triumph of life, with its potential of joy? . . . Do you agree?"

"I agree," I answered.

If you stand in the middle of a field in La Mancha and see about you in every direction the endless terrain of wheatland, you know that the earth is flat and that Columbus was wrong then and the geographers are wrong today when the one contended that it is egg-shaped and the others contend that it is a globe.

I bypass Albacete, our base forty years ago, and drive on toward Tarazona de la Mancha, where those Americans and Canadians for whom there was time enough got a few weeks of infantry training. They became intimate with the fact that even the flattest chunk of sod presents to a soldier, with the precious shelter that any bump in the ground donates to the rifleman.

This square, now surrounded and green with high hedges among which trees are interspersed, used to be a bare, dusty, sun-smitten quadrangle where the battalion lined up, each of the four companies occupying one of the sides. Our final morning there, as we waited for the trucks that would carry us to the railroad and to an unknown front, the women of the town, dressed in black, came to us with goatskins full of wine and water. They did not smile and they did not cry. The inclined their heads in acknowledgment of our thanks as we passed the refreshment from mouth to mouth and returned the empty canteens. Their own sons and husbands were long gone.

The town is sniffing me out. Amnesty is in the air; a multitude of pressures are buffeting each other in the country. For two Sundays in a row—the eighteenth and twenty-fifth of July—the right wing has exploded bombs; nevertheless, the amnesty was decreed. This last Sunday the bombs went off in the hands of their purveyors; decapitation occurred; the severed head ensconced in the limbs of a tree has appeared on front pages throughout the country. Is my outlandish presence—a daytime ghost perhaps of the foreign warriors whom the families of this village once hosted—an omen of a freer time, an added tremor under the crust of thirty-seven years of defeat and torpor?

It is most unusual: women sauntering by with fishnet shopping bags smile if our eyes meet and, at my request, one directs me to a *tienda.*

It is full of women whose murmur stops as I enter. The woman behind the counter smiles at me, and I indicate that I will wait my turn. There is an outburst of protest, and I surrender.

"Please," I say, "I would like mineral water and hazelnuts."

One of the older women pushes aside the beaded curtain of the entrance and comes back with a bottle of mineral water that has been standing in a rack in the shade. She places it on the counter beside the package of hazelnuts that the proprietress has selected.

I am reaching for my wallet when the proprietress asks, "Are you a North American?"

"Yes."

"I knew!" and she looks at the assembly triumphantly. "The moment I saw you in the square I knew! When I was a child, this town was full of North Americans. I can still recognize one, no matter how much time has passed since then. . . . Did you know that North Americans had once been here?"

"Yes," I answer. "I knew."

"They were good people," she says.

Someone murmurs assent. Out of the corner of my eye I see the older woman who fetched the mineral water nodding her head.

The proprietress is a broad-shouldered woman with a resolute air. She stares me full in the face, as if daring herself to challenge me with further assertions.

"They behaved with respect," she continues. "One of them used to come to my house all the time, and he and my grandfather would talk all night. They would read the paper together and teach each other English and Spanish. How they would laugh at each other's accents and mistakes!"

She pauses.

"One day they all left." And now there is a quiver in her voice. "Our friend came to our house for the last time and gave me this souvenir."

She raises her hands off the counter and removes from around her neck a string of beads on which is hung not a cross but a train conductor's tin whistle. It has been hidden beneath the neckline of her dress.

"We do not know what became of him. We used to call him Guillermo."

She puts the necklace on the counter.

I finger the shiny whistle, still warm from its contact with her flesh. This was Bill Miller's whistle, with which he would announce mail call. Random lines from a poem that he cited at one of our amateur entertainments in the church trot through my mind:

> Nobody knows where the hobo goes
> When the snowballs rattle on his spine . . .
> Boom a little saxophone, rap the little drums
> Make a little music for the doggone bums

He was one of our older men, already in his forties. He had been a hobo, following the harvests. As company clerk, he reported our casualties as less than they were; in that way we got more rations while still in battle. A mortar got him in Sierra de Pandols.

"He was killed," I say. "I knew him."

A great sigh fills the *tienda*. The town's surmise about me is at an end. The proprietress picks up the necklace and replaces it around her neck, tucking the whistle out of sight. She waves her palm in negation at my still-open wallet. I glance around. On all faces there is sadness and approval.

"Go with God, señor," she says.

I return to the square, uncap the bottle and swig from it. I have to sit on an unoccupied bench in the sun. Through an opening in the hedge I see the concrete cross that the Falange erected; inscribed on its base is a handful of names, local fascists who fell for God and Spain. Attached to the wall of the church where we used to hold our meetings are the six-foot-high yoke and arrows of the Falange.

An old peasant is standing in front of me.

"Please, señor," he says, and indicates there is room on one of the shaded benches. He and his friends have rearranged their seats.

I walk across, thank them, sit down and offer my water and hazelnuts. They thank me and decline.

He who is their spokesman says, "You can have wine here." He has teeth missing, and so have the others who are now looking into my face and approving the information he is volunteering. "As you leave town," he says, "not in the direction of Albacete, but in the other direction, towards Pozo Rubio, you will encounter our cooperative. There we can give you wine, and a meal. We even have a swimming pool, and you are welcome to bathe."

I regret that I must be back at the *parador* in time to meet friends. It is dusk when we say goodby and, as I drive back, a full white moon, immoderate and intoxicated, dances up from the horizon and holds sway in the cloudless sky and over the horizontal earth. [. . .]

The Aragon will be my last stop. Strange formations succeed each other. Vast sunbaked yellow and brown barren tablelands with fold after fold of hills on the horizon. Bleak hill; rock and sand out of which tufts and shrubs stick up. Suddenly a soothing green oasis; an irrigation system has defeated the surrounding desert. Then repulsive hills again, with massive protuberances of rock in strange shapes; they stick out of the sides of the hills like goiters that deform a sufferer's neck and head. Now, other treeless and grassless hills, low wide-based truncated cones, like great mounds of rock dumped out of sandpails by the children of giants at play. Yet they are a relief to the sight, because they are not afflicted with the tumors of their fellows.

Zaragoza is the city we never took. The way stations were Quinto, Belchite, and Fuentes de Ebro. Quinto was one for the books—the artillery laid down its barrage, the planes came over on time, the tanks and infantry went in. Nevertheless, it took three days of street fighting. Belchite was the real bloodbath. Their orders were to hold us up. The house-to-house and gully-to-gully fighting took six days. We took the town but it was very hard. At Fuentes they stopped us.

I remember the cemetery in Quinto where I started up in the middle of the night out of my spasmodic sleep and saw the spent bodies of my comrades all around me. Quinto was ours, but the huddled forms, wrapped in blankets like shrouds, were contorted into various postures as if they were rehearsing to be the corpses of our next battle. The shelling had ploughed up the graves and shattered the crypts in the cemetery wall over which the damaged cypresses loomed. Coffins, their lids and sides coming apart from the bombardments, rested on the ground at all angles; the moist earth had a sweet subtle smell of exhumation; and skulls and bones were scattered among the exhausted sleepers.

Two men of my age, wearing corduroy jackets despite the heat, with the broad toughened hands of peasants resting on their knees, are sitting in the shade in Quinto's rebuilt square. When I greet them, they answer me courteously. Like the peasants in the square at Tarazona, their opened lips reveal missing teeth.

I introduce myself with the lie that I am a professor of history and wish to get firsthand accounts of what happened in the Aragon during the war. This area was in Franco hands for a long time and, after summoning the inhabitants to witness the execution of the left-wingers and Republicans in the villages, he conscripted the unexecuted. This knowledge I keep to myself. I want to hear what these two have to say.

"Were you in the fighting yourselves?" I ask.

They nod, and one says, "We were in the Nationalist army."

"Are you French?" the second man asks.

"I am a North American."

"North Americans fought here with the Reds," the second man says and nods thoughtfully. "They also fought at Belchite, which you will be interested in seeing. The government left it as a ruin; it is a national monument. Your countrymen were very brave. Spaniards are brave—that is their nature, that goes without saying—but the North Americans were madmen."

I ask them what they think of the amnesty, which has already freed nine military dissidents and several Communists and Basque nationalists.

"We do not know what will develop," the first speaker says after a pause. "What we do know is that we need bread.

"Go to Belchite," he adds. "We do not need more such ruins."

Early the next morning, I set off for Belchite. I feel the throb of my pulse, and my breathing is getting shorter.

It is coming into view—masonry skeletons sprawling across dips of sand and rock, a few dead tree trunks thrusting leafless branches between mounds of rubble.

I drive off the road and park in the shade of a shattered stone barn. A middle-aged couple is picnicking near another ruin. They finish their sandwiches as I get out of my car and drink from the bottle of mineral water I bought this morning. Now they go about folding up their chairs and picnic table; they drop greasy sandwich wrappers on the ground, and flies swoop and buzz at the garbage. They reload their car and drive off without having spoken to each other or to me. I am left alone in the pervading heat, whose torpor is broken only by the drone of flies.

I go into the barn and urinate and a swarm of midges rises from the pool I am making in the weeds. Paul Anderson, the fisherman from Gloucester, used to have kidney trouble. Before each battle, there was a verse he would intone like a prayer:

Overloaded, undermanned, meant to founder, we
Euchred God Almighty's storm, bluffed the eternal sea.

One morning of the fighting in this town I saw him lying as if asleep on the dirt street. I bent over to shake him awake and saw where a bullet had gone through his temple.

I take another swig from the bottle and begin a walk that is a calvary.

In the gullies, in the abandoned rubble-strewn interiors where stubble and weeds have thrust their way through the cracked ground, on the wrecked facades, blood clots spread, then slowly dissolve. They drench in crimson the pitiless sun, which is re-invoking the delirium of heat, thirst, hunger. I see the stiffened corpses, and my brain is shrill with the whine of bullets, the stutter of machine guns, the moans of the wounded, the hoarse curses and shouts of those still alive.

A round-faced, bright-eyed chunky man on a bicycle stops beside me on the dirt street between the ruins. I can see from the tire tracks and hoof marks in the dust that the living make use of this path.

Dígame!" he shouts in a hearty entrepreneurial voice. "Is this your first visit here?"

When I do not answer, he looks at me calculatingly and gets off his bicycle.

"Francés?" he asks, and without waiting for an answer begins his patter. "Moi, je parle. Moi, soldat—ejército, armée, na-tional—Franco, oui? Comprendez-vous? Oui. Oui. Moi, soldat."
He points into an interior whose wooden roof beams are sagging

and where the sunlight is dribbling through the shattered roof on to the uprooted floor. "Ici, les soeurs. Hospital. Enfermería. Comprendez?" His toothless smirk reveals expectation of a generous fee.

"Please, señor," I say coldly. "I do not want your guidance."

Astounded by my hostility and my Spanish, he gapes, then remounts his bicycle and rides off. Once again, the devastation and I are left alone.

Here is the stone house, with walls three feet thick, where machine guns filled every window. Where do Carl Bradley and Charlie Regan lie now, and the nine others with them, who threw the bottles of nitroglycerine into those sandbagged windows, in those tiny moments when our own covering fire forced the fascist gunners to duck and not fire their own guns?

I stumble across a wooden beam at least three inches thick and eight inches wide, which is sticking out of a doorless entrance. Stooping, I finger the hard splintery surface; my fingertips accumulate dust. Perhaps this very beam was one of those we used as battering rams. No doubt we broke down this door; it was not weather that unhinged it. We swept the dark interior with automatic fire; we threw grenades inside and, since this structure had an upper story, we set gasoline-soaked straw afire to smoke out snipers.

Here is the shallow trench where he lay all day under enfilading fire sixty yards from the fascists in the church while the sun tortured us and no food or water could reach us and we had to lie in our excrement and we squirmed deeper and deeper into the dirt and did not dare to raise our heads. We had gotten into that position during the night, and it was not until daylight that we saw where we were.

The church is the ruin that we and they made of it. Some flagstones still lie on the churned ground. The silenced bell dangles in the shattered belfry. Groggy comrades raced and stumbled across the gully and the parapet whose momentary abandonment our shelling had achieved. We reached the rear entrance just as, the shelling having been lifted, the fascists reached the front entrance. Under an enormous dangling crucifix, grenades exploded. They are running! We hold the front door and fire into the town. They are firing at us from windows and alleys; in a moment they will rush. Levick and Eaton fall. But—trust the Finns!—here are Houtijarvi and another nickel miner from Ontario with their machine gun and belts, and here come the guys with sandbags, and we heap them up, and more of us are getting hit, and the low barricade is built, and we are all staggering, and the church is ours.

Beyond the church, *their* barricade, with scores of defenders. They receive supplies from the air and assurances that relief columns are on the way. On this side, ourselves, stupefied with weariness, in anguish from six days of house-to-house combat. Conflagrations leap about, overhead and around us. Doran, who has been demanding that Division send a propaganda truck, sees one headed elsewhere on the road. He races to it in the Brigade car and pulls his revolver on the Army Corps truck driver. The commandeered truck is set up in the ruins. That night it blares its message. It tells them the fascists have taken their land while the Republic is distributing land. And it tells them: "If you hold out, you are doomed. You will all die. There is no escape for you. If you don't come over, you will all be killed in the morning."

A monstrous skull instead of a moon hovered in the sky. Innumerable skeletons spanned the Milky Way. The dreadful utterance worked. There was a firing as they fought with their officers, and then they swarmed over the barricade. Their furious officers escaped through an underground passage to a fortified house, from which they made a sortie, driving women and children in front of them. They encountered our Spanish battalion and the hand grenades of each side ripped flesh without discrimination. One of their commanders used a dagger when his pistol had gone empty, and one of our people grappled with him, wrested the dagger away, and stabbed him in the heart.

I turn the corner of a crumbled wall and come upon a wrought-iron cross taller than a man. Its austerity halts me, and I stand before it, shocked at its fitness in the encircling devastation. Its upright and crosspiece are formed by edges of black-painted round iron bars, and the emptiness within these bars is broken by curved interweaving iron strands that form large uniform circles. Visible through this vacant succession of intertwined horizontal, vertical, and circular iron, there stretches a landscape of endless ruins.

The cross stands embedded in a concrete base on which there is no inscription. The rigidity of the monument avows the stern demands of war. Its nakedness is at one and the same time a homage to those, living and dead, on whom those demands were imposed, and a witness of the desolation of soul and earth that is the real victor in war. This cross without a Christ, with no veneer of wood, with bones of iron, is the skeleton of a cross.

A little further on, a gentler memorial awaits me. A curved flight of steps between two simple brick walls leads to a small open-air chapel. The tall, spaced, thin iron bars that form the gates to the stairs are locked, so I climb up alongside the curving wall and look over its top into the chapel. This memorial in its humility arouses my anger; it is imploring the stern cross for a lessening of its carnage; its timid questioning of the other's austere carriage is hypocrisy.

I am at the end at last: here is the arch that was once the entrance to the old town and on the other side of which I see a neglected treeless square at whose further end there is a row of houses with wash hanging from the balconies.

The side of the arch facing the square has affixed to it a pompous and conventional plaque. An angel in prayerful attitude leans in benediction over a prostrate soldier, and the inscription pays tribute to the heroes who from August 20 to September 4, 1937, defended Belchite against the Red hordes attempting to advance on Zaragoza. These heroes fell for God and for Spain.

Slowly, I walk back through the necropolis. The heat waves shimmer, the blind sockets of the shattered buildings gape sadly into each other's dim recesses, flies drone in and out of the weeds and tufts of grass, and a lizard darts from under a stone across my path.

It is hard to believe, but I have meandered about for two and a half hours. I unlock the car and am drinking from my bottle of mineral water when two young men, bareheaded, their collars open at the neck, and wearing shorts that expose healthy athletic calves, appear around the corner of the crumbling barn and approach me with perplexity in their faces.

"Señor, que es eso, esto pueblo?" one asks me in broken Spanish, and both wave their hands at the ruins.

"Do you speak English?" I ask.

"We *are* English," they answer eagerly. "And you?"

"I'm an American." I offer them the bottle. They thank me and each takes a swallow. They look to be in their early twenties.

"Can you tell us what all this is?" one of them asks. "We have been reading in the papers about entire villages being abandoned, about peasants leaving to search for work in the cities. But this looks the way my parents described London during the blitz."

"This is a bombed-out town," I say. "This is Belchite." I can feel all I have choked down for forty years swelling inside of me. "A battle of the Spanish Civil War was fought here. This is a national monument." I hear how husky my voice has become, and I see that, behind their good manners, the two of them are wondering at my agitation.

They are silent for a moment, then the second youth says respectfully,

"Yes, I have read about the Civil War. Hugh Thomas, you know. Orwell. Those fellows. But why leave the town such an eyesore? If it can't be rebuilt, why not raze it and blot it out?"

Then it pours out of me, the accumulation of defeated compassion, the fury at millennia of continuous and triumphant injustice.

"Because the corpse-chewer Franco wanted it that way," I say, and hear that hoarseness has now completely taken over my voice. "Because he left it this way so as to wag the finger at the Spanish people, and to let them know he was ready to inflict more of the same on them if they dared to challenge their rulers again."

Their sense of delicacy is keeping the two English youths from asking the question that is in their eyes, and which I want to answer anyhow.

"I fought with these people," I say. "So did other Americans. So did hundreds of Britons and Irishmen. Your countrymen were in the same brigade with us, the Fifteenth International Brigade. The Spanish people were our brothers. Our sisters. Our parents. We all understood that, the forty thousand of us who came from every corner of Europe and the Americas. We came from countries as small as postage stamps, and from countries as large as oceans. We came to deliver the future as a gift to the world." ·

The words are flooding out of me. I give them the names of their British and Irish warriors, the quick and the dead, Julian Bell and Malcolm Dunbar, Oliver St. John Spragg and Jock Cunningham, Paddy O'Daire and Frank Ryan, that noble generation of intellectuals and workers. I enumerate the battles in which they fought—the Jarama, Brunete, Purburell Hill. I speak of our crushed hope that we would stop fascism in Spain and prevent the Second World War.

Drained, I fall silent.

Their eyes rove the ravaged landscape, and then one of them says gently,

"You are very moved, and so are we."

And then, for the first time in this exploration and rediscovery that has now come to an end, all I have buried reasserts its fierce life, and I weep.

IRVING WEISSMAN was born in 1913 of Polish-Jewish immigrant parents. In 1937 he went to Spain, where he fought on the Aragon front and at the Ebro. He joined the U.S. army in 1942 and fought in Europe and North Africa. After the war he was a Communist Party organizer in the industrial area of western New York State and then in the coal mining region of southern West Virginia. In 1951, he was one of six defendants in Pittsburgh in one of the many political trials of the 1950s. After the trial and appeals process was over, Weissman rejoined his family in New York and worked in building construction. He retired in the late 1970s and has since devoted much of his time to the VALB. This piece is excerpted from an article in *Massachusetts Review* (Autumn 1978), and is reprinted with permission.

· Studs Terkel ·

Irving Goff: An Interview

As a member of the Abraham Lincoln Battalion, Goff specialized in guerrilla warfare behind enemy lines. He may have been the model for Robert Jordan, hero of Ernest Hemingway's Spanish Civil War novel For Whom the Bell Tolls.

"*I never saw Ingrid Bergman in all the time I was in the war. If I did, I might still be there. [Laughs.] The way Gary Cooper blew that bridge—like blowing a seam in a coal mine. I've blown bridges. You put a detonator in the thing and then you'd better be twenty miles away. You went after bridges and railroads. Usually it'd last five or six days behind the lines.*

"*The biggest guerrilla operation was freeing 135 Asturian miners from a Mediterranean prison fort. Thirty-five of us, plus grenades. Another American and I and two Spaniards got cut off. It was almost like a movie scene. We were swimming toward Africa, while the fascists were pot-shotting at us. The two Spaniards drowned. We saw their swollen bodies later, as we grabbed a rock.*

"*We're in a little crevice, stark naked. The fascists are just above us. We hear 'em talkin'. It's four o'clock in the morning. Icy water hits you. We hug ourselves to conserve whatever body heat there was. We wait till nightfall. We swim some more. We spend another twenty-four hours in tiny caves. No food, no water.*

"*Fascists on one side, the Republican army on the other. Shots going on all the time. We went from rock to rock. We were keepin' our heads below water, just about here, so you could breathe. It took us three days to make it to our lines.*"

I'm a kid from Brooklyn. I was hardly ever in a mountain. What do I know from guerrilla warfare? I learned everything in Spain. I learned from life itself. One time, I'm carryin' explosives on my back and this Spaniard is tellin' me how they work. In two days, I'm behind the lines, blowin' up a train. It had Italian soldiers going to Córdoba. My very first operation. I was never on a plane until I went up for my first jump. I was with OSS then. I was good because I'd been a professional acrobat. You know how to fall and roll and control your body.

Just before Pearl Harbor, Donovan wanted us to work for the British, behind the lines in Egypt. Desert warfare. When Pearl Harbor happened, he said, "Hold everything." Our objective was to go to Spain, organize intelligence, paramilitary work, and protect Gibraltar. Franco had forces in Morocco and could almost lock up the Mediterranean. The State Department stopped it.

Remember Kasserine Pass? That was the big battle in North Africa. A bunch of us Lincoln vets are now with OSS. An anti-Franco Republican fleet was interned there, in a concentration camp at Kasserine Pass. And a lot of International Brigaders were taken out of camps in France to build a trans-Saharan railroad in the desert for the Germans. When we made the landing, they were liberated.

Just at this time, Rommel broke through and there was a massive retreat. We were behind the lines. I'd seen this in Spain. How can you go behind enemy lines without intelligence? You wander into anything. We're under the command of a British major. Courage is not enough. You gotta know what the devil you're doing. We almost walked into an airport, a mile away from Rommel. We would all have been captured. Later on, we were behind enemy lines again, toward Tunis.

Everybody who graduated from the OSS school came out full lieutenants, captains, majors. All us Lincoln guys came out enlisted men. [Laughs.] They considered us all Communists. Because of Spain, we knew ten times more than any of the other guys.

When we first went in, we got civilian pay. We were made enlisted men, but we still would've gotten civilian pay. We wrote a letter to the Treasury: We're in the army, we want army pay.

We got a letter to the finance officer: Are you guys crazy? He couldn't understand that we're in to fight, not make a buck. We didn't want it said we're mercenary. If you're on civilian pay, you can come out of the war with thirty thousand bucks on ya. [Laughs.] That's not why we were fightin'. This major who'd been in class with me, he wouldn't budge without us. [Laughs.] Any goddamn question came up, he'd ask us.

In North Africa, we're seven miles behind the German lines. Three Lincolns and two other guys. Suddenly, the Germans throw a shell over us at our lines. We have no cover. We were supposed to have. Bang! A shell hits near a Lincoln, Felsen. I pull out my sulfa pack, just pour it on his wound. I pull him into a ravine and these tanks come out. They yell, "Hands up!" Tiger tanks, big ones. It is rough, sittin' in front of an 88 tank. I had my nose buried down, I'm close to China practically, I wrapped myself around a sagebrush. Lossowski, another Spanish vet, wrapped himself around a sagebrush. The major, in an Abercrombie & Fitch brown jacket, is visible a mile away. He was silly, but great enough to stand up and divert them to the wounded guy, Felsen, and himself. They took the two prisoners and rolled back. When I met Felsen after the war, we talked of eight German tanks in front of us. Here we are, a handful of nobody. [Laughs.]

When we got back, the remaining officers wrote letters to Donovan: "On our honor as officers and gentlemen, we cannot understand why Sergeant Goff and Sergeant Lossowski and Sergeant Felsen are not made officers." Donovan comes to the front and he makes us all second lieutenants right at the front. [Laughs.] We had a sort of left-handed reputation. When they began to redbait me, Donovan said, "For the work he did in Africa and Italy, he's on the honor roll of the OSS."

Rommel had only three Panzer divisions, no infantry, and he smashed the American lines. A hub-to-hub retreat. If the Stukas came in, they would have knocked the hell out of us. I'm talking about stupidity. We had tanks and half-tracks. They looked like Tinker Toys. Rommel was toying with 'em. No matter what I think of Nazism, as a military man he was brilliant.

There's a myth that he was beaten by Montgomery smashin' him on one end and we smashin' em on the other. Nothing is further from the truth. All the tanks and planes went to Stalingrad. One day, the sky's full of German planes. The next day, you saw nothing. You never saw 'em to the end of the war. All went to Tunis, into Europe. Look at the map. It's not that far to Stalingrad. That's what happened in North Africa. All the rest is nonsense.

We moved from North Africa into Sicily. Donovan's on the boat with us. He's on the beach with us. He's in a foxhole with us. Hell, we hit Anxio on a PT boat together. German plane came down, Donovan's standin' there. He was a great guy, but he had foolish guts. I yelled at 'im, "Get down, general!" He wouldn't get down, and bombs droppin' all around.

The purpose of Anzio was to outflank Cassino. We're really hung up at Monte Cassino. It's twenty miles north of Naples. You have this big mountain range. The Germans were intelligent. They never fought on flat land. When you got to Cassino, they're throwing grenades at you. Tanks couldn't get up there, trucks, artillery, nothing. They bombed the hell out of us for six months, eight thousand casualties.

Lossowski and I are trainin' these young guys how to penetrate the lines and gather intelligence. I'd take 'em with me, come back in a couple of days. We put twenty-two teams across that line. All twenty-two except one were successful.

We had no intelligence. Suddenly you're getting all these reports. The Third Division was ecstatic. The one team captured was in a Gestapo jail, had their nails pulled out, but they didn't talk. We met them in Rome, later on. We didn't lose a man.

Donovan was on the plane with me from Naples to Algiers. He sits down next to me. He's talking about my connection with the Communist Party. Not antagonistic, just curious. "How you makin' out?" He knew all the OSS debriefings here came from me. My prestige with him was pretty high. Jeez, if I asked him for a million dollars, he wouldn't even bat an eye. I told him what the connections were all about and what I had in mind: blowin' up railroads. He says, "We're collaborating with the Communist Party, boy. Isn't that interesting?" He always called me "boy," affectionately. He says, "But in your connection, make sure the Communist Party doesn't come out to win the war. I'll do the best I can to win this war." He was fine, and left.

In Naples, the Communist Party had 150,000 members. All

during the Mussolini time, twenty-two years, the railroad workers maintained an illegal, left-led union, underground. The Italian partisans, during the Nazi occupation, were slaughtering the
Germans, especially as they were fleeing. Hot water from windows—did you see the movie *Four Days of Naples?* Every sector
of the front was commanded by a guy who fought with the
Garibaldi in Spain. The guy that captured Mussolini and strung
him up by his feet was Moscatalli. He fought in Spain.

North of Rome we're parachuting radio teams to the guerrillas who are known as the Garibaldi Committee of National
Liberation. Their leader was a guy who was head of the
Garibaldi Brigade in Spain. With 'em was this guy, Italian, who
spoke with an Oxford accent. He was spectacular. He and a few
of these guerrillas captured a German tank division in the Alban
Hills. The British were slow comin' in. So he walks out in a
ragged outfit and says in his Oxonian English, "What're you
standing there for? I've got 'em all, take 'em." He did it without
any tanks, just submachine guns. He turned 'em over and the
British made a big to-do about it.

The army took Rome. Now you have Florence, Siena, and the
German army in the north. By this time, the guerrillas are a
massive force. We had eighteen radio teams, speaking German,
French, English, Italian in northern Italy. Every day. Never lost a
team. The intelligence we sent was called by Allied headquarters the best from any source. We had house by house. Guys
would come back with intelligence a foot high. We had an
overlay map of all the German positions. The American army
knew where every German was.

General Alexander, the British head at Allied headquarters,
put out a bulletin: all Italian partisans go home and wait until
final offensive. Then they'll coordinate all the activities. Anybody with an elementary knowledge of guerrilla warfare knows
this is impossible. A guerrilla army has to be constantly on the
move, searching for intelligence. You send 'em home to sit on
their fannies, it's stupid. You can't suddenly assemble a force
that's now 300,000 and expect it to function. I told OSS that. I
didn't know that Churchill and Roosevelt were meeting in
Quebec on a battleship and saying the end of the war is in sight
and so on.

I sent out a radio communication that it's necessary to mount stronger and stronger attacks on the German positions. All railroads, all bridges, all ammunition dumps, any kind of factories—we need an enormous amount of intelligence. Eighteen radio teams. [Laughs.] Jesus Christ, I can't believe it myself.

They called me down to Caserta, the top OSS base. They wanted to know what I was up to. I said, It's an all-win-the-war message. How can you fault that? The major agreed. So I went away and forgot the whole thing. Never knew any of the stuff going on with the top officers. There was a guy, Scamperini, one jump ahead of an idiot. He analyzed that everything I was doing was subversive and scheming rather than an all-out-win-the-war effort. Let's face it, they wanted us guys out.

Toward the end of the war, I wrote up a mission to go to China. I got an immediate answer: accepted. Donovan said he'd put us on the first boat. Don't forget, we still had Japan. Two days later, the final offensive had started. You gotta understand that the partisans captured the German army. Kesselring surrendered to them. The message of surrender came through my radio from two different places. I offered to parachute in with some OSS guys to pick up Kesselring. [Laughs.] They gave it to Allen Dulles, who was head of the Swiss desk, and he sent somebody in. They didn't want us. I didn't expect it. Hell, they held up my captaincy for six months.

Donovan backed us up all the way down the line. He called me to Washington. The war was over May 8. May 10, I was on the U.S.S. *West Point*. And Milt Wolff was with me. The mission to China never came off.

Donovan tells me there's a twenty-million-dollar appropriation before Congress to wind up OSS work. A few months earlier, we were asked to write reports of what the future of the OSS should be. It turned out to be the CIA. Donovan was supposed to head it up. But now he's under attack for having communists in his organization. They're putting the heat on him.

He calls me in: "They're holding up the appropriation. We can't finish our work. I'm forced to let you go." Me and the other Spanish vets in the OSS. He gave us a letter attesting to our loyalty in action. I still got it home.

We were shipped to Fort McQuade. It was an AWOL camp. I was supposed to train them for Japan. The commanding officer is reading my record and he couldn't figure out why the heck I was sent here. We did nothing at McQuade except get fat. Didn't do anything. Didn't train anybody. When the bomb dropped, the guy said, "Do you wanna be discharged a little early?" I said sure.

They presented me with the Legion of Merit. And then I was attacked by the FBI, and whoever wanted to get in the act, for being with the Lincoln Brigade, a red. Me and the other guys. Legion of Merit? Oh, it's around the house somewhere.

IRVING GOFF was born in Brooklyn in 1911. He was always an athlete and won tumbling and diving championships. He was a member of the Young Communist League, and when the war broke out in Spain in 1936 he took to the streets to raise funds for the young Republic. He volunteered for the International Brigades and served with their Fourteenth Army Corps, the guerrilla unit. In World War II he was one of the Lincolns who served in the OSS. He has since worked as an organizer for the Communist Party, and at various other jobs. This piece is from Studs Terkel, *The Good War* (New York: Pantheon, 1984), and is reprinted with permission.

· Alvah Bessie ·

The Dead Past

For all of thirteen years
we have made speeches
in dusty half-filled halls, in private houses
    (a handful there),
called meetings, passed out leaflets
picketed the consulates with picket signs that read:
    NO DEALS WITH SPAIN
    SAVE THE PRISONERS IN FRANCO'S PRISONS
    LONG LIVE THE REPUBLIC and
    MADRID WILL BE THE TOMB OF FASCISM!
For thirteen years . . .

                 and there are those who say:
    Why live in the past? Why so much emphasis
    on what is dead and gone and lost and dry
    when the present is here, the future bursts the clock,
    so many things to do, so little time?

Is it the past and is it dead and gone
and was Spain lost or does the battle sound?
And is it dry or is it only the tears that are dry
on the faces of children, light streams through
dirt on cheeks and lips, and isn't the blood still wet
on the dirty concrete floors of the cells
in the model prison on the hillside?

334

There is a village I remember
where in the house on the narrow street
there were only the grandfather and his wife
and the daughter-in-law and the children
       (the one son dead in battle
       the other son dying in hospital)
and I lay crippled—not by wounds but
by the absurdity of rheumatism in battle,
where every night before I went to bed
       (their bed, they sleeping
       on the flagstone floor)
the old woman rubbed my legs and arms

with an old woman's remedies and when
every time I left the house
       I found a present on return:
       (a handful of hazelnuts,
       a glass of wine, dried figs
       or fresh figs)
a present for a stranger in a foreign land
because they knew why I was living in their house
and wanted to say (but did not have the words):
       We love you for coming
       for fighting
       for suffering for us
       (if only from rheumatism)
Are they dead and gone and dry (they were dry then);
The children had never seen a toy
in all their born days and did not know
what to do with one I imported for them
from Barcelona . . .
       are they lost
because the cause was lost (or said to be
by important people who knew better than
these poor *analfabetos* who knew only how to love
and how to fight?)
       Too much emphasis?

But tell us now, today
that the war is done,
the wounded healed and the dead are buried;
tell us now that the children's faces
are clean and fat
and their bellies flat instead of swollen
and the jails are empty and cobwebs are spun
in the corners of the cells
and
the blood has finally dried on the concrete floor
and cannot be distinguished from the red dust
of the arid soil;
and tell us the soil is no longer arid
but dark and damp and stirring
with the life of the vines
and the vats of olive oil are full
and the oil cheap and chickpeas plentiful
and meat is to be eaten instead of dreamed about
and the patent leather hats are green with age
in the museums and the fat sodomist
has gone to his reward at the feet of God—
then we will stop talking about
the past and laying so much emphasis
on what is dead and gone and lost and dry,
and return to the present that has grown out of
this past and cannot be separated from it.

This piece appeared in the *National Guardian*, 17 July 1952.

· Jacques Grunblatt ·

Forever in Spain, V

Spain Forever. After my escape from Gurs I returned to Marseilles. One day that summer I received a letter from Oliva in Spain that our son was born. He was born when Franco's victory was complete and the persecution of anyone connected with the Republic was at its height. To celebrate Franco's victory, they made Oliva dance while she was in labor. This letter made me cry as I never cried in my adult life. I considered myself an animal for having abandoned Oliva when our first child was born. Friends in the house tried unsuccessfully to console me.

During August and September 1939, the dark, gloomy clouds of World War II were spreading. In October I volunteered for the French Army. France was quickly crushed by Hitler's hordes. I fled to Marseilles, which was in the so-called Free France.

I was on the run: from Marseilles to Algiers to Casablanca, to get away from Hitler. I crossed the Atlantic and landed in Mexico with thousands of Republican refugees. For some unknown reason my correspondence with Oliva stopped.

I left Mexico for the United States and started a new life. I was married, passed my state boards, practiced medicine and raised a family, but Spain was on my mind. It was still in the grip of that fascist, Franco.

I decided to look for Oliva and our son, Jaime. I wrote a letter to Juan Negrín, the son of the last president of the Republic, but he did not reply. I wrote to our comrade, Alvah Bessie, asking for advice. He said that there was a risk that my son might show hostility, but that the risk was worth taking.

In Spain, although my battalion was a part of the Lincoln Brigade, it was Spanish. It was not until 1976, when the Veterans of the Abraham Lincoln Brigade organized a trip to Italy and I decided to join them, that I got closer to my American comrades.

By 1977 my American family had grown up. I wanted to search for Oliva and Jaime. I told my wife, Hilda, about them and she agreed to help me.

While I rested in my hotel room in Madrid, Hilda searched through the telephone directories looking for Oliva and Jaime Cabezas García; she found eight of them. I called the first on the list. He was a lawyer who said that he knew the family and would help me contact them in two hours. Impatient with the delay, I did not wait but called the next name on the list. Mari Cruz Cabezas, the wife of my Jaime, answered the phone saying that Jaime was working and that she would contact him at work. Jaime returned my call and we agreed to meet in the hotel lobby when he finished his day's work.

We met and embraced. Then I received the first sad news: Oliva passed away in 1974. The next day he met us in the hotel with his wife and three children. We greeted them, talked for a while and then went to his home where we talked and compared pictures. Before long we felt close. The next day we went to the cemetery and placed flowers on Oliva's grave.

Now Spain is not only the place where I did my best to fight for my ideals, but I am physically and emotionally united with my Spanish family. We loved them and our love was reciprocated. My ideals became my life forever. The American part of my family and the Spanish side became one big family. My Spanish grandchildren come almost every summer to visit us. One American son has visited them in Spain. Hilda and I have made several trips to Spain. My hope is that both families will one day see a Spain that will be socialist not only in name but also in spirit.

· George Watt ·

Reunion in Hamme

I was standing in front of the hinged bookcase that had served as camouflage for the passageway to the "Secret Annexe," where Anne Frank and the others hid from the Nazis for more than two years. Suddenly I was struck by the thought that on that cold November day, forty years ago, I was just a two-hour train ride away from Anne Frank. It gave me a feeling of closeness to her world that I did not remember experiencing when I had read the *Diary* and had seen the movie some years back.

I don't in any way mean to compare my experience with that of Anne Frank. I was merely a transient in this underground world while she was a permanent resident. Her ordeal was life imprisonment, which ended in her tragic death at Bergen-Belsen, while my sojourn was only temporary.

My entry into that "world" started on November 5, 1943, when I landed by parachute on a farm in a little village in Nazi-occupied Belgium. I was an aerial gunner on a B-17 flying out of England. On a bombing raid over the Ruhr Valley, that day, our plane was crippled and knocked out of formation by enemy flak. Limping back on our own, toward the English Channel, we got as far as Belgium, only to be jumped by a German Focke-Wulf. Our plane went down in flames. Eight of the ten-man crew managed to bail out. Seven of them landed on one side of the Durme River. I landed by myself on the other.

Five of my crew were immediately captured by the Germans.

Two others, I found out later, were rescued almost immediately by agents of the Belgian underground. On my side of the river, German patrols arrived quickly, and chances are I would have been captured had I not been helped by courageous farmers and workers. They hid me in the field and in their homes. They gave me civilian clothes and money and guided me on the first leg of what turned out to be a forty-five day trek across Nazi-occupied Belgium and France, across the Pyrenees (yes, those Pyrenees again!) through fascist Spain to Gibraltar, and by air back to England.

My wife, Margie, and I were eternally indebted to these intrepid people who risked imprisonment and death to help me escape. We had been out of touch with them since the end of the war and felt for a number of years that we should go back and thank them in person for saving my life.

Well, we finally did it. Last spring, combining a vacation trip to Holland and France, we went back. I'd like to share this exciting experience with you.

On a Saturday, after a seven-day barge trip on the canals of Holland, where we enjoyed the breathtaking beauty of the tulips at their peak, we checked back into our hotel in Amsterdam and found a letter waiting for us. Here's how it began:

> Dear George,
> First of all I'd like to represent myself because you have to know who is writing to you. My name is Monique Inghels. I'm Raymond's daughter. I was three and one-half years old the fifth November 1943, the day you came down with your parachute in the fields of Durmen, the village where I lived with my parents.
> Since that day I know you by name, because daddy told us often enough "the story of George Watt" and each time my brother and I were hanging on his lips.

Raymond was the seaman who helped me get away from the German search parties in Hamme by taking me on the train to Antwerp and to his brother-in-law, the doctor, in Brussels. Unfortunately, I was too late for Raymond. He died about fourteen years ago of lung cancer.

As soon as I read the letter, I called Monique in Hamme and, wouldn't you know, the only time we could see her aunt and uncle, the doctor, was that very same evening. They were leaving for a vacation in Spain the next morning.

There were Rembrandt, Vermeer, Hals, and all the Dutch painters we had come to see. We made a hurried visit to the Rijks-museum and caught the 5:26 train to Antwerp.

At the Bercham station we were met by Monique and her husband, Theo, and by Eduard and Mathilde Lauwaert and a son and daughter-in-law. The Lauwaerts were the first to hide me in their home and Eduard was the prime organizer of the first phase of my escape. He was the one who gave me a pair of shoes, the only suit he owned, and four hundred Belgian francs. Eduard, Mathilde, and I embraced joyfully. Then Monique and Theo drove Margie and me to Brussels to meet the doctor and his wife.

On the way we learned from Monique for the first time that her uncle's name was Jean Proost, and that the Proosts were still living in the same house. We also learned the name of my first "connection" in the Belgian resistance. He was Henri Malfait. Monique thought he was dead.

Madam Proost must have read the flashback in my mind, when she said, after we embraced inside the entrance to her house,

"This is where you stood forty years ago."

Now, as Hedwige was welcoming Margie and me with such warmth, I remembered that first frightened look and thought of the heroism of a young doctor's wife who, despite that fear, risked her life to protect an American airman who was a complete stranger to her.

Doctor Proost, a handsome, gray-haired man, looking considerably younger than his seventy years, came down the stairs and after we embraced, pointed to the room on the ground floor where he said Raymond and I had stayed in hiding all of that day.

The first thing that he told us when we were comfortably settled in their upstairs dining room was that Malfait was alive. I was overjoyed. As we began to relive that day forty years ago, Doctor Proost told us a few things I did not know, namely: that I was Malfait's first "client"; that Proost's wife, Hedwige, was in the beginning of her pregnancy when I had arrived with Raymond; that a three-volume book, written in French, was published a few years ago, dealing with the Belgian resistance, and in it were recounted the incidents around my rescue. He further revealed to us that he knew Malfait through his (Proost's) sister who had worked with Malfait as typist for the underground newspaper, *La Belgique Libre*. This was a stronger connection than he had originally indicated to me. At that time, he had merely told me that he had occasionally received an underground paper from this young man and thought he might know something about the "White Brigades."

Doctor Proost recalled how we plotted my route to the French border on a map printed on the silk handkerchief that came with my escape kit. And he remembered going out on his bicycle in a cold downpour to look for Malfait.

Toward the end of the visit, Margie said we were Jewish. Well, it was like telling the Proosts they had just been anointed in heaven.

"All these years I thought I helped save an American flyer and I was happy," Doctor Proost said, his face lighting up with a beautiful smile. "Now that I know I helped save a Jewish American flyer, I feel even happier."

Sunday morning we went to the Lauwaerts' house. This was the first house in which I had stayed when Mathilde Lauwaert brought me in from the cold dark outhouses where I was forced to wait until they put their kid to bed. On the front of the house a large American flag was draped over one window, and an equally large Belgian flag was draped over the other. All of the Lauwaerts' children and grandchildren, Monique and Theo and Yvonne Inghels, Raymond's widow, were there along with a number of villagers.

The secretary of the village presented me with a plaque bearing the Hamme coat-of-arms. Margie was presented with a bouquet of flowers. The secretary made a short speech and I made a short speech. I said that I had come back after forty years to thank each one of them in person for the heroic acts performed by them on my behalf and on behalf of liberty. I singled out Eduard and Mathilde, Raymond and the Ducolumbiers. The Lauwaerts presented me with a book written in Flemish. It dealt with the resistance in that region and they showed me the six pages that told the stories and legends around my rescue. The title of the section was "Zijn verjaardag"—His Birthday. November 5, the day on which I was shot down, was indeed my thirtieth birthday! The book also contained a photograph of the remains of my Fort, which had crashed in a cemetery in nearby Lokeren.

When Matilde showed me one of my dog tags, I felt the oddest sensation. There was my name and serial number and Margie's name and address, and it had been hidden in their house all through the occupation and kept all these years!

But I really flipped when Monique handed me a silk handkerchief with a finely embroidered floral pattern and told me this was a piece of my parachute.

"You keep it," I said.

She said no, she had another one. Her mother's sister had made two of them.

Then, after a four-hour dinner in a pleasant restaurant, we all, four carloads of us, repaired to the field where I had come down. On the way we stopped to see the farmer who owned the land. I had dubbed him the "stump" because, just before I landed, when the ground was rushing up at me, I saw a tall stump standing in the field. The stump turned out to be the farmer who knew only Flemish and he stood grinning at me without saying a word, while I tried desperately to make myself understood. He's quite old now and as he came hobbling on two canes toward me, I recognized him at once. His face was fuller, but unmistakably, he was the "stump." When he learned who I was, he gave me the same broad smile, but this time he talked a blue streak. He seemed to remember everything that had happened and quite a bit more.

We tried to get to the spot where I had landed. But what with the children, and with the women wearing high heels, and with the fields being muddy and rutty, and with Eduard having an asthma attack, we had to call off the expedition, to try again another time.

The next morning, I spoke to the children at the elementary school and they rewarded us with a delightful song in English, which they had rehearsed for two hours that very morning. That evening, Monique drove Margie and me to Brussels to see Malfait.

The visit with Malfait and his wife was the most poignant of all the time we spent in Belgium. Malfait was a twenty-three-year-old university student and member of the Catholic Youth Movement at the time I came into his life. He was editing and distributing *La Belgique Libre,* an underground publication, and was in the process of being assigned to the "Lifeline," the sector of the resistance that had as its responsibility the rescue of allied flyers and other military personnel caught behind the enemy lines.

As we sat down in his living room, Malfait asked me, "Did you know you had a gun in your back, when we left Doctor Proost's house?"

Startled, I said "No."

"I thought you might be a German spy," Malfait continued. "I was prepared to shoot you if you made one suspicious move."

This was certainly a shock to me. I always thought when he had radioed the answers on the questionnaire back to London that headquarters had confirmed my authenticity; otherwise, why would he have taken me to his house? Now Malfait told me that he had not gotten a reply from London by the time he came to take me from Doctor Proost's house. He had to get me out of there because too many patients came unannounced into the doctor's house.

Henri had to get permission from his chief to take me to his parents' home, temporarily, till another place could be found. But he was permitted to do so only under one condition. And that condition was that he carry a gun and shoot me at any suspicious move made by me, or if the reply from London came back negative.

When I remember how files and communications used to get snafued in the army, I shudder all over again at the thought that I could have been killed by someone from my own side!

Three months after his encounter with me, Henri was arrested by the Gestapo and placed in the Fort Breendonk concentration camp, situated near Antwerp.

The indescribable horrors and bestiality of the Nazis came alive for us as we listened to Henri's account of torture by repeated "drownings" and beatings (lifting his right trouser leg to show us the forty-year-old deep, ugly welts on his shin); of his stay in solitary confinement in a small, dark cell where he was handcuffed to the wall for unbearably long stretches of time; of his receiving the death sentence in April 1944.

Instead of being executed, he found himself transferred to Buchenwald, where he remained for a year until he was liberated by the Americans.

Impulsively, I said I will go to Breendonk. Henri expressed surprise, but he was pleased. He told us his cell number and suggested what we should look for. He later presented me with a photograph of himself with a group of concentration camp internees taken on the day of liberation, and another of himself, a short time afterward, somewhat fattened up.

I wish I could go on to tell you more about this remarkable man, who came out of the camps broken in body but not in spirit, but I still have more to tell about the trip.

At this time, I should also tell you that I had taped the entire interview with Malfait. But alas, to my absolute horror, this priceless tape, along with three others (six hours of recording) and all my two hundred shots of undeveloped film, and sixty pages of written diary containing names and biographical sketches and impressions, were stolen from the locked trunks of our rented car in Nice, shortly before we left France. Of course they took the camera and tape recorder, but that's only money. The documents were irreplaceable.

Well, to get on with the story. A lot more happened in the remaining two days that we spent in Hamme, including: a radio interview, the search for the "beautiful redhead" to whom I had given my leather flight jacket, the "man with the footprints" (his footprints on the plowed field led the Germans away from the spot where I was hiding), the "man with the cow" (legend has it that the Germans missed me because the farmer hid me behind the rump of his cow, which he was taking to Durmen that day), finally finding the exact spot where I had spent most of that afternoon, and the site of the tram station (which is now a bus stop and parking lot). All of this requires a book. I will just tell you one story about the policeman and call it a day.

Shortly after I had parachuted onto the field, while I was

talking to the villagers, a Belgian policeman suddenly came upon us. I have often told the story of the Belgian cop, whom I described as patriotic because he later gave me the chance to escape.

I said to Monique, when we arrived, "I want to see this wonderful, patriotic man."

"Patriotic? Wonderful?" Monique burst out. "He was an evil man. He was a collaborator!"

In all the years when I told this story to anyone who would care to listen, I related how I suddenly mustered my fighting spirit and made an impassioned plea to the Belgian cop not to turn me over to the Germans. I told him the Americans are on their way to liberate Belgium from the Germans, and that we are fighting in a common cause. I described him as shaken and wrestling with his conscience, and then giving me my chance to escape. I gave myself most of the credit for his action. The story I now got from the villagers gave me some new insight, which downgrades my own role in this drama.

The villagers had argued very forcefully with the officer, Leon Famaey, for my release. But the final blow, just before I spoke to him, was delivered by Suzanne Famaey, the sister of Leon. She denounced him and told him the occupation will not last forever, and you'll have to live with these people. If you turn him in you will not be able to live in this village and you will not be able to live with your own family!

While I thought he was responding to my eloquence, he was, in truth, wrestling with two fears, his fear of the Nazis and his greater fear of the retribution of the villagers.

All the rest of the story—of my parachute and Famaey's encounter with the Nazi field commander—checks out the same. It's a great story, but unfortunately it is too long to recount here.

I must tell you about one postscript to the story, something that I did not know till this visit. After the war, Leon Famaey was brought before the tribunal to be tried as a collaborator. He was charged with a number of offenses against the people. He had one defense. On November 5, 1943, at great risk to himself, he saved an American flyer by not turning him over to the Germans. And so he was exonerated.

"You, George, saved his life," Monique said. "If not for you he would have gone to jail, lost his job and been run out of the village."

The next day we exchanged gifts with the Lauwaerts, the Inghels, and neighbors, and after prolonged goodbyes Margie and I set out with Monique to carry out the promise I had made to Malfait.

I have read about the camps, seen pictures, and heard personal accounts of life in the campus. But none of this prepared me for what I was to experience at Fort Breendonk.

To get to Malfait's cell, we had to walk over wet cobblestones through a long, dark, dank, cold tunnel. I looked through the peephole into Cell No. 7, where Malfait had been kept. It was no more than five feet wide and six feet long. It was one of sixteen cells in a room no more than fifteen by forty feet. The barracks room was approximately the same size but slept forty-eight people on three-tiered straw mattresses! Then we saw the torture chamber. Believe me, we couldn't get out of there fast enough!

We didn't plan it this way. But the return visit to Belgium was neatly packaged between our opening visit to the Anne Frank House in Amsterdam and the closing visit to Fort Breendonk concentration camp in Antwerp. For Margie and me, however, the reunion was anything but gloomy. It was overwhelmingly full of love and joy that comes with the recognition that farmers and working people in a small village, by their courage and resourcefulness, had been able to outsmart the Nazis and score a victory over a monstrous evil enemy.

This is not the "story of George Watt," as Monique had written. The heroes of this story are the people of Hamme and Durmen and the resistance fighters of Belgium and France who risked everything including their lives in the struggle for freedom.

It is much too early to forget.

GEORGE WATT was born in New York City in 1913, the son of Polish
Jewish immigrants. He was New York State executive secretary
of the American Student Union before joining the International
Brigades in July 1937. He first served with the Mac-Paps and
then became the last political commissar of the Lincoln Battalion. During World War II he was a paratrooper in the armed
forces, was shot down, and escaped with the help of the anti-
Nazi underground. After the war he worked for the Communist
Party. He was tried and convicted in the Cleveland Smith Act
trial, but his conviction (and that of a few others) was reversed.
He left the Communist Party in 1958 and became an offset
printer, social worker, community organizer, and administrator
of a community health center until his retirement in 1982.

· Maury Colow ·

Ambulances for Nicaragua

Once a volunteer, okay, but twice a volunteer? Old soldiers have an expression for that. Abe Smorodin, Bill Susman, and finally Abe Osheroff called—all urging me to take off for Nicaragua "literally yesterday." Osheroff, who was to head the delegation, was down with some tropical bug and Susman was completely wrapped up in our fiftieth anniversary affair. And so off went the volunteer to a place where people were dying for the right to determine their own way of life.

We had raised funds enough to buy nine ambulances. Now a group of Vets and their associates from the East and West coasts would formally present the ambulances. All of our delegation paid their own way and all arrangements were made through VALB. Hon Brown was head of the West Coast delegation and my job was to scout ahead, help arrange the itinerary, and do public relations before the groups arrived. So off I went to perform miracles—and not of my usual style. I found myself walking into a bar for a beer, spotting someone who "looked like" a newspaper person, and boldly introducing myself and my mission. It gave me butterflies but I did it, I did it.

Reception was great. Sympathetic and helpful. I was interviewed, scrutinized, examined, and came to be known as the man from the Lincoln Brigade. We did get some coverage. AP, UPI sent out releases. I'm told radio reports went out to all of South America and Spain. (This was one more time we should have been rich enough to have a clipping service. We'd have a better picture of the results.) We did get NBC—Channel 4, local San Francisco news, to do a story. Their reporters followed us everywhere and we helped get them into places they could not have gone without us.

The Hotel Intercontinental where I stayed was the center of the news media. Also all volunteer work groups that came to Nicaragua passed through its lobby. I had made myself and our cause so obvious that I had a chance to talk with many group leaders. I learned that some of the groups came to pick coffee, or to work otherwise in agriculture, or in hospitals and in building construction. An International Brigade without rifles!! They came from the Scandinavian countries, France, Italy, Spain, Germany, Argentina, and there were also hundreds of Americans. It was energizing; it was spiritual, it simply was beautiful. They all knew and admired our ambulance campaign.

To whomever I spoke (news reporters, radio and TV people) I kept repeating that our trip to Nicaragua to present the ambulances was the beginning of our fiftieth anniversary commemoration of the Spanish Civil War. A delegation was at hand when our group arrived on January 9, tired and beat from the long trip. After much discussion, I got our itinerary approved the same night that the groups arrived. And it was a crowded schedule.

The formal ceremonies where Milt Wolff would hand over the keys to the ambulances took place at the Concepción Palacios, the Ministry of Health complex in Managua, on Saturday, January 11 at 3 P.M. I drummed up as much interest as I could among the press and especially with the heads of various volunteer groups. I'll admit to being somewhat disappointed since officially this was kept to a minimum, a sort of formal procedure. I had hoped for a more open and public affair. The Toyota ambulances looked great, powerful four-wheel drive, huge tires, searchlight to navigate the roads, etc. Inside, room for a doctor, paramedic, and wounded—and equipped with oxygen and first aid supplies. Painted on the sides: Abraham Lincoln Brigade in Solidarity with the Nicaraguan People. Some of the ambulances had Doctor Edward K. Barsky's name. The drivers enthusiastically jumped aboard and drove the ambulances about, blasting the sirens.

We jammed into a small conference room for the formalities, with Marie Victoria Urquijo, in charge of the foreign relations department of the Ministry of Health, Doctor Benjamin Barreto, vice-minister, and Mirna Cuadra, assistant in the foreign relations department. We exchanged greetings; some of the press attended. Milt Wolff participated and our hosts were impressed with "El Lobo." During the discussion I spoke about Bill Gandall, who had been a U.S. Marine during the time of Sandino. It was like a bomb exploded. Bill then told how he came to Porto Cabezo with the Marines, referred to himself as a stupid kid who followed orders and took part in raids on villages where they burned and pillaged. And then told of how he grew and changed and ended up fighting in Spain. You cannot imagine the reaction. From then on Bill had newspaper, radio, and TV interviews from all over the world. He made a vital contribution, full of life and drama.

We did a little of the tourist bit. Managua is surrounded by seven volcanos. We visited one. Impressive. Went for a short ride on a boat that could have passed for the *African Queen*. Lake Nicaragua is huge, full of small sharks and snapping alligators. We saw none.

I got word that we were to leave very early on Sunday for a Cara al Pueblo (Face the People). This is a kind of open-air meeting, usually attended by high government officials. Some two hundred people, including us, were present. Daniel Ortega arrived without fanfare; no siren escort but followed by a tough looking group, obviously body guards. He made a few comments greeting the VALB vets. This gathering made me think of 1778 after our own revolution and one of our town hall meetings. People raised their hands and aired their grievances—i.e., a road that was promised and never completed. Ortega or others would respond and very often propose a way to settle the problem then and there. Then thanking the speaker, a rifle was handed to him as a token of participation. The table was loaded with some real hot rifle repeaters. Another incident at the meeting: A man said, "This is a mixed economy, right? Well, I'm a small landlord and my land was taken away from me and now I'm one of the farmhands. But, Mr. President, they are botching things up. Our production is less than before. Why don't I get back my land, I promise I will increase production for I am a good organizer." There was an immediate conference among the ministers and Ortega told him he'd get back his land and gave him a rifle as a token of appreciation. While the parallel can't be tightly drawn, to me this was democracy at work.

Monday we delivered our first ambulance to Matagalpa. Since Region VI was a more active war zone, a second ambulance would be sent up later. Formalities over, we headed for the Apanas military hospital. . . . The physical surroundings were beautiful. Inside the hospital (even by Spanish Civil War comparison) was poor, needing everything from medical facilities, to equipment, to beds. At first the wounded looked confused at this group of Yankees and gringos. After their commander explained, there was applause. Our group spread out among the men and sat down at the beds of the wounded, some of whom were 13 and 14 years old. I asked one soldier his age: 17, he said. I told him I was 18 when I went to Spain. By God, he had a shrapnel infection in his left leg, the same kind of wound I had in Spain. It was hard to break away. Milt Wolff was talking to a small group; Millie Rosenstein to another kid. We boarded our bus with a sense of sadness and an uneasy quiet.

Through a friend, I had been corresponding with Gino Baumann of Estilí. Among other things, he is a scholar of the Spanish Civil War—he's written a definitive study of the South American volunteers. On the Sunday before the groups arrived, Gino found me in the hotel lobby and we talked for hours. He knew we were bringing an ambulance to his city and told me why it's called Estelí. "La tres veces hermosa"—Estelí, three-times beautiful. The name comes from being attacked three times by the contras, who three times got their asses whipped.

In Estelí, delivering the ambulance, we went through the usual formalities and then headed for Gino's estate. He is the representative for the Swiss government aid program. He therefore acts as engineer, agronomist, cooperative advisor, etc. There was no electricity in Estelí: it seems the night before the contras had blown up the power lines. Gino went about repairing his generator, so he had power. He had prepared a feast for us—a 100-pound pig on a spit, fresh bread, pastry, and coffee, and invited leading members of the community to meet us. He also took us to visit a cooperative farm where much of the work was done by hand. There was a desperate need for equipment and for little generators. We had an interesting discussion. . . . One of the vets asked how would you feel about working again under a landowner. The farm group's leader (tough, lean, but vocal) stood a moment in silence, his eyes became narrow slits, his jaw set and then: "Never, never. It would be better to die." I had heard this in Spain so long ago. For a split second we spanned stretches of time. Back to Gino's where we lunged at that 100-pound pig. We drank rum, rum, and rum. And there was lots of warm, intimate conversation; an evening we'll all remember.

Up at 6 A.M. and breakfast at 7. The comrades who were housed by the people of Estelí came in and Gino, our host, offered a huge plate of eggs and fresh bread. We boarded our bus at 8 A.M. for the long trip to Boaco. We left cheering Gino for his warm hospitality. He stood in the doorway looking lonely as he waved us off.

On the trip to Boaco, Vets kept commenting at how familiar the landscape looked—this like Jarama, this like the Aragon, this like the Estremadura. We delivered one of our ambulances at Boaco and were greeted by the usual delegates and representatives of the Ministry of Health, plus all the Americans working at our housing project, which Abe Osheroff organized. We were touched and surprised to be greeted by a bunch of kids and women dressed in white with red and black bandanas around their necks. It seemed like the whole town had come out and we were moved. While we talked, each of us was approached by a child who kissed us and tied a bandana around our necks. A huge bouquet of flowers was handed to me while I spoke to the group. What a shot for a Hollywood movie! Now we headed for the brigade housing project, some twenty-eight kilometers away. Our bus traveled to a point and then we took four-wheel drive jeeps and a huge Russian truck to the project since it was impossible for the bus to get up that road. The project is roughly at an elevation of 4,000 feet, beautifully located, near good coffee-picking terrain, with a breathtaking view. There were more than twenty houses built—some occupied by Nicaraguans, some empty, and some housing the Americans who are part of the working crew. We talked; they greeted us; told us how tough it was to bring materials up to the project and how the road we traveled was made by their carting stuff up that hill. They told us how slowly but surely they had gained the support of the local peasants. And now warm goodbyes, especially to the American volunteers. It was kind of a *déjà vu* experience for me. Two of Abe's sons were there and one looked the "spitting image" of the Abe I remembered from Brownsville, a lifetime ago.

We worried about how vulnerable the project was. The contras were active in the mountains nearby. A new development—becoming more common, I suppose, with the increased U.S. dollars sent to them. We met our bus below and started the long trip back to Managua and our farewell dinner to be held that night.

The top Ministry of Health officials, doctors, and ministers attended our dinner. It was held at some sort of state house where VIPs were feted. There were bartenders running around keeping drinks "fresh." Lots of thanks were heaped upon us. Milt Wolff said a few words of goodbye with a pledge to continue our work. I thanked all for their cooperation and for the opportunity to see their country and meet their people. I offered two ways for us to thank them: one, to attempt in a modest way to bring the truth of Nicaragua to the American people and two, to continue our solidarity in the form of material help. We parted with warm *abrazos*. We felt good. Mission accomplished. We brought the ambulances to the war zones, we met the people, and we kept our pledge made when we left Spain, to continue the fight against fascism on other fronts.

· Minister of Health of Nicaragua ·

Letter to the Veterans of the Abraham Lincoln Brigade

September 24, 1986

Mr. Abe Smorodin
National Secretary
Abraham Lincoln Brigade
799 Broadway, Room 227
New York, NY 10003

Dear Mr. Smorodin:

On behalf of the Ministry of Health of Nicaragua, I should like to thank you and the membership of the Abraham Lincoln Brigade for the various donations sent to Nicaragua. Specifically, I should like to mention the ambulances, which arrived in 1985, and the check for U.S. $17,000.00 received this summer.

Your donations have both a practical and a symbolic meaning. For in many instances they are used to help heal the wounds inflicted on our people because of a policy that seeks the destruction of a revolution that represents the hope of a better future for all Nicaraguans, especially the poor. It is also a reminder to us that we are not alone in the defense of our right to self-determination and strengthens the conviction, deeply held by the people and government of Nicaragua, that there is no conflict between our peoples.

We are convinced that the shared desire of the people of

Nicaragua and the people of the United States for peace and cooperation will help us find ways to stop this unjust war and achieve peace.

Sincerely,
Comandante Dora María Téllez
Minister of Health
Republic of Nicaragua

· Edwin Rolfe ·

First Love

Again I am summoned to the eternal field
green with the blood still fresh at the roots of flowers,
green through the dust-rimmed memory of faces
that moved among the trees there for the last time
before the final shock, the glazed eye, the hasty mound.

But why are my thoughts in another country?
Why do I always return to the sunken road through corroded
   hills,
with the Moorish castle's shadow casting ruins over my
   shoulder
and the black-smocked girl approaching, her hands laden with
   grapes?

I am eager to enter it, eager to end it.
Perhaps this one will be the last one.
And men afterward will study our arms in museums
and nod their heads, and frown, and name the inadequate
   dates
and stumble with infant tongues over the strange place-names.

But my heart is forever captive of that other war
that taught me first the meaning of peace and of comradeship

and always I think of my friend who amid the apparition of
   bombs
saw on the lyric lake the single perfect swan.

· Langston Hughes ·

Hero—International Brigade

Blood,
Or a flag,
Or a flame
Or life itself
Are they the same:
Our dream?
   I came.
An ocean in between
And half a continent.
Frontiers,
And mountains skyline tall,
And governments that told me NO,
YOU CANNOT GO!

I came.
On tomorrow's bright frontiers
I placed the strength and wisdom
Of my years.
Not much.
For I am young.
  (*Was* young,
Perhaps it's better said—
For now I'm dead.)

But had I lived four score and ten
Life could not've had
A better end.
I've given what I wished
And what I had to give
That others live.
And when the bullets
Cut my heart away,
And the blood
Gushed to my throat
I wondered if it were blood
Gushing there.
Or a red flame?
Or just my death
Turned into life?
They're all the same
Our dream!
      My death!
      Your life!
      Our blood!
      One flame!
They're all the same!